Emergence of Eco-Feminism & Reweaving the World

Emergence of Eco-Feminism & Reweaving the World

S Pandey

MD Publications Pvt Ltd
New Delhi
www.mdppl.com

Published by :

MD Publications Pvt Ltd
"MD House", 11, Darya Ganj,
New Delhi - 110 002
Phone : +91-11- 45355555
E-mail : contact@mdppl.com
Website: www.mdppl.com

ISBN : 978-81-7533-315-4

Published and Printed by Mr. Pranav Gupta on behalf of **MD Publications Pvt Ltd** at Repro India Limited.

PREFACE

In 1974, the term "ecofeminism" was conceived by d'Eaubonne as a connection of the ecology and women. Ecofeminism is a social and political movement points to the existence of considerable common ground between environmentalism and feminism with some currents linking deep ecology and feminism. Ecofeminists argue that a strong parallel exists between the oppression and subordination of women in families and society and the degradation of nature through the construction of differences into conceptual binaries and ideological hierarchies that allow a systematic, however logically unsound, justification of domination by subjects classed into higher-ranking categories over objects classed into lower-ranking categories (e.g. man over woman, culture over nature, white over black).

They also explore the intersectionality between sexism, the domination of nature, racism, speciesism, and other characteristics of social inequality. In some of their current work, ecofeminists argue that the capitalist and patriarchal systems that predominate throughout the world reveal a triple domination of the Global South (people who live in the Third World), women, and nature. This domination and exploitation of women, of poorly resourced peoples and of nature sits at the core of the ecofeminist analysis. Although ecofeminism has been called misandrist, in proposing a patriarchy as the root cause of many world problems, its view of the oppression of minorities and the Third World recognizes not just women, but also includes most men as oppressed.

Ecofeminism is a relatively new part of the feminist movement, evolving out of political activism over the past three decades. Peace marches, anti-nuclear protests, environmental and animal liberation movements, and world hunger activism have raised the consciousnesses of many. A range of theoretical positions has emerged from this movement, resting on the assumption that there are critical connections between the domination of nature and of women. Particularly, ecofeminists attack patriarchal society's dualistic thinking, wherein one side of the dualism reflects the "self" or the subject, while the second represents the "other" or the object. The object is considered only insofar as it can benefit the subject.

Some of the more common dualisms addressed by ecofeminists are male/female, culture/nature, and mind/body, the former embodying all that is desired and "good" in Western society, the latter epitomizing those characteristics that should be denounced, shunned, or conquered. Ecofeminism seeks to move beyond this dualistic worldview and restructure our notion of power; life-affirming, consensual relationships are to replace "power-over" relationships. The movement wants to create an interconnected community, void of hierarchies, where all beings - human, non-human, and members of the organic world - have their own intrinsic value and are part of the same living organism, the earth.

I am very grateful to Mr. Pranav Gupta, Director of MD Publications Pvt Ltd, New Delhi, for his kind cooperation and support for this book.

S Pandey

Contents

1

Introduction to Eco-feminism

Eco-feminism represents the union of the radical ecology movement, or what has been called 'deep ecology', and feminism. The word 'ecology' emerges from the biological science of natural environmental systems. It examines how these natural communities function to sustain a healthy web of life and how they become disrupted, causing death to the plant and animal life. Human intervention is obviously one of the main causes of such disruption. Thus ecology emerged as a combined socio-economic and biological study in the late sixties to examine how human use of nature is causing pollution of soil, air and water, and destruction of the natural systems of plants and animals, threatening the base of life on which the human community itself deep ends.

Deep ecology takes this study of social ecology another step. It examines the symbolic, psychological and ethical patterns of destructive relations of humans with nature and how to replace this with a life-affirming culture. Feminism also is a complex movement with many layers. It can be defined only as a movement within the liberal democratic societies for the full inclusion of women in political rights and economic access to employment.

It can be defined more radically in a socialist and liberation tradition as a transformation of the patriarchal socio-economic system, in which male domination of women is the foundation of all socio-economic hierarchies. Feminism can be also studied in terms of culture and consciousness, charting the symbolic, psychological and ethical connections of domination of women and male monopolization of resources and controlling power. This third level of feminist analysis connects closely with deep ecology. Some would say that feminism is the primary expression of deep ecology. Yet, although many feminists may make a verbal connection between domination of women and domination of nature, the development of this connection in a broad historical, social, economic and cultural analysis is only just beginning.

Most studies of Eco-feminism, such as the essays in the book edited by Judith Plant, Healing the Wounds: The Promise of Eco-feminism is brief and evocative, rather than comprehensive. Fuller exploration of Eco-feminism probably goes beyond the expertise of one person. It needs a cooperation of a team that brings together historians of culture, natural scientists, and social economists who would all share a concern for the inter connection of domination of women and exploitation of nature. It needs visionaries to imagine how to construct a new socio-economic system and a new cultural consciousness that would support relations of mutuality, rather than competitive power. For this one needs poets, artists and liturgists, as well as evolutionary organizers, to incarnate more life-giving relationships in our cultural consciousness and social system.

A Platform for Deep Ecology Below is what I call "the platform of the Deep Ecology movement", or rather, one formulation of such a platform; it consists of eight common points to guide those who believe that ecological problems cannot be solved only by technical 'quick-fix' solutions.

1. The flourishing of human and non-human life on Earth has intrinsic value. The value of non-human life forms is independent of the usefulness these may have for narrow human purposes.
2. Richness and diversity of life forms are values in themselves and contribute to the flourishing of human and non-human life on Earth.

3. Humans have no right to reduce this richness and diversity except to satisfy vital needs.
4. Present human interference with the non-human world is excessive, and the situation is rapidly worsening.
5. The flourishing of human life and cultures is compatible with a substantial decrease of the human population. The flourishing of non-human life requires such a decrease.
6. Significant change of life conditions for the better require change in policies. These affect basic economic, technological, and ideological structures.
7. The ideological change is mainly that of appreciating life quality rather than adhering to a high standard of living. There will be a profound awareness of the difference between big and great.
8. Those who subscribe to the foregoing points have an obligation directly or indirectly to participate in the attempt to implement the necessary changes. -Arne Naess

Such a range of expertise certainly goes beyond my own competence. Although I am interested in continuing to gain working acquaintance with the natural and social sciences, my primary work lies in the area of history of culture. What I plan to do here is to trace some symbolic connections of domination of women and domination of nature in Mediterranean and Western European culture. I will then explore briefly the alternative ethic and culture that might be envisioned if we are to overcome these patterns of domination and destructive violence to women and to the natural world.

Pre-Hebraic Roots

Anthropological studies have suggested that the identification of women with nature and males with culture is both ancient and widespread. This cultural pattern itself expresses a monopolizing of the definition of culture by males. The very word 'nature' in this formula is part of the problem, because it defines nature as a reality below and separated from 'man', rather than one nexus in which humanity itself is inseparably embedded. It is, in fact, human beings who cannot live apart from the rest of nature as our life-sustaining context, while the community of plants and animal both can and, for billions of years, did exist without humans. The concept of humans outside of nature is a cultural reversal of natural reality. How did this reversal take place in our cultural consciousness? One key element of this identification of women with non-human nature lies in the early human social patterns in which women's reproductive role as child bearer was tied to making women the primary productive and maintenance workers. Women did most of the work associated with child care, food production and preparation, production of clothing, baskets and other artifacts of daily life, clean-up and waste-disposal. Although there is considerable variation of these patterns cross-culturally, generally males situated themselves in work that was both more prestigious and more occasional, demanding bursts of energy, such as hunting larger animals, war and clearing fields, but allowing them more space for leisure. This is the primary social base for the male monopolization of culture, by which men re-enforced their privileges of leisure, the superior prestige of their activities and the inferiority of the activities associated with women.

Perhaps, for much of human history, women ignored or discounted these male claims to superiority, being entirely too busy with the tasks of daily life, and expressing among themselves their assumptions about the obvious importance of their own work as the primary producers and reproducers. But, by stages, this female consciousness and culture was sunk underneath the growing male power to define the culture for the whole society, socializing both males and females into this male-defined point of view. It is from the perspective of this male monopoly of culture that the work of women in maintaining the material basis of daily life is defined as an inferior realm. The material world itself is then seen as something separated from males and symbolically linked with women. The earth, as the place from which plant and animal life arises, becomes linked with the bodies of women from which babies emerge. The development of plow agriculture and human slavery very likely took this connection of woman and nature another step. Both are seen as a realm, not on which men depend, but which men dominate and rule over with coercive power. Wild animals which are hunted retain their autonomy and freedom. Domesticated animals become an extension of the human family. But animals yoked and put to the plow, driven under the whip, are now in the new relation to humans. They are enslaved and coerced for their labor. Plow agriculture generally involves a gender shift in agricultural production. While women monopolized food gathering and gardening, men monopolize food production done with plow animals. With this shift to men as agriculturalists comes a new sense of land as owned by the male family head, passed down through a male line of descent, rather than communal land-holding and matrilineal descent that is often found in hunting-gathering and gardening societies.

The conquest and enslavement of other tribal groups created another category of humans, beneath the familiar community, owned by it, whose labor is coerced. Enslavement of other people through military conquest typically took the form of killing the males and enslaving the women and their children for labor and sexual service. Women's work becomes identified with slave work. The women of the family are defined as a higher type slave over a lower category of slaves drawn from conquered people. In patriarchal law, possession of women, slaves, animals and land all are symbolically and socially linked together. All are species of property and instruments of labor, owned and controlled by male heads of family as a ruling class. Looking at the mythologies of the Ancient Near Eastern, Hebrew, and Greek and early Christian cultures, one can see a shifting symbolization of women and nature as spheres to be conquered, ruled over and, finally, repudiated altogether. In the Babylonian Creation story, which goes back to the third millennium B.C., Marduk, the warrior champion of the gods of the city states, is seen as creating the cosmos by conquering the Mother Goddess Tiamat, pictured as a monstrous female animal. Marduk kills her, treads her body under-foot and then splits it in half, using one half to fashion the starry firmament of the skies, and the other half the earth below.

The elemental mother is literally turned into the matter out of which the cosmos is fashioned (not accidentally, the words 'mother' and matter have the same etymological root). She can be used as matter only by being killed; that is, by destroying her as 'wild', autonomous life, making her life-giving body into 'stuff' possessed and controlled by the architect of a male-defined cosmos.

The Reformation and the Scientific Revolution

The Calvinist Reformation and the Scientific Revolution in England in the late 16th and 17th Centuries represent key turning points in the Western concept of nature. In these two movements the Medieval struggle between the sacramental and the demonic views of nature was recast. Calvinism dismembered the Medieval sacramental sense of nature. For Calvinism nature was totally depraved. There was no residue of divine presence in it that could sustain a natural knowledge or relation to God. Saving knowledge of God descends from on high, beyond nature, in the revealed Word available only in Scripture, as preached by the Reformers.

Populist Calvinism was notable for its iconoclastic hostility toward visual art. Stained glass, statues and carvings were smashed, and the churches stripped of all visible imagery. Only the disembodied word, descending from the preacher to the ear of the listener, together with music, could be bearers of divine presence. Nothing one could see, touch, taste or smell was trustworthy as bearer of the divine.

Even the bread and wine was no longer the physical embodiment of Christ, but intellectual reminders o f the message about Christ's salvific act enacted in the past. Calvinism dismantled the sacramental world of Medieval Christianity, but it maintained and reinforced its demonic universe. The fallen world, especially physical nature and other human groups outside of the control of the Calvinist church, lay in the grip of the Devil. All that was labeled pagan, whether Catholics or Indians and Africans, were the playground of demonic powers. But, even within the Calvinist church, women were the gateway of devil. If women were completely obedient to their fathers, husbands, ministers and magistrates, they might be redeemed as goodwives.

But in any independence of women lurked heresy and witchcraft. Among Protestants, Calvinists were the primary witch hunters. The Scientific Revolution at first moved in a different direction, exorcising the demonic powers from nature in order to reclaim it as an icon of divine reason manifest in natural law. But, in the 17th and 18th centuries, the more animist natural science that unified material and spiritual lost out to a strict dualism of transcendent intellect and dead matter. Nature was secularized. It was no longer the scene of a struggle between Christ and the Devil. Both divine and demonic spirits were driven out of it. In Cartesian dualism and Newtonian physics it becomes matter in motion, dead stuff moving obediently according to mathematical laws knowable to new male elite of scientists. With no life or soul of its own, nature could be safely expropriated by is the male elite and infinitely reconstructed to augment their wealth and power. In Western society the application of science to technological control over nature marched side by side with colonialism. From the 16th to the 20th centuries, Western Europeans would appropriate the lands of the Americas, Asia and Africa, and reduce its human populations to servitude. The wealth accrued by this vast expropriation of land and labor would fuel new levels of technological revolution, transforming material resources into new forms of energy and mechanical work, control of disease, increasing speed of communication and travel. Western elites grew increasingly optimistic, imagining that this technological way of life would gradually conquer all problems of material scarcity and even push back the limits of human mortality. The Christian dream of immortal blessedness, freed from finite limits, was translated into scientific technological terms.

Ecological Crisis

However, in short three-quarters of a century this dream of infinite progress has been turned into a nightmare. The medical conquest of disease, lessening infant mortality and doubling the lifespan of the affluent, insufficiently matched by birth limitation, especially among the poor, has created a population explosion that is rapidly outrunning the food supply. Every year ten million children die of malnutrition. The gap between rich and poor, between the wealthy elites of the industrialized sector and the impoverished masses, especially in the colonized continents of Latin America, Asia and Africa, grows ever wider. This Western scientific, industrial revolution has been built on injustice. It has been based on the takeover of the land, its agricultural, metallic and mineral wealth, appropriated through the exploitation of the labor of the indigenous people. This wealth has flowed back to enrich the West, with some for local elites, while the laboring people of these lands grew poorer. This system of global affluence, based on exploitation of the land and labor of the many for the benefit of the few, with its high consumption of energy and waste, cannot be expanded to include the poor without destroying the basis of life of the planet itself.

We are literally destroying the air, water and soil upon which human life and planetary life depends. In order to preserve the unjust monopoly on material resources from the growing protests of the poor, the world became more and more militarized. Most nations have been using the lion's share of their state budgets for weapons, both to guard against each other and to control their own poor. Weapons also become one of the major exports of wealthy nations to poor nations. Poor nations grow increasingly indebted to wealthy nations while buying weapons to repress their own impoverished masses. In spite of much toted arms reduction treaties between the United States and the Soviet Union, what is happening is more of a unipolar consolidation of military hegemony on the side of the United States, and not a real commitment to demilitarization. Population explosion, exhaustion of natural resources, pollution and state violence is the four horsemen of the new global apocalypse. The critical question of both justice and survival is how to pull back from this disastrous course and remake our relations with each other and with the earth.

Toward an Eco-feminist Ethic and Culture

There are many elements that need to go into an eco-feminist ethic and culture for a just and sustainable planet. One element is to reshape our dualistic concept of reality as split between soulless matter and transcendent male consciousness. We need to discover our actual reality as latecomers to the planet. The world of nature, plants and animals existed billions of years before we came on the scene. Nature does not need us to rule over it, but runs itself very well and better without humans. We are the parasites on the food chain of life, consuming more and more, and putting too little back to restore and maintain the life system that supports us.

We need to recognize our utter dependence on the great life-producing matrix of the planet in order to learn to reintegrate our human systems of production, consumption and waste into the ecological patterns by which nature sustains life. This might begin by revisualizing the relation of mind or human intelligence to nature. Mind or consciousness is not something that originates in some transcendent world outside of nature, but is the place where nature itself becomes conscious. We need to think of human consciousness, not as separating us as a higher species from the rest of nature, but rather as a gift to enable us to learn how to harmonize our needs with the natural system around us, of which we are a dependent part. Such a reintegration of human consciousness and nature must reshape the concept of God.

Instead of modeling God after alienated male consciousness, outside of and ruling over nature, God in eco-feminist spirituality is the immanent source of life that sustains the whole planetary community. God is neither male nor anthropomorphic. God is the font, from which the variety of plants and animals well up in each new generation, the matrix that sustains their life-giving interdependency with each other.

In eco-feminist culture and ethic mutual inter-dependency replaces the hierarchies of domination as the model of relationship between men and women, between human groups and between humans and other beings.

All racist, sexist, classist and anthropocentric assumptions of the superiority of whites over blacks, males over females, managers over workers, humans over animals and plants must be culturally discarded. In a real sense the so-called superior pole in each relation is actually the more dependent side of the relationship. But it is not enough simply to humbly acknowledge dependency. The pattern of male-female, racial and class inter-dependency itself has to be reconstructed socially, creating more equitable sharing in the work and the fruits of work, rather than making one side of the relation the subjugated and impoverished base for the power and wealth of the other. In terms of male-female relations this means, not simply allowing women more access to public culture, but converting males to an equal share in the tasks of child-nurture and household maintenance.

A revolution in female roles into the male work world, without a corresponding revolution in male roles, leaves the basic pattern of patriarchal exploitation of women untouched. Women are simply overworked in a new way, expected to do both a male work day, at low pay, and also the unpaid work of women that sustains family life. There must be a conversion of men to the work of women, along with the conversion of male consciousness to the earth. Such conversions will reshape the symbolic vision of salvation. Instead of salvation sought either in the disembodied soul or the immortalized body, in a flight to heaven or to the end of history, salvation should be seen as continual conversion to the center, to the concrete basis by which we sustain our relation to nature, and to one another. In every day and every new generation we need to remake our relation with each other, finding anew the true nexus of relationality that sustains, rather than exploits and destroys, life.

Finally eco-feminist culture must reshape our basic sense of self in relation to the life cycle. The sustaining of an organic community of plant and animal life is a continual cycle of growth and disintegration. The western flight from mortality is a flight from the disintegration side of the life cycle, from accepting ourselves as part of that process. By pretending that we can immortalize ourselves, souls and bodies, we are immortalizing our garbage and polluting the earth. In order to learn to recycle our garbage as fertilizer for new life, as matter for new artifacts, we need to accept our selfhood as participating in the same process.

Humans also are finite organisms, centers of experience in a life cycle that must disintegrate back into the nexus of life and arise again in new forms. These conversions from alienated, hierarchical dualism to life-sustaining mutuality will radically change the patterns of patriarchal culture. Basic concepts, such as God, soul/body and salvation, will be reconceived in ways that may bring us much closer to the ethical values of love, justice and care for the earth. These values have been proclaimed by patriarchal religion, yet contradicted by patriarchal symbolic and social patterns of relationship. But these tentative explorations of symbolic changes must be matched by a new social practice which can incarnate these conversions in new social and technological ways of organizing human life in relation to one other and to nature. This will require a new sense of urgency about the untenability of present patterns of life and compassionate solidarity with those who are its victims.

2

Deep Ecology and Eco-Feminism

Deep Ecology's Eco-Centric Egalitarianism

The question of the relative merits of deep ecology and Eco-feminism has recently received considerable attention, primarily from an eco-feminist perspective. This question has an obvious significance to anyone concerned with ecophilosophy and ecopolitics since it contrasts two of the most philosophically and socially influential approaches that have developed in response to ecological concerns. For deep ecologists in particular, the eco-feminist critique of deep ecology is of interest for at least two reasons in addition to the direct challenge that it presents to deep ecological theorizing. First, as I argue throughout this paper, the same criticism that can be made of simplistic forms of Eco-feminism can be applied with equal'force to critiques of deep ecology that proceed from simplistic versions of a broad range of social and political perspectives-the "parallels" of my title. Second, addressing the eco-feminist critique of deep ecology provides an opportunity to further elucidate the nature of deep ecology's concern with anthropocentrism.

Before examining the eco-feminist critique of deep ecology, which centers on deep ecology's negative or critical focus on anthropocentrism, it is important to outline deep ecology's positive or constructive focus. Deep ecology is concerned with encouraging an egalitarian attitude on the part of humans not only toward all members of the ecosphere, but even toward all identifiable entities or forms in the ecosphere. Thus, this attitude is intended to extend, for example, to such entities as rivers, landscapes, and even species and social systems considered in their own right.

If deep ecologists sometimes write as if they consider these entities to be living entities, they do so on the basts of an extremely broad sense of the term life-a sense as broad as that implied in such expressions as "Let the river live!" It is ultimately of little consequence to deep ecologists, however, whether one wishes to consider the kind of egalitarianism they advocate as one that extends only toward living entities or as one that extends toward both living and nonliving entities. Either way, the kind of egalitarian attitude they advocate is simply meant to indicate an attitude that, within obvious kinds of practical limits, allows all entities the freedom to unfold in their own way unhindered by the various forms of human domination. There are, of course, all sorts of problems involved in defining such things as how far these practical limits should extend or, in many cases, even where one entity ends and another begins. But, against this, it must be remembered that deep ecologists are not intending to advocate a specific set of guidelines for action; they are only intending to advocate a general orientation. Deep ecologists not only accept but welcome cultural diversity when it comes to effecting the fics of this general orientation.

As Arne Naess puts it, where we draw the limit between justifiable and unjustifiable interference with respect to this general orientation "is a question that must be related to local, regional, and national particularities. Even then a certain area of disagreement must be taken as normal." For deep ecologists, the only overriding consideration is that such limits should always be worked out in the light of the general orientation they advocate. Naess captures the sense of this general orientation while also conveying a sense of the cultural diversity it allows for: "A rich variety of acceptable motives can be formulated for being more reluctant to injure or kill a living being of kind A than a being of kind B. The cultural setting is different for each being in each culture." It is this general attitude of being reluctant, prima facie, to interfere with the unfolding of A or B indeed, to desire that both should flourish-that characterizes the general orientation that is advocated by deep ecologists.

Deep ecologists have generally referred to this general orientation or attitude as one of "biospherical egalitarianism" or, more often (in order to suggest the intended comparison with an anthropocentric perspective more directly), "biocentric egalitarianism." However, because the prefix bio refers, etymologically, to life or living organisms, it has sometimes been assumed that deep ecology's concerns are restricted to entities that are biologically alive. To correct this impression, Arne Naess and George Sessions have, in line with my preceding remarks, often pointed out that their sense of the term life is so broad, that it takes in "Individuals, species, populations, habitat, as well as human and non-human cultures."' To avoid the possibility of confusion, however, I prefer to describe the kind of egalitarian attitude subscribed to by deep ecologists as Eco-Centric rather than bio centric. While there seems to be little reason for choosing between these terms on the basis of their ecological connotations, there are other grounds for preferring the term Eco-Centric to describe the kind of egalitarianism advocated by deep ecologists. First, the term eco-centric, which etymologically means oikos-, home, or, by implication, Earth-centered, is more immediately informative than the term bio-centric, which etymologically means life-centered and so requires an appended explanation of the broad sense in which the term life should be understood. Second, the term Eco-Centric seems closer to the spirit of deep ecology than the term bio centric, because, notwithstanding their broad usage of the term life, the motivation of deep ecologists depends more upon a profound sense that the Earth or ecosphere is home than it does upon a sense that the Earth or ecosphere is necessarily alive (you don't have to subscribe to some ecological form of hylozoism to be a supporter of deep ecology).

In accordance with this extremely broad, Eco-Centric egalitarianism, supporters of deep ecology hold that their concerns well and truly subsume the concerns of those movements that have restricted their focus to the attainment of a more egalitarian human society. Deep ecologists, in other words, consider their concerns to subsume the egalitarian concerns associated, for example, with feminism, Marxism, antiracism, and anti imperialism.' In the eyes of deep ecologists, the emergence of a distinct Eco-feminism, a distinct "green" socialism, and so on, are-at least in their best forms-attempts by feminists, Marxists-cum-socialists, and so on, to redress the human-centeredness of their respective perspectives. Needless to say, deep ecologists welcome these developments and they recognize that Eco-feminism, green socialism, and so on have their own distinctive theoretical flavors and emphases because of the different theoretical histories that inform them. Nevertheless, they see no essential disagreement between deep ecology and these perspectives, providing that the latter are genuinely able to overcome their anthropocentric legacies.

The Eco-Feminist Critique of Deep Ecology

With respect to Eco-feminism and deep ecology in particular, many observers agree that the two perspectives have much in common-notwithstanding their different theoretical histories. However, some eco-feminist writers have begun to perceive a significant tension between their perspective and that of deep ecology. In an evenhanded examination of eco-feminist criticisms of deep ecology, Michael Zimmerman has presented what is probably the clearest formulation of what I take to be the essential eco-feminist charge against deep ecology: "Feminist critics of deep ecology assert that deep ecology speaks of a genderneutral 'anthropocentrism' i.e., human-centeredness as the root of the domination of nature, when in fact androcentrism i.e., male-centeredness is the real root.

There seems to be wide support for the view that this represents the essential eco-feminist criticism of deep ecology. For example, one of the main criticism made by Janet Biehl in her critique of deep ecology is that, "For eco-feminists the concept of anthropocentrism is profoundly, even "deeply" problematical.... By not excluding women from anthropocentrism, deep ecologists implicitly condemn women for being as anthropocentric as they condemn men for being-that is, for presuming to be above nature, for mastering it." Marti Kheel also notes at the outset of her critique of deep ecology that deep ecologists are concerned to "challenge the anthropocentric worldview whereas for eco-feminists "it is the androcentric worldview that is the focal point of the needed shift." Likewise, the first difference in emphasis that Charlene Spretnak refers to in her comparison of deep ecology and Eco-feminism is that of anthropocentrism versus androcentrism. Jim Cheney has claimed, nevertheless, in response to an earlier version of this paper, that it is wrong to regard Zimmerman's formulation as representing the essential eco-feminist charge against deep ecology. For Cheney, "The essential' [eco-feminist] charge is not that deep ecologists focus on anthropocentrism whereas the problem is really with androcentrism; rather, the central concern is that deep ecology is in some sense androcentric."

In comparison to what to be the essential eco-feminist charge against deep ecology, Cheney's formulation of the essential eco-feminist charge seems to represent a significant concession to deep ecology, since it suggests that eco-feminists are not overly concerned about deep ecologists' critical focus on anthropocentrism so long as deep ecologists do not formulate their critique of anthropocentrism in a way that is "itself in some sense androcentric." But whether Cheney's formulation represents a significant concession to deep ecology or not, my response to his charge is simple. The charge that I propose to address is clear-cut and serious ecologists cannot deny that their negative focus is concerned, first and foremost, with anthropocentrism and eco-feminists cannot deny that their negative focus is concerned, first and foremost, with androcentrism. In contrast, the best that can be said about Cheney's claim that deep ecology is androcentric in its very formulation is that such a claim is entirely contentious.' Cheney's own recent attempt in Environmental Ethics to establish this claim is essentially based upon a misinterpretation of deep ecology as resting upon a "rights-based foundation."

More recently, Cheney has abandoned his previous view of deep ecology and accepted that deep ecologists are primarily concerned with the development of a state of being of wider identification and, hence, with the realization of a more expansive Self. This understanding of deep ecology appears to have much in common with Cheney's characterization of Eco-feminism as being concerned with an ethics of love, care, and friendship as opposed to a theory of rights, justice, and obligation.' However, Cheney argues instead that the deep ecological emphasis on the realization of a more expansive Self is a "totalizing view" that represents "the desperate endgame of masculine alienation from nature." What Cheney means by his highly abstract and potentially obfuscating reference to a "totalizing view" is that deep ecologists identify with particulars only in the derivative sense that the logos of the cosmos threads its way through the cosmos, binds it together as a totality, a cosmos. Identification, for the deep ecologist, does not involve seeing or hearing the other or seeing oneself in the other, but rather involves seeing the other sub specie aeternita.

What Cheney seems to object to in deep ecology, then, is not the emphasis identification per se but rather the fact that deep ecologists emphasize identification within a cosmological context-that is, within the context of anti awareness that all entities in the universe are part of a single, unfolding process. There is, however, a fundamental problem with arguing, as Cheney seems to want to, for a purely personal basis for identification. Specifically, emphasizing a purely personal basis for identification that "leaves selves intact"-necessarily implies an emphasis upon identification with entities with which one has considerable personal contact. In practice, this tends to mean that one identifies with my self first, my family next, my friends and more distant relations next, my ethnic grouping next, my species next, and so on-more or less what the sociobiologists say we are genetically predisposed to do.

The problem with this is that, while extending love, care, and friendship to one's nearest and dearest is laudable in and of itself, the other side of the coin, emphasizing a purely personal basis for identification, looks more like the cause of possessiveness, war, and ecological destruction than the solution to these seemingly intractable problems. In contrast, to argue for a cosmological basis for identification is to attempt to convey a lived sense that all entities are relatively autonomous modes of a single, unfolding process, that all entities are leaves on the tree of life. A lived sense of this understanding means that we strive, insofar as it is within our power to do so, not to identify ourselves exclusively with our leaf, our twig, our minor subbranch, our major subbranch, our branch, and so on, but rather to identify ourselves with the tree. This necessarily leads, at the limit, to impartial identification with all particulars.

This distinction between personally based identification and cosmologically based identification certainly represents a difference in theoretical stance between Cheney's conception of Eco-feminism on the one hand and deep ecology on the other. But whether this difference also reflects a basic difference between feminine and masculine modes of approaching the world is a separate issue. On my reading of the literature, I do not see how anyone can why they would want to deny that many women are vitally interested in cultivating a cosmological/transpersonal based sense of identification.The cosmological transpersonal voice is a "different voice" from the personal voice, but it does not seem to respect gender boundaries. Moreover, as the above discussion suggests, whatever one's view of the relationship or lack of relationship between these approaches and gender, a personally based approach to identification is vulnerable to criticism from an Eco-Centric perspective in a way in which a cosmological/ trails personal approach is not. Because this brief examination of Cheney's critique of deep ecology suggests that there are major weaknesses with his claim that the essential eco-feminist charge against deep ecology is actually "that deep ecology is it's, in some sense andocentric," in what follows, therefore, consider the essential eco-feminist charge against deep ecology to be the far more clear-cut and potentially far more serious charge that deep ecology "speaks of a gender-neutral 'anthropocentrism' as the root of the domination of nature, when in fact andocentric is the real root.

Problems with the Eco-Feminist and Other Critiques

Having established the nature of the eco-feminist charge that I am concerned to address in what follows, it is important to note that this charge is not directed at deep ecology's positive or constructive task of encouraging an egalitarian attitude on the part of humans toward all entities in the ecosphere, but rather at deep ecology's negative or critical task of dismantling anthropocentrism. This distinction often seems to be overlooked by eco-feminist critics of deep ecology, who, presumably, are in general agreement with the constructive task of deep ecology. But with respect to the critical task of these two perspectives, the fact remains that in the absence of a good answer to the eco-feminist charge, there is no reason than intellectual blindness or outright chauvinism in regard to issues concerning gender-why deep ecologists should not make androcentrism the focus of their critique rather than anthropocentrism. In addressing this challenge to the critical focus of deep ecology, I first make some general remarks about a certain style of social and political theorizing and then proceed to the essential deep ecological response to this eco-feminist charge. To begin with, deep ecologists completely agree with eco-feminists that men have been far more implicated in the history of ecological destruction than women. However, deep ecologists also agree with similar charges derived from other social perspectives: for example, that capitalists, whites, and Westerners have been far more implicated in the history of ecological destruction than pre-capitalist peoples, blacks, and non-Westerners.

If eco-feminists also agree with these points, then the question arises as to why they do not also criticize deep ecology for being neutral with respect to issues concerning such significant social variables as socioeconomic class, race, and

Westernization. There appears to be two reasons for this. First, to do so would detract from the priority that econfeminists wish to give to their own concern with androcentrism. Second, and more significantly, these charges could also be applied with equal force to the eco-feminist focus on androcentrism itself. How does one defend the eco-feminist charge against deep ecology (i.e., that androcentrism is "the real root" of ecological destruction) in the face of these charges? For deep ecologists, it is simplistic on both empirical and logical grounds to think that one particular perspective on human society identifies the real root of ecological destruction. Empirically, such thinking is simplistic because it fails to give due consideration to the multitude of interacting factors at work in any given situation. (While on a practical level it can be perfectly reasonable to devote most of one's energy to one particular cause-if only for straightforward reasons to do with time and energy-that, of course, is no excuse for simplistic social theorizing.) Such thinking falls, in other words, to adopt an ecological perspective with respect to the workings of human society itself.

Logically, such thinking is simplistic because it implies that the solution to our ecological problems is close at hand-all we have to do is remove "the real root" of the problem-when it is actually perfectly possible to conceive of a society that is nonandrocentric, socioeconomically egalitarian, nonracist, and nonimperialistic with respect to other human societies, but whose members nevertheless remain aggressively anthropocentric in collectively agreeing to exploit their environment for their collective benefit in ways that nonanthropocentrists would find thoroughly objectionable. Indeed, the "green" critique of socialism proceeds from precisely this recognition that a socially egalitarian society does not necessarily imply an ecologically benign society. An interesting example of the failure to recognize this point is provided by Murray Bookchin's anarcho-socialist inspired "social ecology" (I describe this approach as "anarcho-socialist" in inspiration because it advocates decentralism and cooperativeness and stands opposed to all forms of hierarchy).

Bookchin is interesting in this context because, on the one hand, he correctly observes in the course of a highly polemical attack upon deep ecology that it is possible for a relatively ecologically benign human society also to be extremely oppressive internally, and yet, on the other hand, he fails to see that the reverse can also apply-that it is possible for a relatively egalitarian human society to be extremely exploitative ecologically.

For Bookchin, to accept this latter point would be to argue against the basis of his own social ecology, since in his view a nonhierarchical, decentralist, and cooperative society is "a society that will live in harmony with nature because its members live in harmony with each other. Bookchin's presentation of social ecology thus conveys no real appreciation of the fact that the relationships between the internal organization of human societies and their treatment of the non-human world can be as many and varied as the outcomes of any other evolutionary process.

One may certainly speak in terms of certain forms of human social organization being more conducive to certain kinds of relationships with the non-human world than others. Bookchin, however, insists far too much that there is a straightforward, necessary relationship between the internal organization of human societies and their treatment of the non-human world. To this extent, his social ecology is constructed upon a logically facile basis. Moreover, it serves to reinforce anthropocentrism, since the assumption that the internal organization of human societies determines their treatment of the non-human world carries with it the implication that we need only concentrate on interhuman egalitarian concerns for all to become ecologically well with the world-a point I take up again later.

In doing violence to the complexities of social interaction, simplistic social and political analyses of ecological destruction are not merely descriptively poor and logically facile, they are also morally objectionable on two grounds, scapegoating and inauthenticity. Scapegoating can be thought of in terms of overinclusiveness. Simplistic analyses target all men, all capitalists, all whites, and all Westerners, for example, to an equal degree when in fact certain subble for ecological declasses of these Identified classes are far more response struction than others. Not only that but significant minorities of these classes can be actively engaged in opposing the interests of both the dominant culturable for ecological of their class and those members of their class most response destruction. Inauthenticity, on the other hand, can be thought of terms of underinclusiveness.

Simplistic analyses are inauthentic in that they lead to a complete denial of responsibility when at least partial responsibility for ecological destruction should be accepted. Such theorizing conveniently disguises the extent to which the simplistically identified oppressed group also benefits from, and colludes with, those most responsible for ecological destruction (e.g., consider the case of animal destruction for furs and cosmetics consumed by Western and Westernized women, or the case of capitalists and unionists united in opposition to the antidevelopment stance of "greenies"). It can, of course, be argued in response that the hegemony of androcentrism or capitalism, for example, is such that women or unionists effective.

But this surely overplays the role of social determination and to that extent only serves to highlight the charge of inauthenticity. Moreover, attempting to escape the charge of inauthenticity in this way directly contradicts the view of feminists or Marxists, to continue with the same examples, that women or the working class are capable of self-conscious direction of being a class for themselves, a revolutionary class. Yet another kind of objection to simplistic analyses of the kind to which I have been referring is that while claiming to be "ecological" or "green," some of these critics in fact remain anthropocentric-albeit in the passive sense of serving to legitimize our continued preoccupation with interhuman affairs rather than in the aggressive sense of overtly discriminating against the non-human world. Advocates of these approaches say in essence: "Since the real root of our problems is androcentrism or capitalism, for example, we mustfirst get our interactions between humans right (with respect to gender issues, with respect to the redistribution of wealth, and so on) and then everything else will fall into place." Any form of direct concern with the question of the relationship between humans and the non-human world is thus trumped by concerns about the resolution of specific interhuman problems.

The non-human world retains its traditional status as the background against which the significant action-human action-takes place. Not surprisingly, deep ecologists find it particularly frustrating to witness representatives of simplistic social and political perspectives waving the banner of ecology while in fact continuing to promote, whether wittingly or unwittingly, the interhuman and, hence, human-centered agenda of their respective theoretical legacies. I have already commented on Bookchin's social ecology in regard to this point. Some eco-feminist writing is also relevant here. For example, the focus of Ariel Kay Salleh's critique of deep ecology is thoroughly interhuman. "To make a better world," she concludes, men have to be "brave enough to rediscover and to love the woman inside themselves," while women simply have to "be allowed to love what we are. This conclusion follows from the fact that, in Salleh's version of feminism, women already "flow with the system of nature" by virtue of their essential nature." Karen Warren and Michael Zimmerman have referred to this kind of approach to Eco-feminism, according to which women are supposed to be "closer to nature" than men by virtue of their essential nature, as "radical feminism" (in contrast to liberal, traditional Marxist, and socialist feminism) and "essentialist feminism" respectively. Warren correctly notes that "Radical feminists have had the most to say about eco-feminism," and both she and Zimmerman have made telling criticisms of this approach. All I am drawing attention to here is the fact that this kind of "radical" approach simply serves to legitimize and, hence, to perpetuate our entirely traditional preoccupation with interhuman affairs.

In accordance with the approach adopted by essentialist feminists, there is no need to give any serious consideration whatsoever to the possibility that women might, for example, discriminate against men, accumulate rather than distribute private wealth, be racist, support imperialism, or be ecologically destructive if the conditions of their historical subjugation were undone and the possibility of exercising genuine social and political power were available to them. The upshot is that there is no need to worry about any form of human domination other than that of androcentrism. For deep ecologists, it's just another variation on the same old song-the song that reassures us that all will become ecologically well with the world if we just put this or that interhuman concern first. I have objected to simplistic social and political analyses on the grounds that they are descriptively poor and logically facile, that they lend themselves to scapegoating on the one hand and are inauthentic on the other, and that even in their ecological guises, they are passively anthropocentric. Many who align themselves with the perspectives to which I have referred might well personally agree with the points I have made so far and consider that in virtue of this agreement, these objections do not really apply to their perspective. Thus, this kind of reaction can be quite common in the face of the sorts of objections I have made: "How could anyone be so stupid as to think that we eco-feminists are not also concerned about issues concerning socioeconomic class, race, and imperialism?"

The problem is, however, that there is often a large gap between the alleged and often genuine personal concerns of members of a social and political movement and the theoretical articulation of the perspective that informs their movement. The fact that individual members of a social and political movement agree with the points I have made provides no guarantee whatsoever that the theoretical articulation of the perspective that informs their movement does not itself fall foul of these objections-and it is with this theoretical articulation that I have been concerned. By way of qualification, however, I do not in any way wish to assert that any of the objections I have made are necessarily fatal to the theoretical prospects of the social and political perspectives to which I have'referred, since it is possible, at least in principle, for each of these perspectives to be revised or, at a minimum, suitably qualified so as not to fall foul of these objections.

But, that said, one must nevertheless be careful not to underestimate the significance of these objections, since presentations of the social and political perspectives to which I have referred continue to fall foul of them on an all too regular basis. Variations on some of the objections I have outlined would apply just as much to deep ecology if it were the case that deep ecologists were simply saying that humans as a whole have been far more implicated in the history of ecological destruction than non-humans. (The eco-feminist charge against deep ecology implies that deep ecologists are saying precisely this: in turns on the contention that deep ecologists have been overinclusive in criticizing humanity in general for the destruction of the non-human world when the target of their critical attack should properly be the class of men and, of course, masculine culture in general.) However, this is not the essential point that deep ecologists are making, and it is here that we enter into the essential response by deep ecologists to the essential criticism made of their perspective by eco-feminists.

The Essential Deep Ecological Response to the Eco-Feminist Critique

The target of the deep ecologists' critique is not humans per se but rather human-centeredness." It is not just eco-feminist critics who miss this point. Some other critics also miss it in an even bigger way by attacking deep ecologists not simply on the grounds that they criticize humanity in general for its ecological destructiveness, but rather on the grounds that deep ecologists are actually opposed to humanity in general-that is, that they are essentially misanthropic. According to Murray Bookchin, for example, in deep ecology "'Humanity' is essentially seen as an ugly 'anthropocentric' thing-presumably, a malignant product of natural evolution. Henryk Skolimowski also suggests that deep ecologists are misanthropic. "I find it rather morbid," he writes in The Trumpeter, "when some human beings think that the human lot is the bottom of the pit. There is something pathological in the contention that humans are a cancer among the species. This kind of thinking is not sane and it does not promote the sense of wholeness which we need nowadays." In line with my remarks here, Alan Drengson, The Trumpeter's editor and a prominent deep ecology philosopher, intervenes immediately at this point by adding parenthetically: "And it is certainly not the thinking of deep ecologists."

The extent to which people in general are ready to equate opposition to human-centeredness with opposition to humans per se can be viewed as a function of the dominance of the anthropocentric frame of reference in our society. Just as those who criticize capitalism, for example, are often labeled as "Communists" and, by implication, "the enemy," when, in reality, they may be concerned with such things as a more equitable distribution of wealth in society, so those who criticize anthropocentrism are liable to be labeled as misanthropists when, in reality, they may be concerned with encouraging a more egalitarian attitude on the part of humans toward all entities in the ecosphere. In failing to notice the fact that being opposed to humans-centeredness is logically distinct from being opposed to humans per se (or, in other words, that being opposed to anthropocentrism is logically distinct from being misanthropic), and in equating the former with the latter, Bookchin and Skollmowski commit what I refer to as the fallacy of misplaced misanthropy. Committing this fallacy in the context of criticizing deep ecology involves not just a crucial misreading of deep ecology's critical task, but also the oversight of two other considerations that contradict such a misreading.

The first is that deep ecology's constructive task is to encourage an egalitarian attitude on the part of humans toward all entities in the ecosphere-including humans. The second is that deep ecologists are among the first to highlight and draw inspiration from the fact that not all humans have been human-centered either within the Western tradition or outside it. Far from being misanthropic, deep ecologists celebrate the existence of these human beings.

In making human-centeredness the target of their critique, deep ecologists have contended that the assumption of human self-importance in the larger scheme of things has, to all intents and purposes, been the single deepest and most persistent assumption of all the dominant Western philosophical, social, and political traditions since the time of the classical Greeks-notwithstanding the fact that the dominant classes representing these traditions have typically adjudged themselves more human than others-and that, for a variety of reasons, this assumption is unwarranted and should be abandoned in favor of an Eco-Centric outlook. ' Thus, what deep ecologists are drawing critical attention to is the fact that whatever class of social actors one identifies as having been most responsible for social domination and ecological destruction, one tends at the most fundamental level to find a common kind of legitimation for the alleged superiority of these classes over others and, hence, for the assumed rightfulness of their domination of these others. Specifically, these classes of social actors have not sought to legitimate their position on the grounds that they are, for example, men, capitalists, white, or Western per se, but rather on the grounds that they have most exemplified whatever it is that has been taken to constitute the essence of humanness. These classes of social actors have, in other words, habitually assumed themselves to be somehow more fully human than others, such as women, the "lower" classes, blacks, and non-Westerners. The cultural spell of anthropocentrism has been considered sufficient to Justify not only moral superiority (which, in itself, might be construed as carrying with it an obligation to help rather than dominate those who are less blessed), but also all kinds of domination within human society-let alone domination of the obviously non-human world.

That anthropocentrism has served as the most fundamental kind of legitimatron employed by whatever powerful class of social actors one wishes to focus on can also be seen by considering the fundamental kind of legitimation that has habitually been employed with regard to large-scale or high-cost social enterprises such as war, scientific and technological development, or environmental exploitation. Such enterprises have habitually been undertaken not simply in the name of men, capitalists, whites, or Westerners, for example, but rather in the name of God (and thus our essential humanity-or our anthropocentric projection upon the cosmos, depending upon one's perspective) or simply in the name of humanity in general. (This applies notwithstanding the often sexist expression of these sentiments in terms of "man," mankind," and so on, and notwithstanding the fact that certain classes of social actors benefit disproportionately from these enterprises.) Thus, to take some favorite examples, Francis Bacon and Descartes ushered in the development of modern science by promising, respectively, that it would lead to "enlarging the bounds of Human Empire" and that it would render humanity the "masters and possessors of nature."

Approximately three and a half centuries later, Nell Armstrong's moon walk-the culmination of a massive, politically directed, scientific and technological development effort-epitomized both the literal acting out of this vision of "enlarging the bounds of Human Empire" and the literal expression of its anthropocentric spirit: Armstrong's moon walk was, in his own words at the time, a "small step" for him, but a giant leap for mankind."

Here on Earth, not only do examples abound of environmental exploitation being undertaken in the name of humanity, but this also constitutes the fundamental kind of legitimation that is still most often employed for environmental conservation and preservation-it is implicit in every argument for the conservation or preservation of the non-human world on account of its use value to humans rather than for its own sake or its use value to non-human beings. The cultural pervasiveness of anthropocentrism in general and anthropocentric legitimations in particular are further illustrated when one turns to consider those social movements that have opposed the dominant classes of social actors to which I have been referring. With respect to the pervasiveness of anthropocentrism in general, it can be seen that those countermovements that have been most concerned with exposing discriminatory assumptions and undoing their effects have typically confined their interests to the human realm (i.e., to such issues as imperalism, race, socioeconomic class, and gender). With respect to the pervasiveness of anthropocentric legitimations in particular, it can equally be seen that these countermovements have not sought to legitimate their own claims on the basis that they are, for example, women, workers, black, or non-Western per se, but rather on the grounds that they too have exemplified-at least equally with those to whom they have been opposedeither whatever it is that has been taken to constitute the essence of humanness or else some redefined essence of humanness.

While it would, in any case, be contrary to the egalitarian concerns of these countermovements to seek to legitimate their own claims by the former kind of approach (i.e., on the basis that they are, for example, women, workers, black, or non-Western per se), the pity is that these countermovements have not been egalitarian enough. Rather than attempting to replace the ideology of anthropocentrism with some broader, eco centrically inclined perspective, these countermovements have only served to reinforce it. It should be clear from this brief survey that the history of anthropocentrism takes in not only the assumption of the centrality and superiority of humans in general, but also the various claims and counterclaims that various classes of humans have made with regard to the exemplification of whatever attributes have been considered to be quintessentially human. Deep ecologists recognize that the actual historical reasons for the domination of one class by another (and here I also refer to the domination that humans as a class now exert over the non-human world) cannot be identified in any simplistic manner; they can be as complex as any ecological web or the evolutionary path of any organism. However, deep ecologists also recognize that claims to some form of human exclusiveness have tyically been employed to legitimate the bringing about and perpetuation of historical and evolutionary outcomes involving unwarranted domination. In consequence, deep ecologists have been attempting to get people to see that historical and evolutionary outcomes simply represent "the way things happen to have turned out"-nothing more-and that self-serving anthropocentric legitimations for these outcomes are just that.

What the eco-feminist criticism of deep ecology's focus on anthropocentrism overlooks, then, is the fact that deep ecologists are not primarily concerned with exposing the classes of some actors historically most responsible for social domination and ecological destruction, but rather with the task of sweeping the rug out from under the feet of these classes of social actors by exposing the most fundamental kind of legiti'mati'on that they have habitually employed in identifying their position. (This distinction between a concern with classes of just social actors on the one hand and the most fundamental kind of legitiryiation they employ on the other hand should be apparent from the fact that deep ecology has been elaborated within a philosophical context rather than a sociological or political context-which is not to suggest that deep ecology does not have profound social and political implications.) Of course, eco-feminists, green socialists, and so on are also concerned with questions of legitimation, but they are generally concerned with these questions in a different sense than dee ecologists are concerned with them. The primary emphasis of eco-feminists, green socialists, and the other social and political analysts to whom I have referred is on the distribution of power in society and the ways in which that distribution is reinforced and reproduced. In this context, references to legitmation tend not to be to the "bottom line" rationale employed by these powerful classes (i.e., to legitimation in the fundamental or philosophical sense), but rather to the ways in which existing power structures utilize their sources of power to back up existing states of affairs (from overtly physical forms of power such as the police and the military to less tangible forms such as economic power and the manipulation of social status). To the extent that eco-feminists, green socialists, and so on are concerned to expose the fundamental, philosophical legitimation employed by the classes of social actors whose unwarranted degree of power is the focus of their critique, and to the extent that this concern extends out into a genuinely Eco-Centric perspective, it becomes difficult to see any significant difference between what they call Eco-feminism, green socialism, and so on and what others call deep ecology (such differences as remain are simply differences of theoretical flavor and emphasis rather than differences of substance).

Deep ecologists want to unmask the ideology of anthropocentrism so that it can no longer be used as the "bottom line" legitimation for social domination and ecological destruction by any class of social actors (men, capitalists, whites, Westerners, humans generally or even essentialist feminists!)." Thus, those who align themselves with certain perspectives on the distribution of power in human society misunderstand the essential nature of deep ecology if they see it in terms of their perspective versus deep ecology (e.g., in the case of Eco-feminism and deep ecology, androcentrism versus anthropocentrism or if they criticize deep " Rather, just as deep ecology on the basis that it has "no analysis of power. I ecologists have learned and incorporated much from, and should be open to, a range of perspectives on the distribution of power in human society, so those who align themselves with these social and political perspectives can learn and incorporate much from, 'and should be open to, the deep ecologists' critique of the most fundamental kind of legitimation that has habitually been employed by those most responsible for social domination and ecological destruction.

3

Eco-Feminism, Deep Ecology and Human Population

Introduction

A growing number of environmental activists, concerned academics, and writers are identifying their work as 'radical ecology,' or 'radical environmentalism." Utilizing the political distinction between liberal reformism and political revolution, radical ecologists eschew reformist solutions to environmental problems in favor of a revolutionary change in the way humans conceive and interact with environments (including non-human individuals, other species, and ecosystemic communities). A certain school of radical ecological thought, Deep Ecology, has become very popular in Europe and the United States, especially among white, middle-class, male environmental activists and academics.

Eco-feminism, a radical environmentalism which incorporates both ecological and feminist concems, emerged from the global feminist movement of the early 1970s. Its proponents emphasize the many finks among the oppression of women, the degradation of the environment, and other forms of oppression and domination. Ariel Kay Salleh's 1984 article "Deeper than Deep Ecology: the eco-feminist connection" offered an early eco-feminist critique of Deep Ecology. Safleh argued that Eco-feminism offers a depth of analysis and understanding that is lacking in Deep Ecology.

Although I do not agree with her descriptions there of 'women's consciousness' as foundational to ecological feminism, Salleh's recent piece 'The Deep Ecology/Eco-feminism debate,' evidences both a strengthening of her arguments against Deep Ecology and a shift from her earlier focus on a universalist conception of women's consciousness. My analysis here supports her conclusion that Eco-feminism provides a normative and critical environmental theory that is superior to Deep Ecology. Utilizing Deep Ecologist Ame Naess's own definition of 'depth,' I locate the 'depth' of Eco-feminism in the complexity of its considerations of environmental issues and problems. I begin by illustrating the strength and depth of Eco-feminism through a comparison of the approaches of Deep Ecology and Eco-feminism to the issue of human population. By doing so, I hope to fill out gaps in the Eco-feminism/Deep Ecology debate with an example of concrete differences between these approaches to global environmental issues.

Through this illustration, I also hope to defend Eco-feminism against Warwick Fox's claim that Eco-feminism is a shallow environmental theory. Although some of Fox's critique is based on readings of several eco-feminist authors against whom I argue elsewhere, aim to show that even his arguments against those authors are misdirected. There are various interpretations of "Eco-feminism.' Here I take an Eco-feminism' to be the position that environmental and feminist issues are intrinsically linked, and that environmental and feminist philosophies should acknowledge and address these connections. Central to my argument is the contention that Fox, and those who put forth similar arguments, confuse the legitimate eco-feminist analyses of human interactions with each other with anthropocentrism, a concept which Deep Ecologists and other radical environmentalists use to refer to human-centered thinking, or human chauvinism. My main conclusion, echoing Salleh, is that according to Deep Ecologists' own definitions of 'deep' ecological theory, Eco-feminism is actually "deeper than deep ecology'. In sum, I argue that eco-feminist consideration of the size of human population is superior to Deep Ecologists' precisely due to the complexity of eco-feminist analysis of such issues, and hence that Eco-feminism does not offer a simple analysis of ecological and social problems.

Defining deep ecology

I would like to distinguish deep ecology from Deep Ecology, although I shall be considering both here. One term, which I will represent in small-case letters, refers to a general category a type of ecological theory. The term that I will represent in capital letters refers to a particular example of such theory. Both terms were introduced by Norwegian philosopher Ame Naess in his 1973 article 'The shallow and the deep, long-range ecology movement." There he distinguishes deep ecologies from shallow ecologies and sketches out Deep Ecology, an example of an ecological philosophy based on a theory of bio centric, or life-centered, equality. According to Naess, shallow ecology is typified by movements which fight exclusively against pollution and resource depletion. The central objective of shallow movements is to promote 'the health and affluence of people in the developed countries." Movements and theories are considered 'deep" in terms of the 'distance they look in search of roots of a problem, and in refusing to ignore troubling evidence".

At the core of Naess's view is the belief that arbitrarily restricting moral consideration to humans is an example of anthropocentrism, or thinking which is unjustifiably human centered. In sum, deep theories consider the long-range dimensions of ecological problems and solutions, are not anthropocentric, are not reformist, question anthropocentric thinking at its deepest levels, and recommend fundamental change in human attitudes toward the non-human members of the global biota. Although there may be many examples of deep ecologies (some would characterize the Greens, eco-feminists, social ecologists, and bioregionalists as "believers"), in his more extensive works Naess articulates in great detail a particular philosophy which he and later advocates identify as Deep Ecology. So, as radical ecologist Steve Chase writes, the term deep ecology can therefore be seen as one that does double duty, referring on the one hand to a whole class of approaches and on the other hand to a particular kind of approach within this class... a distinctive kind of approach to nonanthropocentrism.

Naess and others have theorized on the meanings of both deep ecology and Deep Ecology. Deep Ecology is an earth or ecocentrism which entails a "deep yes to nature, and thinking of the landscape first". Its biospherical egalitarianism acknowledges the existence in all "ways and forms of life' of an equal right to live and blossom." In Ecology, Community and Lifestyle, Naess puts forth an eight-point platform of Deep Ecology. The writings of Ame Naess have inspired many philosophers and activists to implement and expand this platform. Probably some of the best known advocates of Deep Ecology in the United States are the members of Earth First!, the 'self-proclaimed 'action wing of the Deep Ecology movement". In the 1980s Earth First! gained notoriety throughout the United States for its implementation of militant activism and 'monkeywrenching" techniques in defense of the wilderness. Media attention to their activities, as well as the ever-growing body of work that has been published by Deep Ecologists, has made Deep Ecology one of the more popular activist movements in the United States since the 1960s. A favorite issue among Deep Ecologists, the "population problem," is often cast by them as a central causal factor in the destruction of the biosphere and wilderness areas in particular.

The relevance of the size of human population in the consideration of global environmental destruction and species depletion cannot be denied by environmentalists. However, I believe the positions of leading Deep Ecologists on the human overpopulation issue provide a stunning example of Deep Ecology's failure to probe deeply into the causes and factors creating environmental problems. Here I will lay out and criticize some Deep Ecological views on human population and use them as a point of contrast from which to consider eco-feminist alternatives.

Deep ecology on human population

Part of Naess's eight-point Deep Ecology platform is a commitment to reduced human population. His fifth principle states, 'The flourishing of human life and cultures is compatible with a substantial decrease of the human population. The flourishing of non-human life requires such a decrease". Elsewhere he asserts that, 'it is recognized that excessive pressures on planetary life stem from the human population explosion'. Naess's principle rests on the belief that human population must be reduced because of the limitations of the Earth's 'carrying capacity.' He has the following to say about a United Nations study of optimal human population, which asks:

"Given the present world-wide industrial and agricultural capacity, technological development, and resource exploitation, how many people could be supported on earth today with the standard of living of the average American? The answer is just 500 million." Agreed, but the question raised refers only to humans. How about the other living beings? If their life quality is not to be lowered through human dominance, for instance agriculture, are not 500 million too many? Or are cultural diversity, development of the sciences and the arts, and of course the basic needs of humans not served by, let us say, 100 million?... Some brush the question away as 'academic," "utopian." They immediately think of the difficulties of reduaion in a humane way [emphasis mine].

Naess is dissatisfied with the study's anthropocentric focus on human well-being and neglect of other living beings, and hence rejects its numerical recommendations. Furthermore, he finds fault with those who dismiss the question because they think it unrealistic and because they think humanely. From a Deep Ecological perspective, thinking humanely is problematic insofar as doing so is human centered. Of course, if humaneness is merely kindness and compassion, it is not anthropocentric to reflect or act humanely. Naess seems here to conflate humaneness with human-centeredness, as though application of the ethics of human interactions with each other is anthropocentric. Is this merely a matter of interpretation? It is true that the overall tone of Naess's work evidences benevolent foundations; his reader would be surprised to find that he would condone inhumane methods of population reduction. My point is to identify a vagueness, or a lack of clarity in Deep Ecological thinking concerning human interactions with each other.

Despite Naess's apparent benevolent sensibilities, the writings and recommendations of a number of Deep Ecologists have sometimes verged on the inhumane, and others have put forth the view that phenomena such as the global AIDS epidemic and Third World famine are 'necessary solutions' to the "population problem." George Bradford has ruminated on the implications of the varying political perspectives of Deep Ecologists, a truth illustrated in Dave Foreman's claim that "Earth First! is not left or right; we are not even in front'. If Deep Ecology has room for such a broad range of political perspectives, and demands few positions on human social matters, it may not provide a sufficiently substantive foundation for considering interpersonal ethics. This is relevant to its adequacy as an environmental ethic, as the ethics of human interactions with each other determine, are determined by, and are necessarily related to the ethics of human interactions with our environment and its members. Eco-feminists argue that these ethical spheres are inseparable.

A central, and related, problem with Deep Ecology is evident in Deep Ecologists' one-dimensional characterization of the population problem.' Naess and other Deep Ecologists, in their relative silence concerning the issues underlying population size, appear to register the ill-effects of an enormous human population as part of a battle between the human species and the Earth. In this scenario, 'humans,' due to their lack of appreciation of the ontological status of "nature,' selfishly reproduce more of their species than can be supported by a healthy, whole, biosphere. Sorely lacking is critical analysis of the universe of human social factors, many of which are related to issues of gender and oppression, contributing to the size of human population, and of the assumptions about the nature of human impact on environments that ground many scientific theories about 'carrying capacity" and 'standard of living." In contrast, eco-feminists might consider the "carrying capacity" of the planet to be, not a biological fact, but an estimate that depends on our assumptions about how humans will impact on the land, other species, and the biota in general. Conceptions of 'carrying capacity' are often based not on ecosystemic givens but on ideological inclinations. A large, low-impact human community may be more environmentally feasible than a smaller high-impact community if the large community is based on ecologically sound principles and practices. Human lifestyle and 'standard of living" are not biological givens, and any theory which posits recommendations for the future of human communities must be specific about the ideal types recommended or assumed, as well as the problems inherent in present human communities. Deep Ecology does not provide such a theory. Deep Ecologists' characterization of the facts of human population and the simplistic solutions recommended by some Deep Ecologists mark its analysis as shallow. Dave Foreman, Deep Ecologist and founder of Earth First!, writes:

> There are far too many human beings on Earth.... Although there is obviously an unconscionable maldistribution of wealth and the basic necessities of life among humans, this fact should not be used as some leftists are won't to do to argue that overpopulation is not the problem. It is a large part of the problem.... Even if inequitable distribution could be solved, six billion human beings converting the natural world to material goods and human food would devastate natural diversity.

Note Foreman's reduction of human beings into mere 'convertors,' and 'leftists' into simple-minded egalitarians. It is nonsensical to attempt to understand human population size without considering the specific ways in which natural objects are converted, exactly who is demanding and benefiting from such conversions, which humans are paying the price for those demands, and whether there is a history of resistance among the oppressed. Despite the fact that the imperatives

"No Exploitation' and 'Self-Realization' are emphasized in Naess's philosophy, and Foreman recognizes that social factors contribute to population, neither believes attention to these factors, especially those concerning exploitation and oppression of humans, is central to understanding and undoing environmental destruction.

Eco-feminists, on the other hand, make the connections between human, women, environmental exploitation central to their position and aim toward an analysis that is inclusive of the many, related forms of domination. An eco-feminist analysis of the causes and effects of a large human population rests not only on ecological facts about the devastation of non-human populations by that human population, but also on feminist analyses of scientific models, human reproduction and sexuality, race and ethnicity, histories of class oppression and economic exploitation, gender roles and the fly, and the psychological disempowerment of the oppressed. Examples of such work covers a broad range, from the Unity Statement of the Women's Pentagon Action, in which eco-feminist activists marked connections among women's reproductive freedom, militarism, depletion of resources, and racism, to Karen J. Warren's essay 'Taking empirical data seriously,' in which she argues that environmental theories and movements cannot ignore the overwhelming scientific evidence of connections among the oppressions of women, people of color, people who are poor, children, and nature.

The careful attention in eco-feminist work to the details and complexities of environmental issues illuminates huge, problematic gaps in approaches like Naess's and Foreman's. Deep Ecologists tend to view humans as an undifferentiated, monolithic species, and hence to regard environmental destruction as resulting from "human' action, 'human' attitudes, or even a 'human' teleology which aims inevitably toward total dominion over and exploitation of the non-human realm. Anarchist George Bradford points out how Deep Ecology 'takes the technocratic reduction of nature to resources for an undifferentiated species activity based on supposed biological need', and social ecologist Murray Bookchin remarks on Deep Ecologists' tendency to regard human beings as a species "rather than as beings who are divided by the oppressions of race, sex, material means of life, culture, and the like". In fact, when we take into account the differences mentioned by Bookchin, it seems plausible that members of different classes, cultures, or genders have different ethical responsibilities with regard to their roles in reducing human population. It is not unreasonable to argue, for example, that members of high-impact technological societies have a greater moral obligation than less destructive societies to minimize their own growth. Bookchin's point also makes clear that the presumption of one universal "standard of living" ignores important human particularities.

In addition to questioning some basic presuppositions in Deep Ecological characterization of human population, such as the notion that it is unproblematic to talk of 'human' as an undifferentiated species and hence disregard the particularities of gender and other specificities, eco-feminist analysis probes more deeply by asking basic questions about the history, context, and institutionalization of population growth and density patterns. Instead of beginning where Naess starts, with the question of the carrying capacity of the planet, a primary question for eco-feminists considering the issue of human population should be, 'Why do women bear many children, even in areas or communities where high population density impacts on individual lives very directly, through overcrowding, shortages of food and other necessities, poor health and hygiene, and the obvious destruction of local land and species?". In order to answer such a question, Eco-feminism entails consideration of at least the following complex and intersecting factors.

Sexism

Although women must be a central focus of any study or analysis of human population size and growth, it is imperative that this be done in a way that does not 'blame the victim.' The systematic oppression of women and girls in patriarchal societies cannot be ignored by environmentalists concerned with the problems associated with a large and growing human population. Women are devalued in nearly every society on the planet, and this devaluation is conceptually related to devaluation of the natural environment and its members.

One consequence of women's oppression is sexual disempowerment. That is, many women are unable to refuse sex with male partners. Glorification of male sexual prowess and virility, a recurrent expression of sexism, associates male social prestige with reproductive capacities and the abundance of offspring. When women cannot refuse heterosex and men demand it for reasons which supersede their desire for space and abundant local species, women's sexual disempowerment feeds population growth, even in squalor.' Furthermore, until women control their own reproductive lives, it will be nearly impossible to decrease the human reproduction rate by instituting birth control programs which are targeted primarily at females, as the vast majority so far have been. Such attempts at population control place responsibility in the hands of women who are often not, in fact, responsible for reproductive decision-making. Women's sexual empowerment is a feminist imperative; it is also an ecological one if one is to take overpopulation seriously.

Motherhood

Many feminist theorists have written about the oppression of women through the institution of motherhood. Others have attempted to reconceptualize aspects of mothering away from the sexism and labor divisions under which motherhood has been constructed. Proponents of either approach to motherhood agree that when female identity is bound intricately with motherhood, or when motherhood is presented as the only or best way to have meaningful lives, women's life options are severely limited. The acts of bearing and caring for children get packed with meanings and importance that make the rejection of motherhood difficult, if not impossible. An eco-feminist analysis of the matter of human population, which centers so dramatically on issues of human reproduction and its meanings in social and political contexts, must include an analysis of the many forms of motherhood and their relations to women's oppression.

Racism and class or caste oppression

These forms of oppression intersect with women's oppression in ways that make issues of reproductive freedom even more complex for women of color, poor women, and women living in the 'Third World.' The legacy of industrial imperialism includes a disastrous level of poverty among people of color which has led to increased birth rates. In some societies, having many children is tantamount to creating a large familial work force. Economic stresses in such contexts intensify the immediate need for children and hence overshadow the supposed importance of 'family planning.' A global history of racist and other imperialist, genocidal policies inevitably results in a justified lack of trust toward Western health care providers and birth control programs. Feminist analysis of oppression and its stance against all forms of oppression entails a conunitment to multiculturalism and against racism and classism. This position grounds eco-feminist concern with environmental racism and environmental classism or the fact that certain forms of ecological destruction occur disproportionately in locations occupied by people of color and people who are poor. The coincidence of overpopulation, poverty, and race cannot be treated as a trivial matter by theorists and activists interested in population. Connections must be explicitly analyzed and addressed.

Cultural factors

How do cultural beliefs and values, which are often dictated by male members of society, contribute to and/or create context in which human reproductive capacities and the practice of having children are highly prized or left unquestioned? Certain forms of birth control may be religiously prohibited or considered by members of some cultures to be a sign of collusion with upper classes or imperialists. The history of the birth control movement in the

United States and England, and its powerful opposition (whose influence is still felt in the opposition to sex education in US schools) is indicative of how cultural norms and mores can have great effects on the distribution and acceptance of birth control methods, even in 'developed' countries. Presumptions about the value of the traditional nuclear family, such as the belief that it is the only or best child-rearing option or human bonding unit, lie beneath much reproductive behavior and attempts to understand or change that behavior. Any theory which purports to offer understandings of and alternatives to ecological problems resulting from a large, high-impact human population must seriously examine the social and ecological value of family units. These presumptions, and their relation to institutions of gender, are of central concern to many eco-feminists, and are mostly left unquestioned by Deep Ecologists.

Health issues and sexuality

Because of the intersections of the oppression of women and of all human physical 'nature,' females are often alienated from their own bodily functions and processes. In industrial societies, where gynaecology and other allopathic medicines have replaced more holistic medical models, somatic alienation is augmented by epistemic alienation from ancient wisdom about human, and particularly female, bodies and health care. This alienation and lack of knowledge puts the power over women's bodies into the hands of professionals and feeds nonprofessional women's ignorance about birth control as well as nonheterosexual options. Such purposeful ignorance enabled a long global history of women being offered unsafe, impractical, and disempowering birth control methods and health care. Of course, women's health and sexuality has also been a primary site for the exercise of patriarchal and racist political power. As Ronnie Zoe Hawkins has argued, reproductive choice is an ecological and an eco-feminist issue.

Finally, in societies which create mystique and taboo around sexuality, active heterosexuality is constructed as a way to become adult, to prevent boredom, or to rebel against authority. Heterosexual intercourse is often conceptually separated from its likely consequence: pregnancy. Talk of population reduction must occur in the context of discussions of the many aspects of human reproduction, heterosexuality and heterosexism among them.

The depth of Eco-feminism

Warwick Fox argues that Eco-feminism is shallow because it is 'logically and empirically simplistic,' positing that 'one particular perspective of human society identifies the real root of ecological destruction". Eco-feminists, he believes, do not look at the complex network of factors which result in ecological destruction. He concludes:

Logically, such thinking is simplistic because it implies that the solution to our ecological problems is close at hand all we have to do is remove "the real root" of the problem.

But does a focus on human social concerns imply anthropocentrism? Not if that focus occurs within a wide lens, enabling a consideration of how social concerns are interrelated with environmental and ecological problems. Eco-feminists do focus on issues of human oppression, but this focus is not exclusively central to eco-feminist thought. In fact, Karen J. Warren points out that a basic implication of nearly all eco-feminist projects is that to treat human social concerns and environmental issues as disparate is to misconceive the character of such issues since they are intrinsically, historically, practically, and conceptually related. Given the intricate interrelatedness of so-called feminist and environmental issues, especially evident in conceptual connections, eco-feminist activism aims at all times to dismantle the oppressive frameworks which harm humans and non-humans similarly. In 'Eco-feminism and feminist theory,' Carolyn Merchant illustrates how eco-feminists from a variety of perspectives prioritize political issues in which female and ecological degradation intersect in very obvious, material ways. These include:

Women who argue that male-designed and -produced technologies neglect the effects of nuclear radiation, pesticides, hazardous wastes, and household chemicals on women's reproductive organs and the ecosystem.

Other eco-feminist movements confront examples of environmental destruction which affect disproportionate numbers of poor women and women of color. Such eco-feminist analysis of and attention to the intersections of oppressions imply that Fox's claim that Eco-feminism recommends working on interhuman problems to solve environmental issues is a simplification of eco-feminist analysis. His simplification rests on a lack of attention to various forms and mechanisms of oppression, devaluation, and degradation, and a consequent ignorance of the intersections of and relationships among systems of domination. The stance of prominent eco-feminists on the value of non-human entities is clear, as are their positions on human-centered thinking. Susan Griffin writes, just as the Earth is not the center of the solar system, so the biosphere is not centered on the human species nor circumscribed by human culture.

And in 'Loving your mother: on the woman-nature relationship,' in which Catherine Roach is critical of environmental theories which naturalize the relationships between women and nature, the following critique of anthropocentrism is offered:

> Any understanding of the world that posits an important or unbridgeable difference between the realm of the human and the non-human risks creating a gulf between the two in which the human is more highly valued than the non-human.... Such an understanding must be rejected as environmentally unsound.

According to Arne Naess's own criteria, Eco-feminism is not shallow insofar as it is anti-anthropocentric and acknowledges the moral value of non-human entities apart from their usefulness to humans. Although eco-feminists do place primary emphasis on the role of patriarchy in the creation and propagation of ecological oppression, patriarchal thinking is not necessarily considered the root cause of anything. In fact, patriarchal attitudes and practices interact with other systems and logics of domination and oppression, such as racism, anthropocentrism, classism, and heterosexism to form a decentered matrix of oppressive attitudes, theories, and practices. Every aspect of this matrix has been constructed within a complex network of historical, economic, political, and environmental factors. Those eco-feminist writers who have explored the complexity of the connections and relationships among various oppressions and social constructions, who are largely ignored by Fox, do not claim that 'woman's perspective' provides the perfect vantage point to determine the causes of ecological destruction because they realize, and in fact assert, that no such unitary perspective exists.

The arguments of many prominent eco-feminists do rest on the fact that the perspectives of females, people of color, and members of other historically disenfranchised groups are virtually missing from the history of academic thought, and also that certain theoretical and ethical insights may be gained by giving attention to these many perspectives and voices. Although Arne Naess asserts that a theory is deep insofar as it refuses to ignore 'troubling evidence" about the roots of ecological destruction, Deep Ecologists tend to ignore the troubling fact that anthropocentrism and other oppressive attitudes toward the non-human realm actually feed and are fed by human oppression and subjugation. Deep Ecologists ignore a significant facet of the matrix of oppression and domination in so far as they ignore the extent to which human interactions with each other determine and are determined by human interactions with the non-human realm.

Concluding thoughts

Given the complexities of an eco-feminist analysis of the problem of human population, the formation of practical solutions and an ethics that addresses the many facets of the problem will be equally complex and multifaceted. One imperative that emerges is the, recogrution of the ethical necessity of women's empowerment. Such an imperative cannot emerge from a one-dimensional Deep Ecology analysis which views anthropocentrism as the sole root of environmental destruction and which posits humans as an undifferentiated species. Women must be empowered with regard to their own bodies, their role as creators of culture, about their role and power in sexuality, and about their self-creation of identities other than as mother. An ethic that addresses the complexities of the human population problem will include an acknowledgment and analysis of the empowerment of women and the need for economic empowerment of the poor, and will offer a thorough critique of genocidal and racist programs and policies.

A medical ethic which addresses the need for safe, practical, nonpaternalistic health care options for women and the poor is a necessary aspect of any theory which addresses the issue of human population. Some Deep Ecologists, and even some eco-feminists, have argued that Deep Ecology and Eco-feminism are theoretically similar, share common goals, and/or are in agreement concerning the positive program of radical ecology. But the differences between the two are not superficial, and they mark serious disagreement concerning the basis of ethics, contextualization of ethical issues, and the interrelationship of ethical issues seemingly confined to the human sphere with those that obviously involve non-human entities.' Deep Ecology and Eco-feminism differ greatly as theoretical systems or paradigms, and hence as ethical frameworks. However, if what I have said is correct, then there is a respect in which Eco-feminism is a kind of deep ecology. It is not shallow; it is anti-anthropocentric, acknowledges the moral value of the non-human realm, and engages in extensive, if not bottomless, questioning about the many factors which contribute to our present environmental dilemmas.

4

Ecological Feminist Philosophies

Introduction

One measure of the strength and importance of the feminist movement is the extent to which philosophers from a broad spectrum-from conservatives to radicals or from historians of ancient philosophy to deconstructionists-now see the discussion of gender issues as an important part of their discipline. Using a parallel yardstick, the environmental movement has grown rapidly in strength and importance: the range of philosophers who address environmental issues is probably as broad as that discussing gender.

Given this rapid and dramatic rise of philosophical concern for environmental issues, we should expect and welcome serious disagreements about both the underlying conceptual and historical reasons for human destruction of the environment and the proposed solutions. The focus on the debate between deep ecology and Eco-feminism, two of the several philosophies that criticize and attempt to supplant the prevailing environmental philosophies. The controversy between deep ecology and Eco-feminism has been going on for nearly a decade. On the positive side, many thinkers from these two camps have helped each other understand better their own views and those they oppose, and they have deepened their own and our understanding of the difficult issues we face. In contrast, some of the exchanges have been rather rancorous: some deep ecologists have accused Eco-feminism of shallowness, anthropocentrism, short-sightedness, and environmental naivete, while various eco-feminists have called their accusers sexist, shallow, ahistorical, stoical, and even fascist. An attempt to show how and why deep ecology and Eco-feminism are at odds, and whether and how these differences could be overcome. To conclude with a discussion of the key issues and differences that need further attention if the "versus" in the title of this essay is to be replaced by a more compatible relationship.

According to Arne Naess, who coined the "deep ecology" label and who is looked upon by most deep ecologists as a seminal thinker in this tradition, deep ecology has eight basic characteristics, the first four of which he claims are conceptually fundamental: " The well-being and flourishing of human and non-human Life on Earth have value in themselves. These values are independent of the usefulness of the non-human world for human purposes. Richness and diversity of life forms contribute to the realization of these values and are also values in themselves. Humans have no right to reduce this richness and diversity except to satisfy vital needs. The flourishing of human life and cultures is compatible with a substantial decrease of the human population. The flourishing of non-human life requires such a decrease". Naess and the many deep ecologists who agree with him begin by asserting the fundamental equality and inherent value of all beings and then draw inferences for human action from their original anti-anthropomorphism. Warwick Fox sums up deep ecology as wanting to encourage an egalitarian attitude that "within obvious kinds of practical limits, allows entities the freedom to unfold in their own way unhindered by the various forms of human domination".

This central concern with "Eco-Centric egalitarianism" leads deep ecologists to oppose, above all else, the historical Western propensity to place humans at the center of the moral universe. Deep ecologists trace most environmental destruction to the anthropocentric attitude that says non-human nature has no value in itself, humans create what value there is, and humans have the right to do as they please with and in the non-human world as long as they do not harm other humans' interests. Thus deep ecologists criticize the human centeredness of prevailing Western attitudes and ethics by claiming that there are no good reasons in general for valuing a member of a species or a whole species over another individual or species or over any given ecosystem. They are not against human flourishing, but deep ecologists believe that this flourishing can generally occur without the destructive domination of non-human nature by humans, and insofar as it can, it should. Naess and other deep ecologists believe we need an ethic that is not a mere extension of existing humanist ethics. Animal liberationist Peter Singer, for example, argues that we can provide a theoretical basis for vegetarianism by extending utilitarianism to include all sentient beings.

Deep ecologists criticize Singer and other "extensionists" for holding onto "an increasingly arbitrary perspective in an age when the ecological imagination can shift reference points within the system and imagine the world to some extent from the standpoint of the muskrat and its environment". Extensions of human-centered ethics perpetuate an unjustifiable bias humans have toward their own. Thus, just as an ethic that begins with men as distinct from women is sexist, utilitarianism and other Western ethics are speciesist." Deep ecology tries to begin with a foundation that does not arbitrarily set "man apart". Hans Jonas puts the difference between shallow and deep ecology this way: "Only an ethic which is grounded in the breadth of being, not merely in the singularity or oddness of man, can have significance in the scheme of things".

The critical side of deep ecology, then, is aimed at anthropocentric domination of nature. The alternatives to anthropocentrism it recommends vary, depending on the non-domination-of-nature tradition to which particular deep ecologists turn. We will look at some of these frameworks briefly at the end of this essay; for now three points are important. First, given the very general nature of the change in attitude deep ecologists desire-from anthropomorphism to egalitarianism-we find greater diversity in the prescriptions given by deep ecologists to solve the problems caused by anthropocentric philosophies and practices than in the diagnosis of the sources of the problems.

Deep ecologists are more unified in their analyses of the problem than in their recommended solutions. Second, while no specific prescription necessarily follows from the diagnosis, a type of alternative is demanded-one that eliminates anthropocentric domination. Finally, while the alternatives offered by deep ecologists are fairly diverse, they tend to be characterized as proposing that we seek a higher unity in the diversity of the world: for example, Naess often turns to Buddhism for a higher Self that transcends the ego-self of the individual; Fox talks of the transpersonal; and Devall and Sessions look to the unity of Spinoza's philosophy.

When we examine the disputes between deep ecology and Eco-feminism, it is crucial to separate their critiques of anthropocentric and androcentric environmental frameworks from their positive alternatives, for disapproval of one or several of deep ecology's positive frameworks is not to dismiss that movement's analysis of the domination of nature. On the other side, a dismissal of antianthropocentrism is to reject deep ecology. I hope to show that Eco-feminism at most modifies deep ecology's negative analysis, and that while the tendency of eco-feminist solutions is perhaps contrary to the standard interpretations of deep ecology's images of unity, they are not logically incompatible with the negative side of the deep ecological framework, and they may not be incompatible with certain versions of the positive side either.

Eco-Feminism

Finding a spokesperson for Eco-feminism is more difficult, and this difference from deep ecology is not insignificant. While both men and women are to be found within each of these varieties of environmental philosophy, most deep ecologists are men, while women make up the strong majority in Eco-feminism. Part of the eco-feminist critique of deep ecology is that the masculinist nature of deep ecology can be seen in its rather unified program as well as in its use of language and logical style. I will return to this issue briefly at the end of this essay; for now bear in mind that the diversity of thought seems much greater in Eco-feminism than in deep ecology. As a starting point I will use Ynestra King and Karen J. Warren as examplars of eco-feminist thought: they have both written a number of influential articles on Eco-feminism, and they both identify strongly with this movement, as illustrated by their ardent defenses of Eco-feminism against feminist as well as deep ecologist critics. Warren says that Eco-feminism is based on the following general claims: " There are important connections between the oppression of women and the oppression of nature. Understanding the nature of these connections is necessary to any adequate understanding of the oppression of women and the oppression of nature. Feminist theory and practice must include an ecological perspective. Solutions to ecological problems must include a feminist perspective".

She further contends that what feminism today needs is to be "transformative," to move beyond the current debate over the four leading versions of feminism (liberal feminism, traditional Marxist feminism, radical feminism, and socialist feminism) "and make an eco-feminist perspective central to feminist theory and practice". Eco-feminism contains both a critique of the dominant "patriarchal conceptual framework" and offers a feminist framework that is "grounded in familiar ecological principles." The former, according to Warren, is one which takes traditionally male-identified beliefs, values, attitudes, and assumptions as... the standard; it gives higher status or prestige to what has been traditionally identified as male" than to what has been traditionally identified as "female".... A patriarchal conceptual framework is characterized by value-hierarchical thinking. Such thinking gives rise to a logic of domination which serves to legitimate inequality when, in fact, prior to the metaphor of Up-Down one would have said only that there existed diversity.

For Warren, the eco-feminist critique of patriarchy is grounded in ecological principles: "Everything is interconnected with everything else; all parts of an ecosystem have equal value; there is no free lunch; 'nature knows best'; healthy, balanced ecosystems must maintain diversity; there is unity in diversity". Warren believes this critique must embrace feminism because otherwise "the ecological movement will fail to make the conceptual connections between the oppression of women and the oppression of nature.".

Warren sharpens this analysis in a recent article by showing the parallel structures between the domination of nature by humans and the domination of women by men. Her version of the logic of the domination of nature has five steps:

- Humans do, and plants and rocks do not, have the capacity to consciously and radically change the community in which they live.
- Whatever has the capacity to consciously and radically change the community in which it lives is morally superior to whatever lacks this capacity.
- Thus, humans are morally superior to plants and rocks.
- For any X and Y, if X is morally superior to Y, then X is morally justified in subordinating Y.
- Thus, humans are morally justified in subordinating plants and rocks.

Warren next shows how women can be substituted for plants and rocks in this argument and how women are identified with nature and men with mind. Thus becomes: "Women are identified with nature and the realm of the physical; men are identified with the 'human' and the realm of the mental". She goes on to argue that the second and fourth premises are unwarranted value assumptions and that without them the arguments for domination of nature and women fail. Warren contends that this eco-feminist analysis not only exposes and successfully criticizes the domination of nature but also shows that the same logic is used to dominate women.

Therefore, she argues, feminism is ecological, and those who oppose naturism are simultaneously against sexism. King emphasizes a further dimension of Eco-feminism by showing that Eco-feminism is naturally closely aligned with the peace movement and other struggles to end domination of people as well as nature. In a classic essay she calls Eco-feminism "cultural feminism," which rejects both the denial of the nature/woman link and the belief that women are more natural" than men. King claims that "both these positions are unwittingly complicit with the nature/culture dualism. Women's oppression is neither strictly historical nor strictly biological. It is both". Moreover, King believes that, gender is a meaningful part of a person's identity.... As women we are naturalized culture in a culture defined against nature. If the nature/culture antagonism is the primary contradiction of our time, it is also what weds feminism and ecology and makes women the historic subject. Without an ecological perspective which asserts the interdependence of living things, feminism is disembodied.

Eco-feminism's critique of predominant Western environmental attitudes is at least in part quite like that of deep ecology: the central fault is an attitude, logic, and practice of dominating nature. Deep ecology's anthropocentrism and Warren's naturism appear to be the same. The central difference between their negative analyses seems to be that while deep ecology focuses exclusively on human domination of nature, Eco-feminism insists that a proper analysis must also emphasize the intimate logical and historical connections between the various forms of domination-the same logic and attitudes of superiority and practices of domination humans display in their relations toward the non-human dimensions of the world are found in men's relations to women and in imperialistic, racist, and classist structures and practices. Some eco-feminists claim that deep ecologists reveal their male chauvinism when they at most allude to the connections among these various forms of domination, and they emphasize the deeply masculinist nature of all these interconnected forms of domination by proposing that the central problem is androcentrism rather than anthropocentrism.

The Conflict Between Deep Ecology and Eco-Feminism

The eco-feminist criticism of deep ecology that it is androcentric. I will also examine the counterclaims by some deep ecologists that Eco-feminism is shallow-that it does not get to the heart of environmental issues because it focuses on the connections among the various forms of domination rather than on the domination of nature itself. At the core of deep ecology is the call for a new sensibility. Modern humans have lost touch with nature and thus with their own natures-we no longer feel the rhythms of nature within ourselves, we have split ourselves from the world, and we live at a distance from what is natural, leaving us fearful and able to deal with the world only on our own terms. We have become insensitive to ourselves and others by losing our natural sensibilities. Deep ecologists thus look to premodern and/ or holistic traditions for suggestions about how to experience the world-to American Indians, Buddhism, Spinoza and others, or to the science of ecology.

In short, their critique focuses on the bifurcation of humans and nature that has its sources far back especially in Western history and deep within many inherited philosophies, and the basic strategy deep ecologists recommend for ending the domination of nature is to somehow reverse this dualism, to join together what humans have split asunder. As we have seen, eco-feminists agree that domination of nature is much the issue, and many of them would further agree that historically the dualism of humans and nature is a major part of the mental substructure undergirding that domination. But they would not agree that this is the whole story. Warren, for example, says that "deep ecology makes a big conceptual error in supposing that the way to reduce a bad dualism is to affirm the neglected or historically undervalued member of the pair. The bad dualism is the problem, not simply what got undervalued." She raises a parallel challenge to radical feminism, which wants to frame "the feminist debate over ecology in terms of the question 'Are women closer to nature than men?' In order for the question to be meaningfully raised, one must presuppose the legitimacy of the nature-culture dualism".Eco-feminists such as Warren are concemed that nature has become a disconnected abstraction for deep ecologists, with the result that although they are devoted to "nature," they relate to nature in a way parallel to that of the dualists they oppose-nature is a lost part of one's self that needs to be rejoined. Jim Cheney puts it this way:

> In discussing naturalism, it is natural and to a large extent unavoidable to rely on the familiar terminology of philosophical tradition to explain it. Since a considerable amount of that terminology is the product of dualism, the question arises as to whether this language can be used effectively to convey the different perspective of naturalism. Although philosophy has always involved a great deal of innovation in new terminology, the defenders of ordinary language argue that philosophical meaning can be adequately expressed in everyday terms. But what if the ordinary view of the world which is embedded in ordinary language is what one wants to avoid and wants to correct?

Throughout his article Cheney tries to paint a different picture of how we might conceive of our relationships with humans and non-humans alike. He turns for his inspiration to the rich material to be found in recent feminist literature about friendship, love, care, and gifting. Cheney believes deep ecologists reveal their ties to the patriarchal traditions they are trying to overcome by the sources and images they use for "reversing" the bifurcation of culture and nature. Despite its sincere concerns, deep ecology remains androcentric, and androcentrism is the real culprit. Thus deep ecology does not, according to this eco-feminist criticism, transcend the perspective it criticizes.

While there are intimate ties between analysis and solution, let us begin sorting out this dispute by differentiating deep ecology's diagnosis from its prescriptions to see just where and how eco-feminists find deep ecology lacking.

Warren's analysis of the logic of domination concentrates on the diagnosis, while Cheney's alternative to deep ecology's images of unity is concerned mainly with prescriptions. At first glance Warren's analysis seems to add to or extend the basic critical analysis of deep ecology. Warwick Fox quotes "one eco-feminist-cum, deep ecologist" who read Warren's 1987 article and wondered "why she doesn't just call it [Warren's transformative feminism] deep ecology?". For what Warren does, says Fox, is to show that the logic of domination that deep ecology sees as the source of naturism has its parallels in sexism, racism, and classism.

According to Fox, anthropomorphism is what deep ecologists call this logic and attitude in human/nature relationships. He further contends that deep ecologists encourage an attitude of egalitarianism toward all entities in the ecosphere-including humans". Moreover, deep ecologists "completely agree with eco-feminists that men have been far more implicated in the history of ecological destruction than women. However, deep ecologists also agree with similar charges derived from other social perspectives: for example, that capitalists, whites, and Westerners have been far more implicated in the history of ecological destruction than pre-capitalist peoples, blacks, and non-Westerners". Human centeredness, not a particular group of humans, is the target of deep ecology; thus, Fox claims that contrary to Cheney and other eco-feminists, deep ecologists are not androcentric. Is Fox correct in his contention that the crucial difference between deep ecology and Eco-feminism is a matter of focus-that deep ecology has its eye on environmental relations while Eco-feminism is more concerned with how the logic of domination is also played out on women? Not according to Warren. She believes that the gendered nature of the logic of domination is more than an accident of history. She believes that feminism should be ecological at its core because the domination of nature and the domination of women are parts of a whole, and she believes that any satisfactory environmental philosophy must be feminist for the same reasons.

She gives three arguments for the latter claim: for the sake of historical accuracy we must "acknowledge the feminization of nature and the naturalization of women as part of the exploitation of nature"; the oppressive dual dominations of women and nature at least in the West are "located in a patriarchal conceptual framework," and to ignore this connection is to give, at best, "an incomplete, inaccurate, and partial account of what is required of a conceptually adequate environmental ethic" and at least in contemporary culture the word feminist helps to clarify how the domination and liberation of nature are conceptually linked to patriarchy and its demise. Warren adds that "without the addition of the word 'feminist', one presents environmental ethics as if it has no bias, including male-gender bias, which is just what eco-feminists deny: failure to notice the connections between the twin oppressions of women and nature is male-gender bias". This exchange between Fox and Warren, who are in many ways quite close in their concerns and analyses, helps to pinpoint what seems to be a critical difference between Eco-feminism and deep ecology with regard to their diagnoses of the philosophical sources of environmental destructiveness. Warren and Cheney talk about this difference by emphasizing that the logic of domination is accompanied by a set of values:

The third feature of oppressive conceptual frameworks is the most significant. A logic of domination is not just a logical structure. It also involves a substantive value system, since an ethical premise is needed to permit or sanction the "just" subordination of that which is subordinate.

According to this eco-feminist criticism, Fox, like Naess and other deep ecologists, emphasizes an abstract equality between humans and all other beings, while Eco-feminism is against the logic of domination and the particular historical values that result in the domination of a particular set of entities. Fox defends deep ecology against this line of criticism by arguing that anthropocentrism is the most "fundamental kind of legitimation" that has been used to justify domination, whether of nature, of women, or of particular groups of people or non-humans. He believes that "these classes of social actors have not sought to legitimate their positions on the grounds that they are, for example, men, capitalists, white or Western per se, but on the grounds that they have most exemplified whatever it is that has been taken to constitute the essence of humanness.... They have... habitually assumed themselves to be somehow more fully human than others, such as women, the 'lower' classes, blacks, and non-Westerners". Fox further defends deep ecology as non-sexist by pointing out that eco-feminists can be guilty of overemphasizing the domination of women and its link to the domination of nature. Since the logic of human centeredness can be used to justify domination of anything or anyone deemed lacking the magic essence, why don't eco-feminists give equal weight to the domination of people of color, aboriginal people, or poor people? In Fox's view:

> There appears to be two reasons for this. First, to do so would detract from the priority that eco-feminists wish to give to their own concern with androcentrism. Second, and more significantly, these charges could also be applied with equal force to the eco-feminist focus on androcentrism itself.

At the very least, this exchange and others like it in the literature serve to warn us to be careful to understand these philosophies before criticizing them; but such debates also highlight that the process of exchange itself is formative of the positions. Given these caveats, what are we to make of the current exchange? Is deep ecology sexist? Is deep ecology's analysis fundamental? Is Eco-feminism simplistic on both empirical and logical grounds" ? My answers to these questions will in certain ways support both contingents. First, I think that Warren's analysis of the logic of domination shows that at least one eco-feminist understands clearly that what Fox calls "human centeredness" is the problem: the logical strategy is to place some person in domination over other persons or entities based on the in-group possessing a special quality exclusively or more fully than the others. Thus I do not see that Fox levels a telling criticism of Eco-feminism by insisting that anthropocentrism is fundamental; eco-feminists don't disagree, as far as that logical point goes. Second, while it is important to understand the logic of domination, it is also important to understand how, where, and on what it has been used.

To simply insist that the logic of anthropomorphism is the problem is like criticizing technology for extending human control over nature without looking at which technologies are used in which ways to do what for or to whom. Furthermore, just as uses of technologies can be good or bad, not all forms of domination are bad, and not all bad forms are equally bad. To ignore the particular uses of the logic of domination is to be guilty of a historical and possibly essentialist philosophizing. Thus it is no accident that the characteristics of Eco-feminism given by Warren emphasize context and process. Third, the supposed sexism of deep ecology is no simple matter. Fox and others are quite emphatic that the scope of their Eco-Centric egalitarianism includes all humans as well as non-humans.

In theory, they are not androcentric or misogynistic. Is this a situation where, as Warren claims, not to be for us is to be against us? Fox does not think so-he sees nothing in the logic or values of deep ecologists that precludes them from being concerned about sexism. But that is not the same as being actively concerned about the actual victims of dominance, nor is it to be sensitive to the particular uses to which the logic of domination has been put. Deep ecologists perhaps do not deserve to be put into the same camp as those who practice the logic of domination on women, but they are guilty of complicity if they do not recognize the particular dominations of the day and work to alleviate them at least by revealing the common logic and values of sexism and naturism. In summary, while I can see why a deep ecologist might wonder why Warren does not call herself a deep ecologist since she begins with the logic of domination, at least with regard to the negative analysis of naturism, I think one could as easily wonder why deep ecologists like Fox don't call themselves eco-feminists. For Eco-feminism not only comprehends the problem of anthropocentrism, but adds the crucial dimension of history the actual ways in which the logic of domination has been used against particular beings and systems. A central tenet of eco-feminist thought is the rejection of either/or thinking; thus a good eco-feminist would say that both anthropocentrism and androcentrism are the problem.

Fox contends that eco-feminists can be guilty of the same transgressions of which they accuse deep ecologists if eco-feminists assert that androcentrism is the problem and mean that men are by nature or in history the only ones who have used or can use the logic of domination. I believe Fox is correct about this, as does Warren: "matriarchy is not the solution to patriarchy any more than saving nature and letting humans die is the solution to the problem of environmental destruction. As demonstrated by the foregoing quotations from Warren and King, however, eco-feminists take pains to distinguish themselves from radical feminists in denying the very strategy Fox accuses eco-feminists of being tempted to adopt.

Furthermore, it is important to note that the culprit is patriarchy, not all men, and the evidence from historians and anthropologists alike indicates that male dominance is ubiquitous if not universal. Another of Fox's charges is that eco-feminists need to avoid overemphasizing the oppression of women and ignoring the domination of people of color, poor people, and aboriginal peoples. I believe Fox is again correct in asserting that this exclusion could happen as eco-feminists attempt to link feminism with ecological concerns; but again, the evidence from even the few quotations above shows that this warning has been heeded. If anything, deep ecologists are less prone than eco-feminists to take seriously the connections between the domination of nature and other forms of domination. The most serious challenge deep ecologists raise to eco-feminist thought is that it is "shallow." Arne Naess says that a philosophy is deep when it has "ultimate premises" from which a system of belief and action flow. Fox contends that eco-feminists show their lack of "depth" when they criticize deep ecology for not seeing that the root cause of environmental destruction is androcentrism rather than anthropocentrism.

Empirically Eco-feminism is simplistic because it fails to give due consideration to the multitude of interacting factors at work any given situation. Such thinking fails to adopt an ecological perspective with respect to the workings of human society itself. Logically, such thinking is simplistic because it implies that the solution to our ecological problems is close at hand-all we have to do is remove "the real root" of the problem-when it is actually perfectly possible to conceive of a society that is non androcentric, socioeconomically egalitarian, nonracist, and non imperialistic with respect to other human societies, but whose members nevertheless remain aggressively anthropocentric in collectively agreeing to exploit their environment for their collective benefit in ways that nonanthropocentrists would find thoroughly objectionable.

Fox seems to be asserting that the nature/woman connection is an historical accident that, if it had not been made by patriarchy, would leave Eco-feminism indistinct from other feminist philosophies. The ecology-feminism link is accidental because it does not flow from the philosophical foundations of Eco-feminism; instead, eco-feminists are concerned about ecology because history has linked women to nature. Is this criticism sound? We have already seen that the eco-feminist critique of "shallow" environmental perspectives shares deep ecology's rejection of human centeredness and that it adds a crucial historical dimension. Thus if Eco-feminism is shallow in its critique, deep ecology is as well.

Furthermore, deep ecologists should be careful not to confuse abstractness with depth. For a critique to be historical and include details of the sort Eco-feminism adds to the analysis of the logic of domination is not to destroy the purity of a conceptual discussion, it is to tie that discussion to the real world. The fact that particular women have suffered from an "application" of the logic of domination should be understood by deep ecologists as a reminder that only in Platonic realms of ideas are logics separable from historical realities, rather than as a lack in eco-feminist thinking. Eco-feminism is, I believe, on solid ground against the deep ecologist's challenge that it is shallow, if we are speaking of Eco-feminism's critique. What of the depth of various eco-feminist alternatives to naturist frameworks? And can deep ecology respond adequately to eco-feminist challenges to its "unity" solutions to the dualism deep ecology finds at the heart of anthropocentric environmental frameworks?

Positive Images of Environmental Relations

While space does not permit a thorough examination of the positive environmental philosophies proposed by deep ecology and Eco-feminism. The following points help clear the way for well-focused discussions of the crucial issues. The most serious challenge by eco-feminists to deep ecology's "unity" alternatives to anthropocentric environmental frameworks seems to be that these proposals remain trapped within the dualistic mode of thinking they reject-in seeking unity nature becomes an abstract and glorified "other" with which one becomes unified in some kind of self-transcending love. The major challenge deep ecology raises to Eco-feminism's "solidarity" proposals is that they are shallow-they do not encompass the breadth of perspective necessary to transcend the anthropocentrism they should oppose and suggest how both of these criticisms mainly miss the mark, and that the real work to be done is in articulating and justifying environmentally egalitarian communities.

What eco-feminists like King and Warren seem to object to in the deep ecology unity proposals is the assumption that the best way to solve our environmental problems is to rejoin the poles of a faulty duality. For not only does this strategy accept this dualism as definitive of how we relate to the world, but in seeking this unity, differences-the crucial and manifold features of the world-become obliterated. Is this accurate the deep ecology quest to transcend dualism and its unhappy consequences logically entail or otherwise imply destruction of difference? Naess says that his environmental philosophy, Ecosophy T, has as its fundamental norm "Self-realization":

This philosophy has three crucial implications: First, a somewhat extreme appreciation of diversity...; enthusiasm for "the mere" diversity of species or varieties within a genus of plants or animals.... Secondly, a somewhat extreme appreciation of what Kant calls beautiful actions in contrast to dutiful ones... maturity in humans can be measured along a scale from selfishness to Selfishness, that is, broadening and deepening the self, rather than measures of dutiful altruism.... Thirdly, I believe that many-sided, high level Self-realization is more easily reached through a "spartan" life-style than through the material standard of average citizens of industrial states.

If we add to this Naess's statement quoted earlier that we must learn to use our "ecological imagination to shift reference points," and deep ecology is necessarily guilty of the charge some eco-feminists level against it. For throughout the literature of deep ecology there is not only affirmation of Naess's commitment to this "extreme appreciation of diversity" but also much discussion of actual and diverse entities and systems. Thus if unity means obliteration of diversity, then deep ecologists are thinking and acting inconsistently. More likely, deep ecologists do not pay enough attention to the complexity and diversity of human ecology, and furthermore they need to communicate more clearly what they mean by things like "unity" and "Self-realization." I am not saying that deep ecologists have not attempted to articulate their positive philosophies.

The more specific they need to attend to the question of the compatibility of diversity and unity. Naess's idea of imaginative variation of perspective takes us partway toward this goal in that it indicates an understanding that unity is one among many possible standpoints we can take. And just as eco-feminists warn us not to take only a holistic view lest we forget the diversity of the world, deep ecologists believe we have forgotten the whole and the links between the parts. Bear in mind too that deep ecology is urging a shift in attitude as well as in paradigms. Thus, while we should not ignore the values of individuals, we should also train our imaginations insofar as we can to observe, evaluate, and experience from the whole. Finally, Fox's emphasis on egalitarianism helps to clarify this issue for deep ecology. Equality does not mean identity and does not imply ignoring of differences.

In fact, egalitarianism seems to be precisely what eco-feminists desire when they advocate difference but not distinction. Eco-feminism's negative critique is no shallower than that of deep ecology. What of its positive proposals? Recall that "depth" is a kind of code word for being antianthropocentric and also for thinking ecologically. When eco-feminists talk about community, solidarity, and unity in diversity, are they measuring up to this yardstick? First, I believe it is important to avoid beating people up with a yardstick, especially with a vague one. Surely the "breadth of being" deep ecologists wish to be considered in any deep ecology can be discussed in terms of community as well as in terms of unity. If anything, the science of ecology uses the language of community much more than referring to unity or wholeness.

Furthermore, many images of community can focus our attention on the interrelationships among the diverse elements of the whole better than can many images of the whole. The real complaint of those accusing Eco-feminism of shallowness seems to be a caution not to forget the non-human world and the complex and intimate human relationships with it when discussing sexism, racism, and other forms of domination.

There are many perspectives, such as radical feminist or socialist frameworks, in which people end up slighting the domination of nature. While these examples point to a real danger, there is nothing in the logic or details of eco-feminism which would encourage such a lapse, and in fact many eco-feminists take pains to criticize socialist and radical feminism precisely for this oversight. Furthermore, eco-feminists such as Warren insist on the intimate connections between the domination of women, blacks, and others with the domination of nature. The real challenge to eco-feminism, is to articulate notions of community that include, in a comprehensible way, non-human nature. Spotted owls and aquifers are not our literal relatives, at least not in precisely the same ways as other humans can be. How are we to comprehend our relationships with the elements and inhabitants of the non-human world such that they are equal but different? This is the task to which eco-feminists and deep ecologists alike should turn, and the spatial metaphor of depth is not a particularly helpful guide in this part of the project.

5

Feminism and the Mastery of Nature

Mainstream environmental philosophy is problematic not just because of restriction in ethics but also because of restriction to ethics. Most mainstream philosophers continue to view environmental philosophy as primarily concerned with an extension of existing ethical frame- works.

For example, instrumentalism is viewed as a problem in ethics, and its solution seen as setting up a theory of intrinsic value. But this neglects the key further aspects we have been examining, of dualism and the account of the self and of human identity as hyperseparated from nature, the connection between this and the instrumental view of nature, as well as the broader historical and political aspects of the critique of dualism and instrumentalism. As an alternative to this impoverished conception, deep ecology has had some success in broadening the conception of the problem to include issues concerning the human self and questions of human identity and discontinuity from nature. Feminist theory has revealed many of the buried links between conceptions of ethics and conceptions of selfhood, and thus has a very useful contribution to make to the discussion of both these approaches.

In many crucial respects deep ecology does not present a very thoroughgoing alternative to extensions of mainstream ethics. In its dominant forms deep ecology continues to suffer from problems associated with unresolved human/nature dualism and other dualisms. If mainstream environmental ethics suffers from the kind of distortions of difference which attend the problematic of individualism and rational egoism, deep ecology tends to suffer from the obverse kind of distortion of difference associated with incorporation. As we saw in the last chapter, major forms of deep ecology fail to acknowledge difference and continue to conceive nature in ways which reflect dualism and, in some cases, male domination. Although deep ecology contrasts with the mainstream in emphasising connections with the self and the continuity between humans and nature there remain severe tensions between some forms of deep ecology and feminist perspectives. These forms have not satisfactorily identified the key elements in the traditional framework, or noted their connections with rationalism and the master identity. As a result they fail to reject adequately rationalist assumptions, and indeed often provide their own versions of rationalist accounts of self, universalisation and the discarding of particular connections.

The analysis of human/nature and other dualisms are presented here has stressed the importance of affirming both difference and continuity, and of maintaining the balance between them. Respect for others involves acknowledging their distinctness and difference, and not trying to reduce or assimilate them to the human sphere. We need to acknowledge difference as well as continuity to overcome dualism and to establish non-instrumentalising relationships with nature, where both connection and otherness are the basis of interaction. The failure to affirm difference is characteristic of the colonising self which denies the other through the attempt to incorporate it into the empire of the self, and which is unable to experience sameness without erasing difference. Major forms of deep ecology have tended to focus exclusively on identification, interconnectedness, sameness and the overcoming of separation, treating nature as a dimension of Self, for example, in the concept of self-realisation and in the extension of ego psychology to nature. Foundational deep ecologist Arne Naess, whose concept of self- realisation, as I will argue later, also has elements of the relational self, urges a way of thinking and feeling which 'corresponds to that of the enlightened, or yogi, who sees "the same"'; Naess quotes the *Bhagavadgita*:

He whose self is harmonised by yoga seeth the Self abiding in all beings and all beings in Self; everywhere he sees the same. Since ethics is normally viewed as concerned with the relation of self to other, Naess's substitution of the 'maxim of "self-realisation" for an account of ethical relations to nature is a symptom of the death of the other in the theoretical framework of deep ecology. Even though 'the self' in such an account is not to be interpreted as the 'egoic or biographical self' or 'the personal ego', such a framework must lose the possibility of providing a dynamic or interactive account, which requires diversified elements. The loss by the account of the 'essential tension between self and other' appears in the fact that the theory does not see itself as concerned with relations between diverse interacting elements, self and other, humans and nature, but basically only with one element, the self.

In terms of a role in the theory, nature as other is erased, and in Warwick Fox's account seems to disappear entirely as a focus of concern: the appropriate framework of discourse for describing and presenting deep ecology is not one that is fundamentally to do with the value of the non-human world... but rather one that is fundamentally to do with the nature and possibilities of the Self, or, we might say, the question of who we are, can become, and should become in the larger scheme of things.

The proper study of the deep ecologist, it seems, is Tautology, and the other is of concern for what it reflects back about the self; the other is made an 'instrument of self-definition'. The proper comparison for such an account of the liberation of nature is not with a theory of opposition to sexism that is also concerned with the behaviour and interests of men, as Fox claims in response to criticism of this self-preoccupation, but with one that sees it as 'fundamentally' concerned only with the behaviour and interests of men.

It is ironic that a position claiming to be anti-anthropocentric should thus aim to reduce questions of the care and significance of nature to questions of the realisation of the human self. The denial of difference is also reflected in the use by some deep ecologists of a 'transpersonal' version of ego psychology, in which the self as isolated subject incorporates or internalises outside objects in nature, assimilating them to self. Hidden at the foot of the tree of transpersonal psychology lie the liberal-individualist roots of humanistic psychology. As Fox explains, transpersonal psychology arose from humanistic ego psychology through Sutich's conviction that the personal ego was too small, was 'no longer comprehensive enough'. The 'big "Self" ' was the answer. But on an interactive account, the loss of the essential tension between different and alike is characteristic of domination and instrumentalisation, which involves the erasure of the other as an external limit and its reappearance as a projection of self. In the domination framework, the entire dynamic of interaction takes place within the self, rather than between the self and the external other.

The framework on which deep ecology draws here represents such a psychology of incorporation, in which our sense of self can expand to include aspects of both the mind and the world that we usually regard as "other". Even if the direction of travel is reversed so as to absorb self in world rather than world in self, the result is still not a framework which allows for the tension of sameness and difference or for the other to play an active role in the creation of self in discovery and interaction with the world; rather it is one that, like ego psychology itself, conceives the self as a closed system. As Benjamin says of ego psychology:

Within this closed system, the ego invests objects with his desire and takes in these objects to further his autonomy from them. This conception of the individual cannot explain the confrontation with an independent other as a real condition of development and change. It does not comprehend the simultaneous process of transforming and being transformed by the other.

These problems over difference emerge especially in deep ecological accounts of separation, the self and the chameleon term 'identification'. Deep ecology locates the key problem area in human-nature relations in the separation of humans and nature, and it provides a solution for this in terms of the 'identification' of self with nature. 'Identification' is usually left deliberately vague, and corresponding accounts of identification and of self are various and shifting, and not always compatible.' There seem to be at least three different accounts of self involved-indistinguishability, expansion of self, and transcendence of self-and practitioners appear to feel free to move among them. Much of the appeal of deep ecology rests on the failure to distinguish between them.

The Indistinguishability Account

The indistinguishability account rejects boundaries between self and nature. The universe is said to be a seamless whole, and according to Fox, the central intuition of deep ecology is that 'We can make no firm ontological divide in the field of existence... there is no bifurcation in reality between the human and non-human realms... to the extent that we perceive boundaries, we fall short of deep ecological consciousness'. This seems like a firm rejection of human/ nature dualism and hyperseparation, but much more is involved here than the rejection of radical exclusion between humans and nature. Leading deep ecologists go on to deny separation entirely, and to replace the human-in-environment image by a holistic or Gestalt view which 'dissolves not only the human-in-environment concept, but every compact-thing-in- milieu concept'-except when they are talking at a superficial level of communication.

These deep ecologists insist on a cosmology of 'unbroken wholeness which denies the classical idea of the analysability of the world into separately and independently existing parts'.

They are strongly attracted to a variety of mystical traditions and to the Perennial Philosophy, where the self is merged with the other -'the other is none other than yourself'. As John Seed puts it: 'I am protecting the rainforest' develops into 'I am part of the rainforest protecting myself. I am that part of the rainforest recently emerged into thinking'. According to Joanna Macy: 'In the web of relationships... there are no clear lines demarcating a separate, continuous self'. Macy thinks that 'the notion of an abiding individual self... is the foundational delusion of human life'. There is 'no separate experiencer, no permanent self'. There are many problems here. It is not merely that the dissolution of boundaries of which deep ecologists speak stands in need of much more clarification; it is also that it does the wrong thing. The real basis of hyperseparation lies in the concept of an authentic human being, and in what is taken to be valuable in human character, society and culture, as exclusive of what is taken to be natural. Instead of healing this dualism, deep ecology proposes a 'unifying process', a metaphysics which insists that everything is really part of, indistinguishable from, everything else. This is not only to employ overly powerful tools, but ones that do the wrong job, for the origins of the particular opposition involved in human/nature dualism remain unaddressed and unanalysed.

This overreaction results from the confusion of separation and hyperseparation, radical exclusion and non-identity. The confusion is clear in Fox, who proceeds from the ambiguous claim that there is no 'bifurcation in reality between the human and non-human realms' (which could be taken as a rejection of human discontinuity from nature) immediately to the conclusion that what is needed is that we embrace an indistinguishability metaphysics of unbroken wholeness in the whole of reality. But the problem must be addressed in terms of this specific dualism and its connections. Instead this form of deep ecology proposes the obliteration of distinction. It is unclear how such a solution to removing human/nature dualism, by obliterating any human/nature distinction and dissolving self boundaries, is supposed to provide the basis for an environmental ethic.

The analysis of humans as metaphysically unified with the cosmic whole will be equally true whatever relation humans stand in with nature-the situation of exploitation of nature exemplifies such metaphysical unity equally as well as a conserver situation, and the human self is just as indistinguishable from the bulldozer and Coca Cola bottle as the rocks or the rainforest. What John Seed seems to have in mind here is that once one has realised that one is indistinguishable from the rainforest, its' needs will become one's own. But there is nothing to guarantee this-one could equally well take one's own needs for its. And some pronouncements indicate clearly that this is what happens. Thus John Seed's 'I remain in awe of the perennial power of humans joining together in worship of our Earth and the way that the Earth always responds. Of course She hears! For She? It?, is us'.

The question of just whose response counts for both of us has important political implications. The problem points towards a general set of boundary problems encountered by forms of deep ecology which dissolve or expand the self in this way. There is an arrogance in failing to respect boundaries and to acknowledge difference which can amount to an imposition of self. Deep ecologists see themselves as 'empowered to act on behalf of other beings' by claims of merging. One may in certain situations claim without arrogance to act in solidarity with or on behalf of another through one's own understanding of that other's situation, but one may not without arrogance assume that one is that other or knows that situation as does the other, that the other is transparent and encompassable by self without residue. Acknowledging the other's boundary and opacity of being is part of respect for the other. It is the master consciousness which presumes to violate boundaries and claims to subsume, penetrate and exhaust the other, and such treatment is a standard part of subordination; for example, of women, servants, the colonised, animals. Similarly, respecting the needs of the other involves acknowledging the difference as well as the connection between our needs. We need to recognise not only our human continuity with the natural world but also its distinctness and independence from us and the distinctness of the needs of things in nature from ours. As Jean Grimshaw writes of a related feminist account implying the indistinctness of persons (the acceptance of the loss of self boundaries as a feminine ideal):'

> Certain forms of symbiosis or connection with others can lead to damaging failures of personal development... because care for others, understanding of them, are only possible if one can adequately distinguish oneself from others. If I see myself as indistinct from you, or you as not having your own being that is not merged with mine, then I cannot preserve a real sense of your well- being as opposed to mine. Care and understanding require the sort of distance that is needed in order not to see the other as a projection of self, or self as a continuation of the other.

These points seem to me to apply as much to caring for other species and for the natural world as they do to caring for our own species. But just as hyperseparation is confused with separation, so self/other merger is taken to be the only alternative to egoistic accounts of the self as without essential connection to others or to nature. Fortunately, this is a false choice; it is neither helpful nor necessary to opt for merger to realise an account of the ecological self as connected to nature in non- instrumental ways.

The Expanded Self

In fairness to deep ecology, it should be noted that it often tends to vacillate between mystical indistinguishability and the other accounts of self, especially between the merged self and the expanded Self. Vacillation occurs often by way of slipperiness as to the meaning of the identification of self with other, a key notion in deep ecology. This slipperiness reflects the coniusion previously noted between separation and hyperseparation, but also seems to reflect a desire to retain the mystical appeal of indistinguishability while avoiding its many difficulties. Where 'identification' is used equivocally to mean both 'identity' and something like 'sympathy' or 'empathy', identification with other beings leads to an expanded self which encompasses all those we empathise with. According to Arne Naess, 'The self is as comprehensive as the totality of our identifications.... Our Self is that with which we identify'. This larger self is something for which we should strive'insofar as it is in our power to do so'. And according to Fox we should strive to make it as large as possible. But this expanded Self is not the result of a critique of egoism; rather, it is an enlargement and an extension of egoism. It does not question the structures of possessive egoism and self-interest; rather, it tries to allow for a wider set of interests by an expansion of self.

The motivation for the expansion of self is to allow for a wider set of concerns while continuing to allow the self to operate on the fuel of self-interest. This is apparent from the claim that 'in this light ecological resistance is simply another name for self defence'. Fox quotes with approval John Livingstone's statement, reminiscent of knightly vows: 'When I say that the fate of the sea turtle or the tiger or the gibbon is mine, I mean it. All that is in my universe is not merely mine; it is me. And I shall defend myself. I shall defend myself not only against overt aggression but also against gratuitous insult'. Joanna Macy also invokes the Self- interest model in an expanded form, calling on us to be 'a little more enlightened about what our self-interest is', while Arne Naess says: 'The requisite care flows naturally if the self is widened and deepened so that protection of free nature is felt and conceived of as protection of our very selves'. The expanded Self version of deep ecology misconceives identification and arises from failure to question fully the problematic of rational egoism. It continues to subscribe to two of the main tenets of the egoist framework-that human nature is egoistic and that the alternative to egoism is self-sacrifice.' The concept of Self-realisation also inherits the Nietzschean framework of egoist assumptions inscribed into humanistic psychology and the human potentials movement.

Given these assumptions about egoism, the obvious way to obtain some sort of human interest in defending nature is both through the expanded Self operating in the interests of nature, and along the familiar lines of self-interest.' Once the assumptions of rational egoism are questioned it is unnecessary to expand the Self in order to extend consideration to the other. The expanded Self strategy might initially seem to be just a dramatic but harmless way of saying that humans empathise with nature. But the strategy of transferring the structures of egoism is both unnecessary and highly problematic, for, the widening of interest is obtained at the expense of failing to recognise unambiguously the difference and independence of the other. Others are recognised morally only to the extent that they are incorporated into the self, and their difference denied. And the failure to critique rationalism, dualism and the structures of egoism means a failure to draw connections with other contemporary critiques.

One of the effects of the shift in focus towards the critique of dualism and rationalism is to make the connections of the environmental critique with other critiques, especially feminism, central rather than peripheral or accidental as they tend to be seen by deep ecologists. There are places, especially in Arne Naess's more recent work, where the assumptions of egoism are called clearly into question and appeal is made to what appears to be a version of the relational account of self. If 'identification' is interpreted to mean simply 'I empathy' or the assuming of the other's interests as one's own, as Naess suggests in his response to Reed, then the self which identifies with the other will be a version of the relational self, albeit a version which is interpreted in an unnecessarily holistic way as interest-identity, the assumption by the self of all the interests of the other. But the problem for deep ecologists in treating the relational self as a further, fallback interpretation of the Self is that it makes the whole problematic and cumbersome account of ecological selfhood as self-expansion and Self-realisation entirely unnecessary, along with the claim that the Self is the totality of its identifications. And it is also inconsistent with these frameworks, for the relational self framework must readmit the other, which the self-realisation strategy of deep ecology, especially with respect to the dissolution of ethics, depended upon absorbing into Self.

The Transcended or Transpersonal Self

To the extent that the expanded Self requires that we detach from the particular concerns of the 'narrow, biographic self' (a relinquishment which despite its natural difficulty we should, according to Fox, struggle to attain), expansion of self to Self also tends to lead into the third position, and to become the transcendence or overcoming of self, the conquest of 'the personal ego'. Thus Fox urges us to strive for impartial identification with all particulars, the cosmos, discarding our identifications with our own particular concerns, personal emotions and attachments. Fox presents here the deep ecology version of universalisation, with the familiar emphasis on the personal and the particular as corrupting and self-interested ('the cause of possessiveness, war and ecological destruction'), and of particulars as inferior to the larger whole. This treatment of particularity, the devaluation of personal relationships and of an identity tied to particular parts of the natural world as opposed to an abstractly conceived whole, the cosmos, inherits the rationalistic preoccupation with the universal and its account of ethical life as oppositional to the particular. Fox reiterates the view of particular attachments as ethically suspect and opposed to genuine, impartial 'identification', which necessarily falls short with all particulars.

The framework of detachment, impartiality and impersonality which this form of deep ecology takes over so uncritically from rationalist ethics and from some eastern thought, has been seen by many feminists as deeply problematic since, as Gilligan puts it, 'it breeds moral blindness or indifference-a failure to discern or respond to need'. The analogy in human terms of impersonal love of the cosmos is the view of morality as based on universal principles, or the impersonal and abstract 'love of man' detached from any particular caring relationships.

As Marti Kheel writes: 'This preference for identification with the larger "whole" may reflect the familiar masculine urge to transcend the concrete world of particularity in preference for something more enduring and abstract'. Because it carries this extra freight of devaluation of the area of particularity which has been associated with women, 'transpersonal ecology' represents a significant increase in theoretical masculinisation over and above the earlier forms of deep ecology.' Because this 'transpersonal' identification is so indiscriminate and denying of particular meanings, it cannot allow either for the deep and highly particularistic attachment to place which has motivated both the passion of many modern conservationists and the love of many indigenous peoples for their land" (which much deep ecology inconsistently tries to treat as exemplifying its modal). In addition to the love of the land as kin, noted earlier, particularistic care emerges clearly in the statements of many indigenous peoples; for example, in the moving words of Cecilia Blacktooth explaining why her people would not surrender their land:

> You ask us to think what place we like next best to this place where we always lived. You see the graveyard there? There are our fathers and our grandfathers. You see that Eagle-nest mountain and that Rabbit-hole mountain? When God made them, He gave us this place. We have always been here. We do not care for any other place.... We have always lived here. We would rather die here. Our fathers did. We cannot leave them. Our children were born here-how can we go away? If you give us the best place in the world, it is not so good as this.... This is our home.... We cannot live anywhere else. We were born here and our fathers are buried here.... We want this place and no other.

These are very specific and local responsibilities of care. In inferiorising such particular, emotional and kinship-based attachments, deep ecology gives us another variant on the superiority of reason and the inferiority of its contrasts, failing to grasp yet again the role of reason and incompletely critiquing its influence. To obtain a more adequate account than that offered by mainstream ethics and deep ecology it seems that we must move towards the sort of ethics much feminist theory has suggested, which can allow for both continuity and difference, and for ties to nature which are expressive of a rich variety of relationships of care, kinship and friendship, rather than towards increasing abstraction and detachment from relationship.

The Ecological Self and the Virtue of Ethics

A major motivation for the self-realisation account of deep ecology is that it supposedly makes it possible to dispense with appeals to ethics and morality in ecological matters and to replace them with Self- interest, from which care flows naturally. On this deep ecology account, ethics and morality are equated with duty, sermonising and self-sacrifice, in effect Kantian ethics, which operates as a prohibition on desire. But this form of ethics is only one variety of ethical account of relationship to nature, and there are other types of ethical experience and theory which do not take such a prohibitory form. Virtue accounts, for example, are based on a set of commitments inherent in a particular type of identity, and from them care does'flow naturally', that is, it expresses what that individual wants to do, as that particular sort of individual, rather than what he or she is constrained to do through duty. Deep ecology often operates with a covert version of a virtue-based account of the ecological self; thus Naess writes: 'We need not say that today man's relation to the non-human world is immoral. It is enough to say that it lacks generosity, fortitude, and love'. Were the use of such a virtue-based account to be explicitly admitted by deep ecology, it would be unnecessary to incur the many problems of Self-interest, especially the denial of difference, in order to find a basis for consideration of others in nature which flows from the self and is not based on prohibition.

There are many good reasons to avoid building an account of ecological morality on ethics in its usual rationalist conception, and to inspired move in the direction of an ethics of virtue. Rationalist ethical concepts are highly ethnocentric and cannot account adequately for the views of many indigenous peoples. The attempted application of these rationalist concepts to their moral life tends to lead to the view that they lack a real ethical framework. Alternative virtue-based concepts such as care, respect, gratitude, sensitivity, reverence and friendship seem more applicable." Such concepts are more resistant to analysis along the lines of reason/emotion dualism, and their construal along these lines has involved confusion and distortion. They are moral 'feelings' but they involve both cognitive elements, ethical elements and emotion in ways that do not seem separable. These are more local concepts, which allow for particularity and do not require either assimilation or, mostly, reciprocity. They are also concepts many feminist philosophers have argued should have a more significant place at the expense of abstract concepts of mainstream western ethics such as rights and justice.

The feminist suspicion is that no abstract morality can be well founded that is not grounded in sound particularistic relations to others in personal life, the area which brings together in concrete form the intellectual with the emotional, the sensuous and the bodily. Such an approach treats ethical relations as an expression of identity; for example, maternal care as an expression of self-in-relationship rather than as the discarding, containment, or generalisation of a self viewed as self-interested and non-relational, as in the conventional ethics of prohibition or universalisation. From this perspective, rationalist ethics provides an account suited to governing the relations of egoist stranger to egoist stranger, rather than one suited to a richer and more particular form of relationship. If the grounding of virtue in the commitments of identity can provide the terra firma of valuation which floundering ethical theories have long sought, it also provides its own problems. Identities themselves must be subject to ethical assessment, and may be morally problematic; alongside the identity and virtue of the mother must be placed that of the soldier.

Indeed many moral issues are simply displaced on to issues of the morality of being that kind of person, having that identity. But the argument developed in this book has shown that these issues of human identity and relationship to nature are among the key issues which need to be addressed in any new approach to nature. It is not, then, that we need to abandon ethical aspects of environmental philosophy, or opt for an entirely contextual ethics. Rather environmental ethics needs a different and richer understanding of ethics, one which gives an important place to the issues surrounding human identity, allows for ethical concepts owning to emotionality and particularity, and abandons the exclusive focus on the universal and the abstract associated with egoism, and the dualistic and oppositional accounts of the reason/emotion and universal/particular contrasts given in rationalist accounts of ethics.

Deep ecology has some excuse for the identification of ethics with those rationalist forms of it based on the concept of moral rules restraining the rational ego. For this has been the conception corresponding to dominant forms of modern market rationality and social life. Rationalism, the prestige of reason and the kind of egoist and instrumental identity demanded by the public sphere have influenced not only the concept of what morality is and of what is central to it, but also what count as moral concepts. Virtue-based concepts such as friendship, love, respect, care, concern, gratitude, community and compassion are in conflict with the rational instrumentalism of the public sphere, in which they have no place. As the main ethical concepts of society, they correspond to a different conception of moral life which is now, as McIntyre argues, a residue. Excluded from the public, these concepts appear today mainly in the practices and relationships of the private sphere, and of women especially as the representatives of that sphere. Motherhood and friendship represent perhaps the clearest examples of relational selfhood, and an identity expressed in caring practices which treat the other non-instrumentally.

The ecological self can be interpreted as a form of mutual selfhood in which the self makes essential connection to earth others, and hence as a product of a certain sort of relational identity. In expressing that identity, the individual fulfils his or her own ends as well as those of the other. He or she stands in particular relations, which may be those of care, custodianship, friendship, or various diverse virtue concepts, to that other, who is treated as deserving of concern for its own sake, and hence as intrinsically worthy or valuable. The relational self and intrinsic value are, therefore, essential theoretical complements of a virtue account of ecological selfhood. They can be accounted for in ways that enable them to apply to the natural world without problematic assumptions about difference or egoism. On their own, however, they do not delineate the precise content of that relationship, except as one of essential and non-instrumental concern, one of regard for beings for their own sake.

Since virtue accounts are based on a set of commitments inherent in a particular type of identity, an essential further ingredient in putting flesh on the bones of an alternative conception of care for nature is that of human identity. The origins and defects of the traditional western account which defined human virtue in terms of the radical exclusion of the contrast class of nature, and which, as we have seen, treats the human relation to it as one of domination and instrumentalism. Any new conception of human identity would need to make allowance for the variety of human commitments to and human caring relations for the limitless variety of beings in nature, as well as providing for alternative visions and ethical frameworks which may be highly regionalised and particularised. It is unlikely that any single conception would cover a ground of such diversity.

However, if care and friendship are seen as generic or determinable concepts, there is a range of determinate relationships and caring virtues on which such a practice of human virtue in relation to nature might draw. Many of the more specific virtues which might be drawn upon for a new human identity in relation to nature have already emerged from the debate. Some of them are the general virtues of friendship, such as openness to the other, generosity, leaving space for the other, the ability to put oneself in the place of the other and to respond to the other's needs. With nature, as with the human sphere, the capacity to care, to experience sympathy, understanding and sensitivity to the situation and fate of particular others is an index of our moral being. Other virtues would express recognition of specific relations of dependency, responsibility, continuity and interconnection, as well as those of difference and of respect for the independence and boundlessness of the other.

An important ground of certain caring relations would be a locally particularised identity involving commitment to a particular place and its non-human as well as its human inhabitants. This is advocated by bioregionalism. But any attempt to rekindle such an alternative conception of human identity must confront the loss in modern urban life of much of the basis of that identity, and the loss of the particular practices of care through which commitment to particular places is expressed and fostered. For most people in industrial society such virtues are, tragically, indeed a residue.

This is not just a feature of modernity; it is a feature of the mobility and instrumentalism of market society. Although a virtue ethics is usually now exemplified in relations in the private sphere, a private construction of ecological selfhood does not go far enough. Rather such an ethical commitment should be thought of as a form of resistance to dominant instrumental constructions of public and social life. Any attempt to work towards a different conception of the human self and to construe its relations to nature along these lines as non-instrumental will have to confront the problem of the dominance of instrumental relationships in the public sphere.

Although ecological selfhood has private aspects, it cannot satisfactorily be construed as a purely private practice, like personal friendship or motherhood, which does not impinge on the public sphere, or challenge its dominant instrumentalism. Hence ecological selfhood cannot be conceived in terms of the thunderclap of personal conversion to an after-hours religion of earth worship, tacked on to a basically market-orientated conception of social and economic life. Nor, as Poole argues against McIntyre, should it be tied to the attempt to resurrect past social forms. It must be seen rather as an attempt to obtain a new human and a new social identity in relation to nature which challenges this dominant instrumental conception, and its associated social relations. Hence it is a practice of opposition which parallels that of the attempt to retain and expand other non-instrumental forms of social and economic life in the face of relentless instrumentalising pressure. Part of overcoming the influence of dualism in ethics is the dissolution of the false opposition rationalist ethics assumes between particularistic relations of concern and more general moral concern.

There can be opposition between particularity and generality of concern, as when concern for particular kin is accompanied by exclusion of others from care or chauvinistic attitudes towards them. But this does not happen automatically. Emphasis on oppositional cases obscures the frequent and important instances in which care for particular others is essential to a more generalised morality. Special relationships, which are treated by universalising positions as at best morally irrelevant, and at worst a positive hindrance to the moral life, are thus mistreated. For as Blum stresses, special relationships inevitably must form the basis for much of our moral life and concern. Special relationships with, care for or empathy with particular aspects of nature as experienced, rather than with nature as abstraction, are essential to provide a depth of concern.

Under appropriate conditions, experience of and care and responsibility for particular animals, trees, rivers, places and ecosystems which are known well, are loved and are appropriately connected to the self, enhance rather than hinder a wider, more generalised concern for the global environment. This helps to explain why global moral concern should not be and does not have to be abandoned in such a framework. Certainly, we cannot treat the entire universe as if it were our nearest and dearest, although saints sometimes try, and certainly, moral concern cannot exclude strangers and distant others. Moral concern cannot just be particularistic, but at the same time it cannot be based satisfactorily on a universalism which denies and devalues particularised moral commitments and the relevance of personal experience. Nor can they just be tacked on, as some accounts suggest. For we have to address not only the omission of the voice of love and care but also the opposition between the universalising voice and the caring voice, as well as the latter's subordination. And this in turn is part, not just of ethics, but of re-evaluating and realigning the relations of the public and private sphere on which these different voices have been based. Still, there is scope here for a different account of universalisation which is not based on devaluation of the personal and particular.

It would make wider concern a question not of transcending or detaching the self from particular, personal moral commitments, but in part at least of understanding or coming to see the relationship between these particular commitments and local situations and those of distant others. You can come to understand the relationship between your own loss and that of others, the degradation of your own local ecosystem and that of the global ecosystem, the impoverishment of social and natural life-forms and that of your own life and the lives of those you know. Such wider forms of care can be expressed in political consciousness and social action with as much force and validity as in personal relationships.

The implication of this form of empathic generalisation, in contrast to Kantian universalisation, is that the more strongly you feel about your own commitments and attachments the more basis you should have for expanding concern to others. This is not to assume that everyone makes such connections, but rather to shift the moral focus from supposed oppositional relations, between particular and general concern, to the conditions of social and political life which produce such opposition and which hinder such empathic generalisation. These conditions will often be those which construct the other as alien, and include especially the web of dualism and hierarchy.

However, an ethic of care speaks not in one voice but in a number of different political voices, both particularised ones of concern for family and immediate others, and more general forms voicing concern for nature and wider social groups. These voices will not necessarily be in harmony. To expect that they would be so would be to mistake what such voices have to offer us. The voices of care are non-instrumentalising voices, but they can carry widely different political messages. There cannot be a single answer to the question of whether the ethics of care is socially progressive or socially regressive-it is a determinable whose determinates can be either.

The care which women provide in the context of the family in market society typically has an incompleteness and an ambiguity, the more so to the extent that it is controlled and structured by its larger context. Often the ethics of care is contained and adapted to a supportive role, that of supplying the care and the human values omitted from the public sphere and so making life tolerable or possible, or that of providing the co-operatively socialised individuals on which the public sphere relies but which it could not itself provide. Thus familial care can support a conservative value system resisting extension of care to non-familial or 'undeserving' others or working to disadvantage women by denying them equal participation in the public arena; the mother working in the munitions factory can give care for 'the boys' as the justification for work supporting militarism. Or, in the ecological case, a woman can give care for a husband's or son's welfare and employment as the reason why she thinks a logging practice, which will destroy an endangered species, should continue. But despite these ambiguities, the care model has a major contribution to make to understanding alternatives to the dominant instrumental models.

The association of the virtues of personal care with women is historical and contingent rather than essential. It does not reflect women's unique or innate suitability for their practice so much as the exclusion of these non-instrumentalising virtues and practices from the public sphere. It is in these wider contexts especially that the practices and virtues of care, long contained in the private sphere, realise their subversive and oppositional potential. Women indeed have something highly valuable to offer in these non- instrumentalising voices, as 'custodians of a story about human attachment and interdependence', a story increasingly driven from the world at large, both as human care and in the form of care for the earth.

Reconstructing Reason

The resolution of human/nature dualism is closely linked with the resolution of other closely associated reason/nature dualisms, such as the reason/emotion dualism. We have seen how reason/emotion dualism fits the model of denied dependency, especially in the rationalist conception of the ethical. We have noticed how emotion is constructed as the opponent and dualised underside of reason, so that it is identified as an unreliable, unreflective, irrational and sometimes uncontrollable force reason must dominate. We should certainly challenge the narrowing and dominating role of reason. But what is contraindicated by the analysis of reason/emotion dualism is the replacement of the affirmation of reason by the affirmation of the dualised conception of emotion. Emotion, like other areas reason has excluded, can be treated affirmatively, as a crucial and creative element, but in doing this we affirm neither the irrational nor the anti-rational.

Since overcoming dualism does not imply dissolving difference, there may still be a point in recognising a distinction between reason and emotion. But the distinction should not be treated in terms of radical exclusion: emotions need not be treated as so unreasonable, nor reason as so divorced from emotion, as they are in dualistic construction; nor need they be construed as necessarily oppositional, but as capable of a creative integration and interaction. The anti-dualist programme implies a politics which can create a different, non- hierarchical and integrative role for rationality in developing and articulating perceptions, feelings and values, in grounding and establishing a basis for human existence on the earth which is not based on illusions of the master.

In a properly grounded human life, reason could act as the facilitator for the faculties, rather than the dictator, and play this role both in its relation to other elements in individual life and in the many social forms and institutions in which the hierarchical construction of reason is still embedded. An honoured, rather than a denigrated, place could be given to engaged forms of reason which acknowledge and are faithful to their value commitments, and to a conception of social and public life governed by the values of care for and commitment to the other which have been stripped from it and confined to the private. The expulsion of the master identity from the western construction of reason requires not the abandonment of reason itself, but an effort to instal another, less hierarchical, more democratic and plural identity in its place.

Reflections on Identity and Difference

It is a sad irony that the destruction of the natural world appears to be proceeding apace with the construction of moral theories for how we should behave in light of this fact. Unable to trust or draw upon a felt sense of connection, most environmental theorists endorse reason as the sole guide in our dealings with the natural world.

The vast majority of theories that constitute the field of environmental ethics are thus axiological or value theories whose primary purpose is the rational allotment of value to the appropriate aspects of the natural world. Both Eco-feminism and deep ecology share in common an opposition to these value theories with their attendant notions of obligations and rights. The emphasis of both philosophies is not on an abstract or "rational" calculation of value but rather on the development of a new consciousness for all of life. Both Eco-feminism and deep ecology may therefore be viewed as "deep" philosophies in the sense that they call for an inward transformation in order to attain an outward change. Deep ecologists employ the notion of self-realization to describe this inward transformation. As environmental philosophers Bill Devall and George Sessions explain, this process: begins when we cease to understand or see ourselves as isolated and narrow competing egos and begin to identify with other humans from our family and friends to, eventually, our species. But the deep ecology sense of Self requires a further maturity and growth, an identification which goes beyond humanity to include the non-human world.

There is a significant distinction between Eco-feminism and deep ecology, however, in their understanding of the root cause of our environmental malaise. For deep ecologists, it is the anthropocentric world-view that is foremost to blame.The two norms of deep ecology self-realization and biospherical egalitarianism-are thus designed to redress this self-centered world-view. Eco-feminists, on the other hand, argue that it is the androcentric world-view that deserves primary blame. For eco-feminists, it is not just "humans" but men and the masculinist world-view that must be dismantled from their privileged place.

The key to understanding the differences between the two philosophies thus lies in the differing conceptions of self that both philosophies presuppose. When deep ecologists write of anthropocentrism and the notion of an "expanded Self", they ostensibly refer to a gender-neutral concept of self. Implicit in the feminist analysis of the androcentric world-view, however, is the understanding that men and women, under patriarchal society, experience the world, and hence their conceptions of self, in widely divergent ways. Whereas the anthropocentric world-view perceives humans as the center or apex of the natural world, the androcentric analysis suggests that this world-view is unique to men. Feminists have argued that women's identities, unlike men's, have not been established through their elevation over the natural world. On the contrary, under patriarchal society, women have been identified with the devalued natural world, an identification that they have often adopted as well.

One of the most thoroughgoing analyses of the masculine and feminine conceptions of self was formulated by Simone de Beauvoir in her monumental work The Second Sex. According to de Beauvoir, under patriarchal society, women's sense of self is inextricably tied to her status as the "other."

For de Beauvoir, the facts of pregnancy, menstruation, and childbirth have historically confined women to the world of immanence and contangency, a state of being in which life "merely" repeats itself. Authentic subjectivity is achieved to the extent that one raises oneself above biological necessity and hence above the animal world. Men have historically transcended the world of contingency through exploits and projects, that is, through attempts to transform the natural world. Thus, selfhood is an identity that emerges through an antagonistic relation to an "other." In order for women to achieve full human status or selfhood, they must join with men in exploits and projects that express this opposition to the natural world.

De Beauvoir developed her concept of the other from the writings of both Hegel and Sartre. Both of these philosophers considered antagonistic consciousness to be necessary for the establishment of the self. For Hegel, consciousness could only be achieved through recognition from other. If the truth of self-certainty-the sustained sense of oneself as a part of the world -was to be achieved, the other must be overcome. This contradictory need for both recognition from and negation of the other could result in only two possible outcomes: the death of the other or the subjection of the other in the relation of master and slave.

Sartre went on to develop the notion of the antagonistic nature of consciousness with his concept of the "look." The struggle between two consciousnesses thus becomes one of competing looks. When one is looked at, according to Sartre, one becomes objectified; one is no longer the center of infinite possibilities. Each self struggles to attain transcendence by turning the other into an object.

De Beauvoir's contribution to Sartre's thought was to

show that it was women, under patriarchal society, who had been assigned the role of the looked upon other.

While agreeing with much of de Beauvoir's analysis, many contemporary feminists reject the masculine norm of autonomy that she endorsed. The notion of an autonomous self, established through the defeat of a female-imaged other, is viewed by many feminists as a central underpinning of the patriarchal world. Feminists have shown that many of the world's most sacred traditions depict stories of struggle and conquest. Typically, the conquest is of darkness or Chaos, usually symbolized by a female-imaged animal form - frequently a serpent or a snake. Through this struggle against unruly nature, the world of light and order is born.

The psychoanalytic theory of object relations presents a modern-day rendition of the same heroic struggle of the masculine self in opposition to the female world. According to this theory, both boys and girls experience their first forms of relatedness as a kind of merging with the mother figure. The child then develops a concept of self through the process of disengaging from this figure. Unlike girls, boys have a two-stage process of disidentification. They must not only disengage from the mother figure, but in order to identify as male, they must deny all that is female within themselves. The self-identity of the boy child is thus founded upon the negation and objectification of an other. Dorothy Dinnerstein extends this analysis to the masculine mode of interacting not only with women but with all of the natural world. For Dinnerstein, since a child's self-identity is originally viewed as indistinct from the surrounding world, later self-identity is founded not only upon the notion of not being female but upon the notion of not being nature as well. Thus, object relations theory provides another interpretation of why the masculine self is conceived as the negation of both women and the natural world.

If men in our society are socialized to perceive their identity in opposition to a devalued, female-imaged world, we might expect that the process of reinstituting this forbidden identification might be fraught with problems along the way. At the very least, we might expect that such a process of identification would not be experienced in identical ways for women and men. The writings of three prominent male philosophers, who claim that their process of self-realization occurs through the act of hunting and killing animals, are suggestive in this regard.

According to the philosopher/biologist Randall Eaton:

To hunt is to experience extreme oneness with nature.... The hunter imitates his prey to the point of identity.... hunting connects a man completely with the earth more deeply and profoundly than any other human enterprise. Paradoxical as it may appear at first glimpse, the hunter's feeling for his prey is one of deep passion, ecstasy and respect.... The hunter loves the animal he kills.

Let us recall that according to psychoanalytic theory, the boy's yearning to identify with the mother figure is fuelled by his feelings of alienation and the consequent urge to reexperience the original state of union. Eaton's words convey such a longing, which may be viewed as a longing for the original self:

What do I mean at the deepest level when I say I want to know the behavior of the tiger? I really mean that I have affection for tigers and that I want to see the essential nature or being of the tiger. If the truth be known, I want to be a tiger, to walk in his skin, hear with his ears, flex my tiger body and feel as a tiger feels.

Jose Ortegay Gasset, a well-known Spanish philosopher, reflects a similar urge toward unification with the animal, which he sees as a unification with the animal within himself. In his words: "Man cannot re-enter Nature except by temporarily rehabilitating that part of himself which is still an animal. And this, in turn, can be achieved only by placing himself in relation to another animal.

For men such as Eaton and Ortega, the ultimate purpose of the hunt appears to be this reversion to an earlier state of being in which one's separateness not only from women, but from animals, has not yet occurred. Ortega, in fact, refers to hunting as a kind of "vacation from the human condition through an authentic 'immersion in Nature.'" He goes on to explain: "In that mystical union with the beast a contagion is immediately generated and the hunter begins to behave like the game. The erotic undertones of hunting can be found in sensuous descriptions of the hunt. Thus, the prominent environmental writer Aldo Leopold writes that he "tingled" at the recollection of the big gander that sailed honking into his decoys, and Ortega writes of the "exquisite" feel of the air that "glides over the skin and enters the lungs." At other times, both write of hunting in more heated terms, using such words as "hunting fever" and the "drama" and "contagion" of the hunt. Indeed, Ortega goes so far as to assert the "unequalled orgiastic power" of blood, contending that wildlife photography is to hunting what Platonic love is to the real thing.

According to both object relations and Jungian theory it is the ongoing denial of the original union with the mother figure that creates the lifelong yearning to experience this original state. Hunting is, in fact, described by these writers as a permanent or instinctive longing. According to Ortega, sport hunting is "however strangely a deep and permanent yearning in the human condition." And according to Leopold: "The instinct that finds delight in the sight and pursuit of game is bred into the very fiber of the human race. Desire for hunting, according to Leopold, lies deeper than other outdoor sports: "Its source is a matter of instinct as well as competition.... A son of Robinson Crusoe, having never seen a racket, might get along nicely without one, but he would be pretty sure to hunt or fish whether or not he were taught to do so." In other words, a boy instinctively wants to hunt and kill.

It must be emphasized here that all three writers describe hunting not as a necessary means of subsistence but rather as a desire that fulfils a deep psychological need.

At times Leopold is unclear as to whether this instinct is universally held by all humans or only by men and boys. He writes that: "A man may not care for gold and still be human but the man who does not like to see, hunt, photograph or otherwise outwit birds and animals is hardly normal. He is supercivilized, and I for one do not know how to deal with him. In order to understand how the act of identification can coexist with the desire to kill the being with whom one identifies, it is important to understand the ambivalent nature of the hunt. Ortega refers to the "ambivalence" felt by every hunter, an ambivalence that results from "the equivocal nature of man's relationship with animals." As he explains: "Nor can it be otherwise, because man has never really known what an animal is. Before and beyond all science, humanity sees itself as something emerging from animality, but it cannot be sure of having transcended that state completely."

The hunter is thus driven by conflicting desires to both identify with the animal and to deny that he is an animal himself. The "drama" of the hunt thus enables the hunter to experience both the yearning for a return to unity, while ensuring, through the death of the animal, that such a unification is never attained.

Deep ecologists caution that identification must entail a recognition of the "relative autonomy" of the other being, but it is precisely this autonomous existence that the above writers have failed to convey. According to object relations theory, it is only when the boy child transforms his mother into an object that his identity can be formed. In a similar way, animals have become objects in the eyes of these men. In fact, Leopold openly expresses this urge to reduce animals to object status: "Critics write and hunters outwit their animals for one and the same reason-to reduce that beauty to possession. Interestingly, the original title of his famous Sand County Almanac was "Great Possessions."

The significance of the reduction of the animal to object status is that the relationship to the animal becomes more important than the animal itself. The feelings of yearning for union, the urge to "outwit" all these take precedence over the living being that will be killed. The animal is swallowed up in the act of merging. Even the death of the animal is considered incidental-it is a by-product of the more important desire that finds its expression in the hunt. As Ortega explains:

> To the sportsman the death of the game is not what interests him; that is not his purpose. What interests him is everything he had to do to achieve that death-that is the hunt. Therefore, what was before only a means to an end is now an end in itself. Death is essential because without it there is no authentic hunting. To sum up, one does not hunt in order to kill; on the contrary, one kills in order to have hunted.

Deep ecologists argue that a widened identification will ensure that one will want to minimize harm to individual beings, in that they will be viewed as part of the all-inclusive Self. However, it seems clear from the above examples of self-realization that for these men this was not the case. For all three, the killing of animals was an integral part of the process of self-realization. For them, the animal is seen not as a unique, living being but rather as a means to achieve a desired psychological state. The animal is thus reduced to the status of object or symbol.

For all three writers the desire to hunt is clearly of greater importance than the life of the animal they kill. For Leopold, the urge to hunt was strong enough to merit its enshrinement as an inalienable right. In his words:

> Some can live without the opportunity for the exercise and control of the hunting instinct, just as I suppose some can live without work, play, love, business or other vital adventure. But in these days we regard such deprivation as unsocial. Opportunity for the exercise of all the normal instincts has come to be regarded more and more as an inalienable right.

Aldo Leopold is considered by many a pioneer of deep ecology and eco-philosophy. He is perhaps best known as an early promulgator of an ethic of non-anthropocentrism and bio centric equality. What is not widely recognized, however, is how paramount the hunting instinct was to Leopold's philosophy and to the land ethic for which he is so well known.

Right after he writes of the inalienable right for the free exercise of the "normal" instinct to hunt, he goes on to deplore the fact that "The men who are destroying our wildlife are alienating one of these rights and doing a good job of it. In other words, wildlife must be conserved not because of the animals' inalienable right to life but rather because of "man's" inalienable right to hunt and kill! As Leopold elaborates:

> His instincts prompt him to compete for his place in the community but his ethics prompt him also to cooperate [emphasis added].... An ethic ecologically is a limitation on freedom of action in the struggle for existence. An ethic philosophically is a differentiation of social from anti-social conduct. These two are two definitions of one thing. Good social conduct involves a limitation of freedom.

Leopold's land ethic is thus conceived as a necessary restraint for a self that is driven by an inherently aggressive drive. All three of the above writers see such aggression and struggle as a fundamental fact of life. In Ortega's words: "Life is a terrible conflict, a grandiose and atrocious confluence." This notion of life's inherent conflict can be understood as the result of the male's ongoing internal struggle to maintain his self-identity as distinct from the female-imaged natural world. This internal conflict then becomes projected onto the "outside" world. But not everyone's concept of self entails such an aggressive drive. For many women this is, in fact, clearly not the case. Such women's process of identification and widening of the self finds expression in different ways. For many women, identification with animals entails not an aggressive drive but rather the desire to avoid causing them harm. At times deep ecologists would seem to express this feeling as well.

Thus, the Norwegian philosopher Arne Naess writes that: "There is a basic intuition in deep ecology that we have no right to destroy other living beings without sufficient reason. Another norm is that, with maturity, human beings will experience joy when other life forms experience joy, and sorrow when other life forms experience sorrow.' This statement, however, appears to be contradicted by Devall and Sessions, who suggest in Deep Ecology that hunting, along with such diverse activities as surfing, sailing, sunbathing, and bicycling, is "an especially useful activity" that, with the "proper attitude," can help encourage "maturity" of the self. In order to understand this seeming contradiction, we must recall that it is the widest sense of identification that deep ecologists ultimately call for -that is, an identification not with individual beings but rather the larger biotic community or whole. Australian environmental philosopher Warwick Fox expresses this relative prioritizing when he states that: "In terms of the wider identification approach, then, it can be seen that there is a strong sense in which community is even more important than the individual expressions that constitute it since the community itself constitutes an entire dimension of the world with which I identify, i.e., of myself.

And the poet Robinson Jeffers, whom deep ecologists cite with approval, expresses this relative prioritizing in even stronger terms: "I believe the universe is one being, all its parts are different expressions of the same energy, and they are all in communication with each other, therefore parts of an organic whole.... It seems to me that this whole alone is worthy of the deeper love [emphasis added]."

Deep ecologists maintain that this primary identification with the whole is not at the expense of the individual beings since they, too, must be seen as part of the same all-inclusive Self. But, as we have seen, the danger with widening one's identification to the "whole" or biotic community is that one may widen it beyond the reach of individual beings. This preference for identification with the larger "whole" may reflect the familiar masculine urge to transcend the concrete world of particularity in preference for something more enduring and abstract.

Deep ecologists would have us believe that self-relation is a simple process of expanding one's identification to all of the natural world. But when deep ecologists write of expanding the self, eco-feminists must be prepared to examine more deeply the unconscious drives that fuel the self that one seeks to expand. We have seen that women and animals have been utilized as psychological instruments for the establishment of the masculine self. The conquest of the snake, the dragon, and other female-imaged monsters reflects the inner drives and needs of the masculine self. What we witness in the experiences of the writers discussed here is the same conquest mentality now operating on a seemingly "higher" plane. Nonetheless, animals are still used as instruments of self-definition-they are killed not in the name of an individual, masculine ego but instead in the name of a higher, abstract self. But whether one is establishing the self writ small or large, the experience of the animal the loss of her or his life remains the same.

The danger of an abstract identification with a larger "whole" is that it fails to recognize or respect the existence of independent, living beings. This has, in fact, been a major failing of both environmental philosophy and the environmental movement. By alternately raising the ecosystem or an aggrandized self to the level of supreme value, they have created a holism that risks obliterating the uniqueness and importance of individual beings. The disillusionment of many animal liberationists with both the environmental movement and environmental philosophy is a consequence of this fact.

Eco-feminist philosophy must be wary of a holistic philosophy that transcends the realm of individual beings. Our deep, holistic awareness of the inter-connectedness of all of life must be a lived awareness that we experience in relation to particular beings as well as the larger whole.

If, as object relations theory argues, women's self-identity, unlike men's, is not bound up with the urge to negate one's dependence on the natural world, then we should not be surprised to find that women's experiences with nature may differ from those of men. Although it cannot be claimed that no women hunt or perhaps experience their sense of nature in the ways described by the writers discussed here, most people, I think, will recognize such behavior as primarily characteristic of men. Throughout history hunting has, in fact, been an activity that has been pursued by and large by men.

Many women have found other ways to experience their oneness or identification with nature. Charlene Spretnak writes that women often have such experiences through the "body parables" -"reclaimed menstruation, orgasm, pregnancy, natural childbirth and motherhood. It is out of women's unique, felt sense of connection to the natural world that an eco-feminist philosophy must be forged. Identification may, in fact, enter into this philosophy but only to the extent that it flows from an existing connection with individual lives. Individual beings must not be used in a kind of psychological instrumentalism to help establish a feeling of connection that does not, in fact, exist. Our sense of oneness with nature must be connected with concrete, loving actions.

Eco-feminism and deep ecology have suggested, at times, that what each refers to is a consciousness of love. As we have seen, however, love can mean many things and be expressed in a variety of ways. As Eco-feminism develops in relation to other philosophies, it must carefully examine the practical consequences of all abstract ideals. Only then will Eco-feminism know how far our own identification can go.

6

Deep Ecology and Eco-Feminism
The Emerging Dialogue

In the Spring of 1987, a barge loaded with garbage from Islip, New York, made international headlines as it searched in vain for a place to dump its unwanted load. The garbage barge was a striking symbol for and symptom of the behavior of "advanced" industrial societies, which are poisoning themselves and the biosphere by their own wastes. One of today's leading issues is whether we can survive the very industrial practices that we have relied upon for material "progress." Some people, including deep ecologists and eco-feminists, maintain that the set of Western categories responsible for this "progress" must be transformed if we are to learn to dwell upon the Earth in an appropriate way.

In what follows, the deep ecologists, on the one hand, and eco-feminists, on the other, would explain how these Western categories have shaped society in a way that almost inevitably led to the appearance of the garbage barge. But despite apparent similarities in their critical appraisal of Western culture, the deep ecological and the eco-feminist views are not entirely in harmony. Eco-feminists argue that deep ecologists overlook the real source of the domination of nature: patriarchy. In developing a critical exchange between deep ecology and Eco-feminism, my intention is to strengthen and to further the important dialogue that has been initiated between these two opponents of the domination of nature, of our own bodies, and of woman and man.'

Deep ecology, a radical stream of the environment movement, maintains that the environmental crisis is the inevitable outcome of the history of Western culture. A primary distinction between deep ecology and reform environmentalism is that the former is non-anthropocentric in its attitude toward the natural world, while the latter is anthropocentric. It would be incorrect, however, to lump into one undifferentiated group all forms of environmentalism that are not "deeply" ecological. Environmental philosopher John Rodman, for example, differentiates four stages in ecological consciousness: resource conservation, wilderness preservation, moral extensionism, and ecological sensibility.

Resource conservation is the most obviously human-centered version of reform environmentalism. From its viewpoint, we must conserve "resources" because of our obligation to future generations of humanity. Although widespread, resource conservation is by no means universally accepted. Some people argue, for example, that we not only have no obligations to the natural world, we also have no obligations to so-called future generations of people.

Wilderness preservation seems at first glance to be oriented not toward human beings but instead toward protecting the wilderness itself from human "development." Rodman argues, however, that wilderness preservationists remain anthropocentric since they aim at protecting wilderness as the site for aesthetic or religious experiences in the grandeur of unspoiled wild places. Wilderness preservation, then, turns out to be subtly anthropocentric: we are to preserve the wilderness not so much for its own sake as for the sake of the experiences people have in it.

The third version of reform environmentalism is moral extensionism.' According to this approach, the environmental crisis stems in part from our unethical treatment of non-human beings. One way to protect the non-human world from human exploitation is to show that some non-human beings are worthy of moral "concern" and/or legal "standing." But there are problems with this approach, too. For example, the standards used to determine whether a non-human entity is morally "worthy" are all too often derived from criteria considered definitive of humanity, such as sentience, or consciousness. Anthropocentrism raises its ugly head once again.

Rodman's fourth stage of ecological consciousness is ecological sensibility, or deep ecology. While there are various approaches to deep ecology, there is one major issue on which virtually all deep ecologists agree: the industrial pollution, species extinction, biospheric degradation, and nuclear annihilation facing the Earth are all symptoms of anthropocentrism. Only by recognizing that humanity is no more, but also no less, important than all other things on Earth can we learn to dwell on the planet within limits that would allow other species to flourish and to follow out their own evolutionary destiny. Anthropocentric hierarchies would be replaced by bio centric egalitarianism. Disputes would necessarily arise in the face of difficult decisions ("Should these trees be cut down for the sake of building these houses?"), but such disputes would not paralyze human activity. The disputes would take place with the presupposition that all entities concerned have "rights" that must be taken into account during the decision-making process. According to the Norwegian philosopher and naturalist Arne Naess, living according to deep ecological principles would bring about the fulfilment of human existence as well as liberating nature from human exploitation. Humanity's highest possibility is to bear witness to and to participate in the great process of life itself. Supposedly, only deep ecology points the way beyond abuse toward appreciation, beyond anthropocentrism toward a mature humanity living within appropriate limits that enable other entities to thrive as well.

According to the Australian environmental philosopher Warwick Fox, the "central intuition" of deep ecology is that there is no absolute divide between humanity and everything else.' Western humanity tends to think in terms of dualisms, such as that between mind and body, or between humanity and nature. Such dualism leads Western humanity to split off its "dark side"-its mortality, dependence, and finitude-and to project it upon the body and nature, which it then attempts to "dominate" and "control." Deep ecology, by way of contrast, thinks non-dualistically; it looks instead to the rich internal relations that constitute the universe. Deep ecology also proposes an alternative to Newton's atomistic conception of the physical world, a conception that was extended by Hobbes and Locke into the social world. Far from being a social atom that is wholly independent of other people and the natural world, the human being is a "node" in the internal relations that compose everything. A mature humanity would understand its interrelationship with everything else.

Many deep ecologists maintain that their view is consistent with both Eastern religions and mystical traditions within Western religions, namely, that the I and the not-I are ultimately a unity. Such realization also involves direct insight into the limitations of subject/object dualism and its calculating rationality. Rationality, according to deep ecology, is an important way of interpreting the world, but it is often used destructively in the service of the ego striving to deny its mortality by controlling all things. An enlightened humanity would use rationality in accordance with a more profound understanding or sensibility that transcends subject/object dualism. The discovery that all things are internally related would lead us to treat each other as well as the non-human world with profound respect instead of merely as raw material to enhance human power.

Deep ecology, then, seeks to overturn the major Western categories that are apparently responsible for humanity's destruction of the biosphere: anthropocentrism, dualism, atomism, hierarchalism, rigid autonomy, and abstract rationalism. A deep ecologist would see the garbage barge as merely the tip of the waste-and-pollution iceberg that is threatening the biosphere. The huge quantities of poisonous industrial and municipal wastes, the nuclear weapons, the destruction of the living Earth-all are manifestations of what amounts to human self-worship. Having "killed" God, humanity arrogated to itself the Divine position in the Great Chain of Being. Human beings became the origin and measure for all value, truth, and meaning. A "thing" had "value" only in economic or pragmatic terms -in relation to human needs. And because nature reminds us of our dependence on the body, we must conquer" nature to reassure ourselves of our immortality. White Western humanity believes it has the "right" to dump its waste wherever it wants, instead of curbing its lavish consumption and recycling its wastes. The abstract, linear rationality at work in modern economies cannot comprehend the essentially cyclical character of natural processes. Despite the findings of the science of ecology, Western society plunges blindly ahead toward disaster in the name of infinite progress. Science can be an important part of the solution to anthropocentrism, but only if it is freed from its current enslavement to economic and nationalistic interests.

Deep ecologists agree that reform environmentalism - including stiff international laws against pollution, annihilation of species, expansion of human population, destruction of rain forests and marshes, nuclear power and nuclear weapons, and so on -is necessary in the short run. In the tong run, however, mere reformism will not be sufficient to prevent the destruction of the Earth. Only a revolution in humanity's understanding of itself and its place within nature will bring about the dramatic changes in human behavior that are necessary at this critical juncture in human and terrestrial history.

Eco-Feminism

At first glance, Eco-feminism and deep ecology share many points in common. Both are critical of atomism, dualism, hierarchalism, rigid autonomy, and abstract rationality. According to feminist critics, however, because deep ecology has been formulated almost entirely by men, it is characterized by unintended patriarchal prejudices. Whereas the deep ecologist speaks of the drawbacks of anthropocentrism or human-centeredness, the eco-feminist speaks of the drawbacks of androcentrism or man-centeredness. According to many eco-feminists, patriarchalism leads to the destruction of the Earth. Because deep ecologists fail to understand the fundamental role of patriarchy in the development of atomism, dualism, hierarchalism, rigid autonomy, and abstract rationality, deep ecologists mean something different by these categories than do eco-feminists. Eco-feminists believe that only when deep ecologists learn to appreciate the effects of patriarchal culture on their own awareness, only when they discover the extent to which their conceptions of self, body, nature, and other are shaped by patriarchal categories, will their ecology become truly deep.

Contemporary feminism is an extraordinarily complex movement. In the late 1960s and early 1970s, many Western feminists saw the problem as women being systematically denied the educational and economic opportunities necessary for them to compete on an equal footing with men. Feminism meant fighting for equal rights in the political and economic arenas. Gradually, however, feminists began to see that it might be unwise for women to emulate roles that had been defined and structured by and for men. Feminist theorists began to emphasize the differences between men and women. Still later, some feminists began to conclude that not only are women different from men, they are better than men. Whereas earlier feminists had insisted that differences between men and women were cultural in origin, some feminists now began taking an "essentialist" position, according to which patriarchal culture distorts or conceals the essential feminine that is the birthright of every woman.

Other feminists have been quick to point out the problems with this position. First, it seems to confirm the misogynist's viewpoint that women are essentially or naturally or biologically different. The misogynist concludes that such "natural" differences make women "inferior," while the feminist concludes that they make women "superior." And any talk of female "superiority" reinstalls the very hierarchy that feminists found and fought against in patriarchy. Some eco-feminists even speak as if men are so flawed that only women can solve the environmental crisis because women are more attuned to the cycles of nature and to their own feelings than are men. But women are also distorted by patriarchy, and some men are deeply appreciative of their relationship to the natural world. Most eco-feminists acknowledge that what is needed is the transformation of women and men. Eco-feminists, however, may be able to make a contribution that many men cannot because the marginal place of women in the history of patriarchy may have protected them from some of the crippling effects that it has had on so many men.

Many eco-feminists agree that the technological assault upon the Earth is the culmination of a direction in human history that took a particularly virulent form in Europe.In the Europe of several thousand years ago, before the emergence of agriculturally based cities and before the onslaught of the Goddess-slaying, Sky-Father-worshipping nomadic horsemen, there was no patriarchy. Society was apparently non-hierarchical, non-authoritarian, and non-dualistic. Human worship was directed at the Goddess, the female divinity regarded by women and men alike as the source of all life and bounty and goodness. Gradually, however, the Goddess was displaced by the new Father God. Feminists have often interpreted this new God as the projection of the male's hierarchical, patriarchal, domineering, and authoritarian attitude. While the Goddess affirmed the goodness and primacy of the body and the Earth, the God affirmed the goodness and primacy of the spirit/soul and heaven. But this is not the only possible interpretation of the Father God.

C. G. Jung and psychotherapist Erich Neumann have argued that the emergence of the Father God was consistent with the development of human consciousness from out of a relatively collective state to one of increasing individuation. They see the solar God as representing the clarity of the free-willed, self-assertive, rational ego-self. For this kind of individuated selfhood to be possible, according to Jung, the heroic ego had to escape from the embrace of the Great Mother, who represents both the organic-bodily and the subconscious domain of human existence. Transpersonal psychologist Ken Wilber, however, argues that the emergence of the Father God amounted to a new level in humankind understanding of divinity, a level consistent with and made possible by the Great Goddess-IO Wilber sees the Great Mother as representing early humanity's conception of "Mother Nature" as the now-bountiful, now-withholding source of life and death, who must be placated by ritual and blood sacrifice, while the Great Goddess represents the insight of a few into the transcendent Divine Unity that constitutes the creative source of all things. That is, the Great Goddess is the unifying principle of transcendence-in-immanence that makes even the Great Mother possible. Unlike the Great Mother, who demands ritual sacrifice, the Great Goddess requires not sacrifice of the body, but instead sacrifice or surrender of the separate self to the Divine Unity which is its source.

Rightly understood, the great Father can be regarded as a further development of the individuating and transcendent principles that first emerged with the Great Goddess. God did not necessarily have to become the basis for patriarchy. But as men became individuated by their identification with the Father God, the terror of individuation led them to construe him as an all-powerful, separate, other-worldly self. Men made God in their own image. This conception of God led men to dissociate themselves from women, from nature, and from their own bodies from everything that reminded them of dependence. Hence, whatever corresponding process of individuation that might have occurred for women in association with the Great Goddess was feared and repressed by the newly individuated men. Men justified their deeds by portraying women as being too bound up with the Great Mother, the Earth, and with the subconscious, prerational, collective, material, and emotional realms. Women were simply "unfit" to follow the path of individuation. Worshippers of the "jealous" Father God destroyed the temples and killed the worshippers of the "false" deities, the Great Mother and the Great Goddess.

Correctly intuiting that in some sense they shared in the eternal presence of what I prefer to call the God/dess, the ancient males mistakenly concluded that their own egos were immortal. Instead of surrendering their separate egos to the eternal God/dess, men embarked on what Wilber has called the "God project." They invented immortality substitutes and symbols, such as money, war, science, art, and other activities of culture. The ego's logical-rational discourse projected an infinite future for unfolding its immortality projects. Hungry for the power that promised immortality, the God-worshipping urban kings invented full-scale war. They projected death and guilt upon the enemy-by slaying the enemy, they would also slay death and guilt. And they projected mortality and limitation on women, whom they regarded as semi-natural beings incapable of participating in the "creative" domain of culture.

The "history of consciousness," then, has turned out to be the story of man's development. The heroic male struggles violently to free himself from the clutches of the subconscious and collective powers of the Great Mother. Only by the matricidal act of slaying the beast does the hero achieve individuation. The fierceness of the ego's repression of the female, the bodily, and the natural is directly proportional to the ego's recognition of its ultimate dependent status. But the anxious ego finally claims to be independent of everything, including t ' he Divine. The ego in effect declares itself to be God.

According to eco-feminists, modern technology is simply the culmination of this male quest to conquer death and limitation by dominating his environment, his own body, his women, and all other "subhuman" types. The garbage barge represents man's refusal to own up to his own wastes, the disposal of which he has usually consigned to women. Organic wastes in particular remind man of his mortality, his connection to the Earth and to woman. By hoping to dump the barge's garbage in the U.S. South and then in Mexico, wasteful patriarchal culture again revealed its exploitative attitude toward the poor and dark-skinned. Even if a woman had ordered the barge to head south, she herself would be a victim of patriarchal thinking. Female bureaucrats, too, can be taught to think in linear terms, to conceive of the Earth not as a living entity with cyclical patterns but instead as an infinite resource for human projects and an endless dumping ground for excrement.

One may readily discern important similarities in the deep ecological and the eco-feminist account of the garbage barge as a symptom of the illness of Western culture. Eco-feminists charge, however, that patriarchal culture is governed not only by the categories of dualism, abstract rationality, rigid autonomy, and atomism, but also by the crucial category of androcentrism or patriarchy. Despite the fact that, except for androcentricism, the same categories are mentioned in the deep ecological critique of Western culture, eco-feminists argue that there are significant differences between the deep ecological and the eco-feminist perspective. That is, because of profound differences in the male and female sense of self, men and women experience the world differently.

Eco-Feminist Critiques of Deep Ecology

One eco-feminist, Ariel Kay Salleh, maintains that deep ecologists propose enforced birth control to solve the ecocrisis. According to her, this drive to control reproduction betrays the long-standing patriarchal desire to dominate the female reproductive process. Moreover, she accuses deep ecologists of speaking in abstract terms, typical of males raised in patriarchy, instead of in terms of concrete, personal relationships to other people and to the Earth. Isolated from others and from nature, the alienated male ego invents deep ecology as another desperate attempt to become reattached to the world he denied during the matricidal process of individuation.

A male philosopher sympathetic to Eco-feminism, Jim Cheney also argues that patriarchal categories can be discerned in the basic program of deep ecology. For example, he notes that Arne Naess speaks about the importance of rights for all beings and about the inevitable conflict among bearers of such rights. But the vocabulary of rights is, according to Cheney, a conception of human beings seen as isolated, autonomous egos who choose to limit competition among themselves by according each other certain inalienable rights that each ego must respect. To conceive of biospheric egalitarianism in terms of rights, then, betrays an atomistic conception of human society that is inevitably linked to androcentrism and patriarchy.

Moreover, even the central intuition of deep ecology-the notion that we are all nodes in the fabric or web of internal relations-may be only apparently consistent with the view that while men think atomistically, women think relationally. What better way to overcome the effects of hierarchal and dualistic thinking than by doing away with atomism and by affirming a "contextual" metaphysics? While sympathetic to the aims of such an approach, Cheney maintains that it fails. For example, how are we to solve disputes among competing claims to rights? Ultimately, if it's a question of a human's right to life versus a squirrel's, won't we resort to some hierarchical consideration that undermines the commitment to bio centric egalitarianism?

The infusion of the web-of-life concept into deep ecological ethics, then, may be seen to promise... a feminist ethical theory while in fact it serves either to flatten all issues of value and obligation into a normative egalitarianism which cannot serve to guide practice without reintroducing hierarchy or to shift the focus of ethical concern to the ecosystem as a whole, the result being a kind of ecological totalitarianism in which the good of individuals is subservient to the good of the whole. The concept of a moral community implied by the idea of a web-of-life in which selves are defined by means of relationships of care and responsibility cannot survive the attempt to fit it into the framework of a rights, whether it be of the individualistic or holistic variety.

Like Cheney, Marti Kheel maintains that we cannot solve the ecological crisis simply by ridding ourselves of metaphysical and social atomism and replacing such atomism with a metaphysical and social relationalism. It is important to remember that relationships can only obtain between individuals that have some measure of importance and reality of their own. If we reduce individuals merely to the status of 11 nodes" in a field of internal relations, we run the danger of removing all obstacles to regarding the nexus of internal relations as being more important than the individual nodes comprising the biome. That is, for the sake of the "overall good" of the whole set of internal relations, individuals could justifiably be sacrificed since after all they are only temporary coagulations of the dynamic patterns at work in the vibrant field of life.

Feminists are calling for a new version of selfhood or individuation, one that avoids isolated egos on the one hand and unconscious blending on the other. Earlier, the masculinist bias in the prevailing Western account of individuation. In their path-breaking analyses of such individuation, Jung and Neumann recognized the destructive character of the patriarchal repression of the female principles of nature and divinity. Most feminists, however, have concluded that Jung and Neumann's history of individuation, despite its critique of the lopsidedness of patriarchal consciousness, is itself so colored by masculinist categories that it cannot be of help in developing an alternative conception of individuation. Recently, however, feminist theologian Catherine Keller has reinterpreted the approach of depth psychology to individuation to make it compatible with her own version of a feminist understanding of individuation.

According to Keller, Jung's major achievement was his "discovery and charting of a collective unconscious." Jung argued that the task of the ego in a person's later life was to reaffirm its relationship with the world, a relationship temporarily denied during the process of individuation:

Sacrificing its own illusory claims to autonomy, the ego's task becomes that of reconnecting with the depth and breadth of life from which it had so early cut itself off. For the mother archetype symbolizes the ego's relation to its own deeper psyche, the transpersonal or collective unconscious. By its very nature, it belies the separate ego of the warrior-hero.... Reintegration of the psyche on the basis of its own transpersonal scope requires the process Jung calls "individuation." Authentic individuality can be gained only when I experience myself as fundamentally connected to all of life: this is the wisdom of the Jungian outlook. An ego-transcending selfhood is massively relational, exposing the individuality of the ego as the sham of individualism and a fabrication of persona... Jung's vision of a radical world-openness suggests the essence of a connective self.

Where Keller speaks of the mother archetype as symbolizing the ego's relation to the transpersonal or collective unconscious, I would distinguish between the transpersonal and the collective unconscious. The transpersonal domain refers to the level of awareness opened up by the Great Goddess; the collective unconscious refers to the domain represented by the Great Mother. An integrated personality would be open to both domains. Both women and men are capable of such integration. Arguing against those feminists who adopt an essentialist view of the nature of woman and man, Keller maintains that women and men alike are originally relational beings. In early childhood, however, the boy is forced to separate in accordance with misguided patriarchal conceptions of individuation. But none of us is ever truly cut off from our relations with the world -the patriarchal quest to total autonomy and independence is an illusion. The task facing women and men today is to develop a non-patriarchal, non-matricidal version of individuation. Instead of slaying the "dragon," we need to integrate this disowned and denied aspect of ourselves:

This is not to step out of our skins, to subordinate gender-specific concerns to supposedly transcendent, humanistic ones, but rather to spin a meaning of self out of our femaleness, without reducing it to anything exclusively "feminine".... We are searching for some path of differentiation in relation. This would permit women to remain faithful to the complex inner and outer connectivity that we may sense as integral to our selves, while liberating ourselves from the accompanying dependency and self-suppression. It would challenge males to modes of relatedness that require not the sacrifice of their maleness but of their ego rigidities and corollary manipulation of women. But then differentiation-becoming uniquely our selves-must not be cast in the category of separation.

Deep ecologists understand the relationship between the separatistic, body-despising, "independent" ego-subject and the ego's quest to control nature by technological means. As an alternative to this separateness and its paranoid lust for power, deep ecologists have appealed to a wide variety of spiritual traditions, including Buddhism. As mentioned earlier, however, critics of deep ecology claim that such mystical traditions tend to "overcome" the dualism between self and other by expanding the self to the status of a transcendental Self which includes everything within itself. The danger of this transpersonal conception of enlightenment is twofold. First, the individual loses his or her integrity as an individual; hence, he or she can then justifiably be subordinated to the good of the "whole." Second, defining authentic selfhood in terms of the identity of self and Self seems to omit what many feminists regard as essential to selfhood: relationship.

While the Self spoken of by mystics and some deep ecologists may appear to be an inflated version of the male ego, I believe that at least some deep ecologists have something more in mind than this. Consider the contributions of the poet Gary Snyder to deep ecology. A long-time student of Zen Buddhism, Snyder takes seriously the Zen critique of the "inflated self" conception of enlightenment. For the Zen practitioner, insight into the Buddha-nature dwelling within all creatures frees a person from the dualistic-abstract domination imposed by the ego. Enlightenment involves entering everyday life more deeply than ever. Being awake means "chopping wood and carrying water." This commitment to everyday life is made possible by the paradoxical insight that as Buddha-nature, one is both this embodied person-inrelationship and the "openness/ emptiness" in which all spatio-temporal events can unfold and thus "be." The more we surrender to the openness at work in us, the more we are liberated from the anxiety and insecurity produced by the illusion of radical separateness.

The isolated ego defends itself against change and dependency; it despises the body as the bearer of limitation, sickness, and death. The Zen practitioner affirms and integrates the mortal-bodily realm and lives from the insight that "this very body is the body of Buddha." This leads to treating all creatures both with respect and with individualized attention. The Zen practitioner learns to care for each creature in a way consistent with its needs and possibilities. There is no abstract table of ethical judgments but a personalized compassion based upon insight into what is needed and into what can be done to help.

Such compassion provides the basis in which to situate the behavior of people toward each other and toward non-human beings. Compassion may begin with the members of one's own family; as it grows it may extend out to all our human sisters and brothers. Finally, it may extend to all beings. One may say that we should care for trees and plants, rocks and waters, animals and people because all things are both fundamentally related to each other and are manifestations of the same life principle. This compassion would be made concrete by reference to one's own particular geographical context and social history. Deep ecologists like Gary Snyder put such compassion into practice by attempting to "reinhabit" the land and to reestablish appropriate humanity-nature relationships in light of the particular character and possibilities of the area in which they find themselves. The bioregional movement, favored by deep ecologists, is an example of the growing conviction that only by living in a particular place, with particular relationships with people and the landscape, can humanity learn to produce goods and dispose of waste in ways that respect all who are affected.

Thus, discovering one's Buddha-nature means entering fully and deeply into one's particular body in particular relationships. Human beings are endowed with a degree of awareness and self-awareness that seems to differentiate us from the organic-biological realm in which animals dwell. Such awareness enables us to form a moral community to begin with, one that has the potential for expanding beyond the immediate limits of our own families and even of our own species.

The emergence of the Great Goddess and Father God can be regarded as crucial stages in the evolution of human awareness. The patriarchal perversion of this evolution, however, has led to terrible suffering for human and non-human beings alike. And yet, mystics in all religious traditions have known that no matter how profound our cosmic-transcendental insight might be, our understanding of ourselves and of the world in which we live is always a human understanding.

This insight, I assume, is behind Cheney's statement that "non-human nature must be located in the ethical space of the moral human community. At first glance, some deep ecologists might say that such talk smacks of anthropocentrism. In their desire to curb anthropocentrism, deep ecologists have often relied upon metaphysical schemes that argue for the relative unimportance of humanity in the cosmic scheme of things. On the basis of such metaphysics, deep ecologists have developed moral principles such as bio centric egalitarianism, which are to curb the human tendency toward hubris. Eco-feminists, however, are wary of metaphysical and moral principles that downplay the role of humanity in the world. Perhaps they retain a sense of their connectedness with others in a way that leads them to have fewer suspicions and doubts about "human nature." And perhaps they also retain a more profound relationship with their own bodies, so that they take seriously the idea that "this very body is the body of Buddha." To be sure, some deep ecologists maintain that humanity has a crucial role to play in the scheme of things, as the witness and participant in cosmic evolution. Nevertheless, they sometimes have difficulty in formulating humanity's place in the world, partly because they are so concerned about lapsing into anthropocentrism.

Eco-feminists maintain that since we are human beings, we can only understand how to behave toward non-human beings in terms of principles and insights that are derived from the particular character of our humanity. According to

Cheney, maintaining the human/non-human distinction appropriately "does not maintain moral hierarchy; it builds moral community. Only within a fully textured moral community can people become aware first of how they can care for other people and for themselves and then how they can care for non-human beings. The atomistic individualism of patriarchy destroys much of the fabric of the human community. Such a damaged community is incapable of understanding the needs of its own members, much less of the non-human world. Before we can respond to the needs of the non-human world appropriately, we need to reestablish the fully textured human community in such a way that we learn to care for each other once again. Eco-feminists argue that then, and only then, will we be capable of extending our concern appropriately to the needs of non-human beings. Cheney maintains that, just as an answer to the question of what one's responsibilities are to one's friends is a highly contextual matter involving a detailed under standing of the precise threads of connectedness and intimacy involved, so an answer to what might be our moral relationship to the non-human environment depends upon a complex understanding of what it means to be a human being, what it is to respond to another as a human being, and an understanding of how those complex webs of relationships that constitute the human moral community might expand to include the non-human. This sort of expansion of the moral community is not the extension of moral privilege to non-human creatures just because they happened to resemble us in desirable ways.... Rather, it is simply a matter of trying to come to an understanding of what it might mean to care, to respond to something in the non-human environment as a member of one's moral community.

From the eco-feminist perspective it makes no sense to speak of caring for non-human beings apart from our capacity to care for each other. The moral context in which we can become concerned about non-human beings is made possible by particular human beings with needs and the capacities to take care of those needs.

This capacity for a deeply textured understanding of our particular human and environmental situation is by no means restricted to women, though under patriarchy far fewer men than women have retained this capacity in a healthy way.

Cheney concludes that Eco-feminism involves a highly contextual attempt to see clearly what a human being is and what the non-human world might be, morally speaking, for human beings-i.e., what kinds of care, regard, and responsiveness might be possible for us in relationship to the non-human world.... The limits of moral regard are set only by the limitations of one's own ability to respond in a caring manner, which, in turn, are a function of the depth of one's own understanding of the human moral community and the clarity and depth of one's understanding of, and relationship to, the non-human world or elements of that world.

The danger of this approach to humanity's place in nature is that it may be used to reinforce the relative lack of concern that many feminists have traditionally displayed toward environmental issues. It may be true that our capacity to care for non-human beings is at least partly grounded in the human community that we must reproduce and sustain in everyday life. Feminists have understandably focused upon the needs of those members of the human community who have suffered most from the history of patriarchy. Nevertheless, increasing numbers of feminists are discovering the needs of the non-human world and their capacity to care for it, even as they continue to repair the human world.

Conclusion

It appears then that the emergence of concern for the non-human world has coincided with the rediscovery of the Great Goddess in particular and of the Divine in general. In the quest to rectify the mistreatment of women, many feminists tended to neglect both the Earth and the Divine. To more and more women and men alike, however, it is becoming clear that the Divine cannot be identified with the patriarchal understanding of divinity. Moreover, we are beginning to realize that our capacity for caring for other human beings is somehow related to our capacity to appreciate the divinity at work in all of us. By appreciating the Divine God/dess, the origin and destiny of all things, we also appreciate more fully both our own bodies and the Earth upon which those bodies so depend. Surrendering to the Divine, we simultaneously surrender to and affirm our own embodiment.

This Divine God/dess is simultaneously and paradoxically transcendent and immanent. Perhaps this concept of a post-patriarchal God/dess is necessary for women and men alike to develop a form of individuation that does not involve dissociation from the body, from nature, and from woman. This God/dess may then provide the understanding and compassion necessary for women and men to care for each other in a way that encourages us to care for other people and for the Earth as well.

An attempt have been made to develop a dialogue between deep ecology and Eco-feminism. No doubt, masculine bias and phrasing color the writings of many deep ecologists, but a generous and compassionate interpretation of their work reveals an authentic concern to heal men and women and to heal the Earth that has been wounded by men and in some cases by women. Women and men alike have been distorted by the effects of patriarchy. What we need now is cooperation and trust, not animosity and suspicion, between deep ecologists and eco-feminists. We need each other in our common search for a way to be mature and complete human beings, so that the Earth can be freed from the burden of domination and exploitation.

7

Critical and Constructive Contributions of Eco-feminism

The earth-body and the womb-body run on cosmological time. Just as the flow of earth's life-giving water follows lunar rhythms, so to follow the tides of a woman's womb. No culture has failed to notice these connections or the related feats of elemental power: that the female can grow both sexes from her very flesh and transform food into milk for them, and that the earth cyclically produces vast bounty and intricate dynamics of the biosphere that allow life. Cultural responses to the physical connections between nature and the female range from respect and honor to fear, resentment, and denigration. Whatever the response, it is elaborately constructed over time and plays a primal, in forming role in the evolution of a society's worldview.

The central insight of eco-feminism is that a historical, symbolic,and political relationship exists between the denigration of nature and the female in Western cultures. The field has grown immensely since the term was coined in 1972 by Francoise d'Eaubonne in *La feminisme ou la mort*. Women have come into Eco-feminism in the United States from several directions, including the environmental movement, various types of alternative politics, and the feminist spirituality movement. In recent years, a number of eco-feminist anthologies, as well as hundreds of articles, have been published.

Historical Background

With regard to European cultures, considerable archaeological evidence indicates that both the earth and the female were held in high regard in the Neolithic settlements prior to the Bronze Age. Ritual figurines of a stylized sacred female with incised patterns of water or with the head of a bird, for instance, reflect perceptions of inherent interconnectedness with nature and seemingly "obvious" honoring of the elemental power of the female. After 4500 B.C. the archaeological record reveals a radical shift. Graves were no longer roughly egalitarian between the sexes but suddenly followed the barrow model of burial, wherein a chieftan is surrounded by the bodies of men, women, children, animals and objects that he owned or controlled. The westward migrations of nomadic Indo-European tribes from the Eurasian steppes imposed in old Europe a warrior cult, the addition of fortifications around settlements, a patriarchal social system, andthe transferral of the sense of the sacred from nature and the female to a distant sky-god, although not all societies followed this pattern, of course.

From the Bronze Age onward, the denigration of nature and the female in European societies fluctuated but never disappeared. The Pythagoreans codified their influential table of opposites in which the female is linked with the negative attributes of formlessness, the indeterminate, the irregular, the unlimited-that is, dumb matter, as opposed to the principles of fixed form and distinct boundaries. Aristotle considered females to be passive deformities. The intellectual prowess of the male, he felt could reveal and categorize all forms and functions of organisms in nature. Later, the medieval cosmology ranked men above women, animals, and the rest of nature, all of which were considered to be entangled with matter in ways that the male spirit and intellect were not. The advent of modernity created by the succession of Renaissance humanism, the Scientific Revolution, and the Enlightenment shattered the holism of the medieval synthesis by framing the story of the human apart from the larger unfolding story of the earth community. The "new mechanical philosophy" of the Scientific Revolution in the sixteenth and seventeenth centuries perceived the natural world as a clock work that could be fully apprehended and mastered by human intellect. The practitioners of empirical science used metaphors that express heady delight in assaulting nature in order to learn "her secrets."Eco-feminists and others have noted that similar metaphors and attitudes were used in the "trials" that preceded witch burnings and other torture during the era of the new rationalism.

Dualistic Thinking in Western Philosophy and Culture

The dualistic thinking that has shaped so much of the Eurocentric worldview is perhaps the central concern of eco-feminist philosophical and political analysis. Countless ramifications follow from the Eurocentric notion of "the masculine" being associated with rationality, spirit, culture, autonomy, assertiveness, and the public sphere, while "the feminine" is associated with emotion, body, nature, connectedness, receptivity, and the private sphere. The reductionism of this orientation is accompanied by several assumptions that are essential to patriarchy: that the cluster of attributes associated with the masculine is superior to that associated with the feminine; that the latter exists in service to the former; that the relationship between the two is inherently agonistic; and that a logic of domination over nature and the female should prevail among humans in the "superior" configuration.The Eurocentric construction of masculinity hence is a reactive and unstable posturing to appear "not-nature" and "not-female." The patriarchal core of the Eurocentric worldview is the culturally imposed fear that nature and the elemental power of the female are potentially chaotic and engulfing unless contained by the will of the cultural fathers.

Eco-feminists feel that the above analysis is relevant to identifying problematic assumptions in philosophical and political situations that have evolved within the Eurocentric orientation. In the area of eco-feminist philosophy, two topics that have received a good deal of attention are the critique of "manstream" environmental ethics and the dialogue between Eco-feminism and deep ecology.

Eco-feminist Critiques of Environmental Philosophy

With regard to the field of environmental ethics, eco-feminists maintain that many of its leading philosophers are largely blind to their patriarchal assumptions and hence can only replicate the logic of domination, albeit embedded in various versions of an ecological worldview. Eco-feminist philosophers reject the assumption that clinging to the rationalist concept of the self and the instrumental view of nature that dominates Western philosophy is a viable way to frame a post-patriarchal environmental ethics. The Kantian-rationalist framework is based on oppositionally construed reason: intellectual facility that is sharply distinct from the "corrupting" influences of the emotional, the personal, the particular. Because the self is believed to be discontinuous from other humans and the rest of the natural world, moral progress is possible via a progression away from personal feelings to abstract, universalized reason. This approach results in strong opposition between care and concern for particular others and generalized moral concern. Eco-feminists have identified this false opposition as a major cause of Western maltreatment of nature, noting that concern for nature should not be viewed as the completion of a process of universalization, moral abstraction and disconnection, discarding the self, emotions, and special ties.

Eco-feminists also challenge the Eurocentric concept of rights as a basis for philosophical frameworks of environmental ethics. "Ethical humanists" and "animal liberationists" attempt to establish the relative values of various parts of nature via such criteria assentience, consciousness, rationality, self-determination, and interests. A being possessing one of these characteristics is said to have "intrinsic value" and hence the right to "moral consideration."Eco-feminists generally regard this approach as static, arbitrary, and lacking a holistic apprehension of the natural world. Another objection to the use of rights theory is that it requires strong separation of individual rights-holders and is set in a framework of human community and legality. Its extension to the rest of the natural world often draws upon Mill's notion that if a being has a right to something not only should he or she have that something but others are obligated to intervene and secure it. Such reasoning gives humans almost limitless obligations to intervene massively in all sorts of far-reaching and conflicting ways in natural, balanced cycles to secure rights of a bewildering variety of beings. Eco-feminists feel that a more promising approach for an ethics of nature would be to remove the concept of rights from the central position it currently holds and focus instead on less dualistic moral concepts such as respect, sympathy, care, concern, compassion, gratitude, friendship, and responsibility.

The Eco-feminist Dialogue with Deep Ecology

The response of eco-feminist philosophers to the body of thought known as deep ecology has drawn attention to its gender-blind assumptions in condemning anthropocentrism without taking seriously the formative dynamics of androcentrism, or male dominance. Most eco-feminists acknowledge common ground with deep ecology's rejection of rationalist value theories and an environmental ethic grounded in abstract principles and universal rules believed to be discoverable through reason alone. Most eco-feminists also appreciate deep ecology's rejection of the Eurocentric sense of discontinuity between humans and nature. However, eco-feminists are wary of assumptions that may lie embedded in the concept of the "ecological self," which was formulated by the founder of deep ecology, Arne Naess, and which refers to the aspect of one's being that is continuous with the large Self rather than the individual self. It is sometimes described by Naess's colleagues inways that could be interpreted to result in the obliterating of all particularity, a worrisome notion to the sex that has been socialized in patriarchal culture to sacrifice their own self-definition to the needs of husbands and children. Other eco-feminist concerns include issues of differentiation, bio-centric egalitarianism, and concepts of caring.

Political Analysis and Activism

In this area, eco-feminists have astutely critiqued the masculinist bias in the daily functioning of the environmental movement; played an important role in the growing challenge to the modern model of "development" for the Third and Fourth Worlds; and been a leading force in campaigns for animal rights and opposition to several aspects of reproductive technologies. Most eco-feminist activists are engaged with grassroots political work, whether or not they identify themselves with any particular party, movement, or ideology. Many eco-feminists work in the Green politics movement, often within Green parties, because the democratic, community-based,and the ecological Green political vision includes eco-feminist concerns and aspirations. Its ideal of community-based economics, in which wealth and ownership are spread as broadly aspossible, stands in stark contrast to the increasing centralization of power and control in the hands of huge corporations.

The experience of most feminists who have entered the environmental movement either in institutionalized organizations or alternative groups has been painfully disillusioning. The historical link noted by eco-feminist theory between patriarchal attitudes and the logic of domination over nature, women, and people of color has yet to be acknowledged in practice by most male activists. In the Green politics movement this situation is often somewhat better than in environmentalist organizations because feminist values are among the core values, at least in principle. Hence Greens are ideologically committed to eliminating patriarchal behavior. When that fails to occur, women leave the Greens, as they have demonstrated in several countries. Sometimes they return when conditions improve.

An example of the political issues addressed by eco-feminists is their vocal opposition to policies that reduce women of the Third and Fourth Worlds to "resources" in the emerging global economy. A leading eco-feminist critic, Vandana Shiva, who is an Indian physicist, maintains that "maldevelopment" is a new project of Western patriarchy, one that results in the death of the"feminine principle." She asserts that the modern model of development being imposed by the West is inherently patriarchal because it is fragmented, "anti-life," opposed to diversity, dominating, and delights in "progress" based on nature's destruction and women's subjugation. Eco-feminists insist that Third and Fourth World women themselves must have control over decisions about whether to opt for local self-reliance or integrate into the global economy. Unfortunately, enormously powerful banks and transnational corporations in the "developed" world are furthering "maldevelopment"via centralized, large-scale projects that are usually capital-intensive, energy-intensive, and disruptive of local self-reliance and ecological integrity.

Spiritual Dimension

In addition to the philosophical and political aspects, Eco-feminism contains a spiritual dimension. The eco-feminist alternative to the Western patriarchal worldview of fragmentation, alienation, agonistic dualisms, and exploitative dynamics is a radical reconceptualization that honors holistic integration: interrelatedness, transformation, embodiment, caring, and love. Suchan orientation is simpatico with the teachings of several Eastern and indigenous spiritual traditions on nonduality and the relative nature of seemingly sharp divisions and separations. To refer to the ultimate mystery of creativity in the cosmos itself organizing, self-regulating dynamics - spiritual traditions draw on metaphor and symbol. Those may be female, male, or non anthropomorphic, such as the Taoist perception of The Way. Eco-feminists are situated in all the major religious traditions, and most see good reason for women to use female imagery in references to "the divine," or ultimate mystery in the cosmos. Particularly, in patriarchal societies, the choice offemale metaphors is a healthy antidote to the cultural denigration of women. Those eco-feminists drawn to Goddess spirituality appreciate the nature-based sense of the sacred as immanent in the earth, our bodies, and the entire cosmic community-rather than being located in some distant father-god far removed from "entanglement" with matter. The transcendent nature of creativity in the cosmos, or the divine, lies not above us but in the infinite complexity of the sacred whole that continues to unfold.

Goddess spirituality is not the sole tradition that contains these understandings, and even religions that are somewhat hostile to them are being persistently challenged by their own eco-feminist members.

Conclusion

In summary, Eco-feminism is a movement that focuses attention on the historical linkage between denigration of nature and the female. It seeks to shed light on why Eurocentric societies, as well as thosein their global sphere of influence, are now enmeshed in environmental crises and economic systems that require continuing the ecocide and the dynamics of exploitation.

Eco-feminism continues the progression within traditional feminism from attention to sexism to attention to all systems of human oppression to recognition that "naturism" is also a result of the logic of domination. Eco-feminism challenges environmental philosophy to abandon postures upholding supposedly gender-free abstract individualism and "rights" fixations and to realize that human relationships are constitutive, not peripheral.

Hence care for relationships and contextual embeddedness provides grounds for ethical behavior and moral theory. Politically, eco-feminists work in a broad range of efforts to halt destructive policies and practices and to create alternatives rooted in community-based legitimacy that honors the self-determination of women as well as men and that locates the well-being of human societies within the well-being of the entire earth community. Spiritually, eco-feminists are drawn to practices and orientations that nurture experiences of non-duality and loving reverence for the sacred whole that is the cosmos.

Eco-feminism is a global phenomenon that is bringing

attention to the linked domination of women and nature in order that both aspects can be adequately understood. Eco-feminists seek to transform the social and political orders that promote human oppression embedded in ecocidal practices. The work consists of resistance, creativity, and hope.

8

Eco-Feminism, the Environment, and Social Movements

In 1974, the term "Eco-feminism" was conceived by d'Eaubonne as a connection of the ecology and women. In 1978, Susan Griffin's *Woman and Nature: The Roaring Inside Her* poetically acquainted others with the idea, but the diffusion of the idea did not become apparent until after the meltdown at Three Mile Island when six hundred women attended a conference called "Women and Life on Earth: A Conference on Eco-feminism in the Eighties".

Eco-feminism is a joining of environmental, feminist, and women's spirituality concerns. As the environmental movement along with environmental crises raised the consciousness of women to the decay of the earth, they began to see a parallel between the devaluation earth and the devaluation of women. Women began to see the link as not a false construction of weakness, but as a strong unifying force that clarified the violation of women and the earth as part of the same drama of male control.

One of the areas where Eco-feminism is found lacking in the traditional paradigm of social movements is the area of action. The common view is that social movements engage in protest and direct action; however, Eco-feminism calls for consciousness raising, healing, and a communion with nature. There is little direct action. Some call for concern and to be involved in crucial issues. Others call for intellectual work to form a holistic conception of Eco-feminism. Furthermore, there is no group of eco-feminists, no declared leader, and no vague form of organized activity. A few organizations have included the word "Eco-feminism" in their title, such as Eco-feminists for Animal Rights, but they are not a subgroup of the larger Eco-feminists. In addition, most groups that can be identified as eco-feminist in nature do not identify themselves as eco-feminist.

Eco-feminists do participate in the formation of ideology and recruitment in that conferences and books are explicitly for the development and spread of eco-feminist thought. The message has spread. More and more people identify themselves with Eco-feminism, conferences are held, articles are written, and books are published and bought. But, Eco-feminism has not resulted in collective action in the way Black Power as a philosophy did. This issue is one that is shared by many environmental groups, and, through an examination of Eco-feminism, new ways of thinking about other such groups can also be pursued.

This clash of popular belief on what constitutes a social movement comes out of a similar, growing debate on the nature of social movements. Developments, such as Eco-feminism, are a growing phenomena and present a challenge to movement theory in all fields. Rhetorical analysis is the key to understanding phenomena like Eco-feminism because their manifestation is rhetorical. The purpose of this paper is to go about meeting that challenge by uncovering what Eco-feminism is and, at the same time, add to movement theory by constructing a valid, useful means for analyzing the rhetoric in such phenomena. In order to construct this theoretical argument, a discussion of an alternative view of social movements will be followed by a proposal for analyzing the rhetoric of these phenomena which will allow an analysis of the nature of Eco-feminism.

Movements as Meaning

The structural analysis offered by the rhetorical tradition is not particularly helpful explaining a movement such as Eco-feminism because these phenomena are more ideological than structural in nature. It is not structure but meaning that is important in the analysis of this type of movement.

Cathcart provides the rhetorical definition of movements which can serve as a starting point to developing a rhetorical analysis of these type of movements. Cathcart directly opposes the old definitions growing out of other fields and formulates a rhetorical definition based in dramatistic theory. He believes that the place to find movements "is not a historical place, but a dramatistic situation where moral strivings for a salvation bring human agencies into contact". Cathcart further argues that "*reciprocity* or *dialectical enjoinment* in *the moral arena...* defines movements and distinguishes them from other dramatistic forms". Cathcart's rhetorical definition of movements focuses on stasis as a way to locate movements and drama as the key to analyzing it.

McGee makes a similar argument. Central to McGee's conception of social movements is his critique of traditional view of movements as a phenomenon with structure. McGee contends that social movements inherently have structure because they are undertaken by people in society, but structure should and cannot be the focus of a rhetorical study. McGee argues, a consciousness is presumed by the concept "movement" which *requires* meaning, order and pattern in human experience even when these regularities must be manufactured. A theory of movement, therefore, must determine the identity and meaning of the consciousness which inspires us, as citizens and scholars, to seek and see "movement" when we look at historical and social facts.

McGee insists that theory be totally reconceptualized and the new theory based in "movement existing as a figure or meaning within the ground/context of human communication". In conceptualizing movements as meaning the theorist will need to prove rather than presume the existence of movements ... by observing changes in the "ideographic structures of social norm systems".

Both McGee and Cathcart conceptualize movements

based on rhetorical theory rather than formulations from other fields; however, as other disciplines move toward understanding movements as symbolic rather than structural, rhetorical theory needs to respond. Indeed, the alternative views indicate that understanding the symbolic meaning of movements is the appropriate approach to movements. McGee contends that a rhetorical study is the key to uncovering the meaning aspects of movement.

Analysis of Meaning

In undertaking an analysis of movements, McGee suggests using his concept of ideograph and/or the "treatises in critical science," by Habermas, Feuer, Gouldner, Eco, and Foucault. While further study might point toward developing methods based in their theories, an alternative starting point is the idea of symbolic action. Creating meaning through symbolic action forms a basis for communication theory. Symbolic action, is as Cathcart argues, dramatistic in nature. Cathcart presents a dramatistic view based on a Burkeian approach, but, McGee's conception, seems more in line with Bales, Bormann, and Fantasy-Theme Analysis.

The connection is apparent in how McGee establishes the existence of movements. McGee argues, When people use new words-or obviously attribute new meaning to old words-we can assume that consciousness of their environment has "moved" by measure of the difference in descriptors themselves or in meanings.

The place where McGee finds movements is the place where Bales and Bormann identify dramatizing. Bales observes, One's feelings fuse with the symbols and images which carry the feeling in communication and sustain it over time. One is psychologically taken into a psychodramatic fantasy world, in which others in the group are also involved. Then one is attached also to the other members. Bales not only provides a connection to consciousness but also to the formation of identity within groups.

Symbolic convergence theory adds to the idea of identity

formation and consciousness. The theory contends that individuals' meanings for symbols converge to create a shared reality for participants. Bormann elaborates, If several or many people develop portions of their private symbolic worlds that overlap as a result of symbolic convergence, they share a common consciousness and have the basis for communicating with one another to create community, to discuss their common experiences, and to achieve understanding.

This creation of shared consciousness through shared definitions of symbols is exactly what McGee argues establishes the existence of a movement. Since it is symbolic convergence theory which merges and aides in the explanation, it is only natural to use fantasy-theme analysis to uncover how consciousness operates within the movement. In addition, Bormann's references to rhetorical movements throughout his initial article on fantasy-theme analysis make it clear that he conceived that it be used for the study of movements.

Fantasy-Theme Analysis

Fantasy-theme analysis centers around the belief that people chain out fantasies which form together to create an acceptable view of reality-a rhetorical vision. A rhetorical vision is a "symbolic drama that contains a dramatic scene, dramatic characters, plotline, and a sanctioning agent". Each element acts to create a common symbolic reality to be shared by a large group of people. The base unit of communication is the fantasy theme which is a complete dramatic statement. These themes vary then to the extent in which each element is important in the scenario. Overall rhetorical visions powerfully draw people together as "meaning, emotion and motive are contained in the rhetorical vision, and people caught up in the vision will act it out as their sense or understanding of social reality dictates".

Another important concept for this study is that of saga. The idea of sagas grew out organizational research. A saga is "a collective understanding of unique accomplishment in a formally established group". Dottlich establishes a connection between saga research and fantasy-theme analysis. His argument is that both are constructed similarly. For example, Clark writes,

> The organizational motif becomes individual motive, much more than a statement of purpose, a cogent theme, a doctrine of administration, or a logical set of ideas. Deep emotional investment binds participants as comrades in a cause.... An organizational saga turns an organization into a community, even a cult... Sagas create a uniform commitment to organizations by providing something on which to pull everyone together. Within a group, different rhetorical visions may be found united by a uniform commitment to an overarching saga.

Fantasy-theme analysis requires uncovering fantasy themes within rhetorical artifacts, in order to construct a rhetorical vision of the group. The most important fantasy themes are identified and then used to develop the rhetorical visions. In this case, the rhetorical visions will then be used to determine the depth and strength of the saga. The interaction of these elements determines reality for the group and provides insight into group motives, cohesion, values, and style. This provides a basis for a rhetorical criticism of the vision.

A Rhetorical Analysis of Eco-feminism

An analysis of the essays in the collection yielded three distinct rhetorical visions linked together by a saga. Each vision grows out of distinct differences in the groups which came together under Eco-feminism. While each vision decidedly results in a separate strain of eco-feminist thought and action, they are linked together three dimensionally under the saga of Eco-feminism. In the discussion of these three visions, the way they construct their view of the past, present, action, and future will analyzed.

Spiritual Vision

The spiritual vision constructs the earth as a sacred being known as the Goddess or Gaia. Starhawk portrays the dramatic scene in broad strokes, our primary understanding is that the Earth is alive, part of a living cosmos. What that means is that spirit, sacred, Goddess, God-whatever you want to call it-is not found outside the world somewhere-it's in the world: it is the world, and it is us. Our goal is not to get off the wheel of birth nor to be saved from something. Our deepest experiences are experiences of connection with the Earth and with the world. Those sharing the vision undergo a sacred experiencing of the earth as they share and celebrate a glorious past where women were valued equally with men.

Past- Adherents to this vision have shared an analogy that depicts the creation of the world as a process of birth, just as women give birth daily.

Not bombs, not explosions, not abhorrence; rather she sees the event for what it is, a birthing moment, the Great Birth. The elementary particles rushed apart in their trillion degree heat, yes, and became stars, yes, and all of this a swelling, an egg, a mysterious engendering that is the root reality behind all the various facts.

The vision sees creation as a beautiful, nurturing, intensely natural moment and one in which women continually engage. Because women weave life like the earth was weaved, women have a unique unity or special connectedness to the earth. In the past, that connectedness was acknowledged and valued.

Adherents share fantasies that dramatize an age that 5,000 years ago where the earth was a matriachate, based on the worship of the Goddess. Women and men were equally valued. These societies were "not warlike. They were not societies where women were subordinate to men. And they did not see our Earth as an object for exploitation and domination". This golden age was a "partnership society," where no one was dominated or dominator and "diversity is not equated with inferiority or superiority". Women who share this vision see the golden age of the matriarchate as a kind, inclusive alternative to patriarchal society and religion. Mara Lynn Keller dramatizes the past as follows: "The Mother

Earth Religion did not glorify the sacrifice of her children, but celebrated their birth, enjoyment of life, and loving return to her in death". However, waring, dominating, patriarchal society intruded on this utopia and it was destroyed.

The "connection between the demise of the Goddess, the rise of patriarchy, and the rape of the environment" provides the basis for this vision. Science and technology as tools of men and the dominator society are villainous agents in the exploitation of the Goddess Earth. Those who share this vision personify patriarchy as the embodiment of human science and technology which is "inherently progressive, which systematically denigrates ancestral cultures, and which asserts that human beings are entitled to dominion over nature". Such fantasy types serve to arouse strong abhorrence of science and technology so that even the enlightenment is looked upon as evil. In the end, the dominator society took over and raped and plundered earth and women at will.

Present- In developing the present scene the dominator society is depicted as continuing without any signs of stopping or slowing. In fact, the rush to development has put more and more peoples and animals under its control and pushed the evergiving earth to the point of crisis. There is some recognition of the crisis for people in developing nations, but overall concern is for the animals of the world. All life is connected; "the destinies of the oak trees and all the peoples of the Earth are wrapped together". But more importantly is that all life is sacred. The destruction of any living being is a disaster.

While they are concerned about pollution, these women dramatize the loss of species, the wearing of furs and feathers, and the needless death of animals for food as signs of the destruction of the earth. King contends,

No part of living nature can ignore the extreme threat to life on Earth. We are faced with worldwide deforestation, the disappearance of hundreds of species of life, and the increasing pollution of the gene pool by poisons and low-level radiation.

The earth as the Goddess and the animals as kin are calling to these women. In a series of dramatic fantasy types Quinby portrays the present in terms of "The cries of factory farm animals, the suffocation of fish in poisoned waters, the sounds of flood waters rushing over deforested land-these are also voices we need to heed". But central is a personified Mother Earth who calls most dramatically.

Now we only have to look, to listen, to our beloved planet to see that tranquility is not the best word to describe her condition. Her volcanic passions, her hurricane storms of temper, her tremblings and shakings, her thrashings and lashing indicate that something other than serenity is goings on. The earth is being exploited and harmed but not destroyed. The earth is eternal and is now entering into a "new consciousness," which we must recognize and join.

Action- This vision seeks to reclaim and renew the golden age of the past. They believe that an earth-centered consciousness needs to take hold upon the earth. There are two levels of action.

The first is a personal experience of beginning a communion with nature. Orenstein argues, that Eco-feminism calls for an *endarkment*-a bonding with the Earth and the invisible that will reestablish our sense of interconnectedness with all things, phenomenal and spiritual, that make up the totality of life in our cosmos.

Women must recognize the Earth as their mother and join in a communion with her. Rituals of the seasons and cycles need to be renewed in order to achieve unity with the nurturing mother. We need to notice the birds and trees, and enjoy our "tour through the natural world". Even in the city, the center of development and patriarchy, the Goddess can be found and worshiped. Women then share these personal odysseys with other women and weave networks of sisterhood. From these networks, other women can be reached and brought in communion with the Goddess. While communion and worship are the main goals, there is a call for these groups then to take action to save the earth. It is not clear what the direct action might be, but it seems to be joining with others, particularly the Greens, in their efforts to save the earth. The action clearly includes prayer and ritual as the main features.

The result of this action would be a new covenant with earth and all living things. All life would be recognized as sacred and valued, and all could live in unity with each other. There would be no dominated or dominator. Society would operate on the basis of equal value for all living things. It would be a "new synthesis, one that will gather together 'both branches and roots' of the human world, a vision of tremendous healing power that rise up from the depths of the unconscious and stretches out to include every galaxy".

Feminist Vision

The main value of this vision is that of justice for all parties. While the present world only allows justice for those who are in power, they conceive a world where all people and their needs are equally valued. This is distinct from the spiritual vision and its valuing of spirituality and equality of all of nature. This vision is, also, distinct because it concentrates on direct action at the local level to make lives better for women. Further, this vision does not construct the past as a glorious world that needs to be reclaimed.

Past- In fact, this vision does not have a developed past. There is an implicit sense that in the past humans were more connected with nature. They point to the developing countries as examples of that connectedness and direct dependence on nature. They argue that men were separated from nature by development and have continued to widen the gap through further development. As a result, men devalued nature and the natural. Women were also devalued and the patriarchal society took hold, devaluing and exploiting the earth and women. The earth is not, in this vision, innately living or sacred. The earth must be valued because people are dependent upon it for life. All life on earth is linked together; therefore, exploiting one life hurts all the others.

Present- Women are hurt most by the exploitation of the earth because they are the most vulnerable in patriarchal society. The main focus is on women who are more at risk because they suffer double oppression of poverty, race, education, or nation. One such group that this vision recognizes as primary victims of exploitation are women in developing countries.

These women are seen as the most vulnerable of the vulnerable and it is these women who are being victimized more and more by Western development. Shiva's contribution deals primarily with the problems of what she terms "Maldevelopment." The argument is that Westernization actually decreases the quality of life for women in developing countries. Traditional agricultural methods are abandoned, cash crops which deplete the delicate ecosystems are substituted for subsistence crops, and natural resources are taken or destroyed. Men must move to the cities to obtain jobs, but it is the women who are now left alone to work longer and harder to acquire less food and needs for their children. As in the case of Somalia, the end result is mass starvation. This vision sees women as worldwide victims of oppression fighting for their very lives and the lives of their children. The focus is not on saving trees, animals, or soil because it is sacred, but rather because it is necessary for the survival of people. King writes, Yet this is not a sentimental movement-lives depend upon the survival of the forest. For most of the women of the world, interest in preservation of the land, water, air, and energy is no abstraction but a clear part of the effort to simply survive. While there is a great concern in this vision for those in other countries, there is also a recognition of similar practices that victimize women within our own country. Quinby notes the disproportionate incidence of cancer among the poor who are forced to take jobs with greater risks of cancer, to live in "cancer-prone cities," and who are least able to afford the exorbitant costs of medical treatment. These conditions are exacerbated in Blacks, falling the heaviest on Black women and children.

These groups are also the groups who have traditionally the least access to power in the patriarchal system. This view holds that not only are these groups forced to work and live in bad conditions while denied medical care, but patriarchal society strives to make their lives worse. The areas where they live become the dumping grounds of patriarchal industrialization. Nelson observes, that incinerators and dumps are not built in the more affluent neighborhoods because those people have political power and access; however, in poor neighborhoods, where most of the people are renters, women and children, and have limited access to political power, opposition is less of a threat.

This vision depicts patriarchal society as operating with malicious forethought. Their argument is that women and children who are poor are subject to these living conditions, which are life shortening and threatening in order to keep them in submission. They also argue that women become a scapegoat for those exploiting the environment. Nelson observes,

> Both the "fetal protection" approach and the "toxic gender gap" perspective are scapegoats of a sort. They allow environmental health to be a "women's problem," something women are particularly vulnerable around and/or worried about. Women's "delicate biology" and "fragile psychology" virtually become the cause of the problem.

When women are not considered the scapegoat, they are used as a signal for polluted areas. Diamond observes, "It has been argued that in an economy built upon a growing trade in toxic material, drugs, and radiation, babies are the best 'canaries' we have-that pregnancy can provide a warning much like the canary did for coal miners".

This vision has a stronger notion of women as direct victims of oppression struggling for their lives and of humans as an important part of the world. King writes, "There is no point in liberating people if the planet cannot sustain their liberated lives, or in saving the planet by disregarding the preciousness of human existence not only to ourselves but to the rest of life on Earth". The vision encompasses a stronger sense of urgency and agency resulting in direct action rather than creating a consciousness of communion with Mother Earth.

Action- Women are capable of taking and maintaining strong stands against the further exploitation of the planet. The call is for all women to act directly at the local level to stop all pollution and all destruction. The result is "resistance politics operating at the microlevels where power is exercised". The collection is filled with heroic, almost epic, tales of women fighting at the local level. King writes about the *Chipko Andolan* movement in India. Women respond to developers bulldozing their forests by wrapping their bodies around the trees. This act of bravery to save the trees is symbolic of the connection of the trees to their lives. Nelson tells of the struggles of women against pollution and toxicity in their environments. Hamilton recounts the successful battle by women in "a poor, residential, Black, and Hispanic community" against the city's decision to place an incinerator in their neighborhood. All of these fantasy themes of direct action are held up as examples to follow in daily life. These are the heroes doing battle where they are oppressed, on their own turf. There is a shared consciousness that battling at the local level is the place where women can be the most successful because they know the power structure, can organize around the problem, and can access power more easily.

Future- The goal of this vision is not the return to a prehistory because it is seen as impossible and undesirable. The goal is to develop a healthy relationship with nature built around the needs of all peoples. King speaks of a "stewardship of evolution," which would focus on the continual and future needs of all humans. The future requires a creation of a new consciousness, where development and progress are not necessarily good and where people and the quality of their lives is dominant.

Environmental Vision

The prominent value in this vision is living in balance or harmony with nature. Instead of exploiting the ecosystem of the earth for our needs, we need to change our lives to live within the system. This vision is a central point between the two previous ones, but it is distinct from both, in that it calls for personal action directly impacting the quality of life as well as political concern. Similar to the feminist vision, it does not place importance in the past.

Past- There is an implicit belief that the past was a time when people lived in balance with nature. People were forced because of lives directly linked to the earth to value it and its resources. The coming of development broke that link for many and the earth's resources were exploited and the earth was wasted.

Present- The exploitation continues into the present, especially in our throw-away society. Catherine Keller sketches a scene in which, the Earth is being wasted-devastated, with a violence echoed by the crude contemporary idiom of "waste the sucker"; it's being used up, its profound resources squandered, its lush abundance consumed, its complex surfaces worn out.

In this vision, it is not that the earth is sacred or that exploitation is harming people now. The focus of this vision is the future. Once it is all used up, there will nothing left for future generations.

The damage and waste come about because of the dominant anthropocentric belief that the world was created for man. This belief holds that God resides elsewhere and all of the earth is man's domain. This view is drawn from the biblical creation story, where God presents all the animals to Adam to name. Man then uses earth for his gain. Zimmerman portrays a counter drama, the huge quantities of poisonous industrial and municipal wastes, the nuclear weapons, the destruction of the living Earth-all are manifestations of what amounts to human self-worship. Having "killed" God, humanity arrogated itself the Divine position in the Great Chain of Being. Human beings became the origin and measure for all value, truth, and meaning....

Although, in this fantasy, all humans are at fault, it is men who are primarily responsible and men continue to act upon that belief in business, science, and technology. Kheel uses hunting as an example. While granting that women hunt, she constructs it as a male need to dramatically act out the conquest of nature. The hunter may appreciate the beauty of nature, but only in the guise of being built for his consumption.

In the same way, this vision links violence toward women and violence toward the earth. The dominant, patriarchal view holds that women, too, are created for the consumption of men. Plant argues, we have painfully seen that it is the same attitude that allows violence toward us that also justifies the rape of the Earth. Literally, the images are the same. We also know that we just as capable, generally speaking, of enacting the same kind of behavior.

While it is men who are responsible for the violence toward women, it is women and men alike who are responsible for the waste of the earth. Women living out their lives in developed society are responsible for the damage they inflict upon the Earth.

The images of the earth are of devastation on an tragic level. The visions are almost hopeless. In their dramatic construction of the present, one gets the idea that there is little left to save, but they do look toward the future. Catherine Keller contends, "Yet this apocalyptic sort of message would not be worth repeating if it weren't also the case that there is still great life and responsiveness in the Earth as well".

Action- The action in this drama is based on the following philosophical view: Only by recognizing that humanity is no more, but also no less, important than all other things on Earth can we learn to dwell on the planet within limits that would allow other species to flourish and to follow out their own evolutionary destiny.

This consciousness is dependent upon all developing the same sort of connection that women have to nature. Human community must be rebuilt on mended relationships with the natural world. The result is personal action focusing on living in balance with nature to help save the planet.

The action is living on the basis of the philosophy. Truly adapting to the needs of nature. This bioregionalist attitude is embedded in the following fantasy theme by Plant: Bioregionalism means learning to become native to place, fitting ourselves to a particular place, not fitting a place to our predetermined tastes. It is living within the limits and the gifts provided by a place, creating a way of life that can be passed on to future generations.

Fitting into the natural balance of nature is mostly a personal struggle, but, through networking with others, it can become an united effort involving many. Russell uses an analogy to reflect the shared vision: "I also saw I had the choice to live as a healthy cell, joining with other healthy cells, to function as part of the Earth's immune system". The result was Eco-Home, where wastes are reduced and recycled, energy conserved, food is grown organically, and investments are made in projects to save the earth. There they live with the world on a limited basis but attempt to spread their lifestyle to others. In this vision, these are the heroes, battling within their own homes to become better consumers and better Earthmates.

Future- The future is dependent upon all adopting this strategy of living with the Earth. We can fit into the ecosystem by recycling resources and utilizing renewable resources. This can only come about through a total change in consciousness. This vision, like the others, promotes an entirely new way of life. Plant offers a vision of that future which would result in an "egalitarian society-a society that would be based on the full participation and involvement of women and men in the process of adaptation and thus in the maintenance of healthy ecosystems". Disputes would be solved on this basis. Zimmerman contends, "the disputes would take place with the *presupposition* that all entities concerned have "rights" that must be taken into account in the decision-making process". As a result, this society would operate on the basis of what is best for the whole of society.

Eco-feminist Saga

These three distinct visions are all linked together under an eco-feminist saga. The consciousness created by sharing the saga includes the base fantasy themes and types of each. The shared fantasies are based in the link between the devaluation of women and nature by men. Men use this linked devaluation to control, despoil, manipulate, and use women and nature for their gain. Western development and industrialization have further separated man from nature, thus continuing and exacerbating the exploitation of both women and nature. All visions call for fundamental change, based in realigning values. In the new egalitarian system, all are equal and no one is exploited for the gain of another. All live together in harmony.

Criticism

The analysis shows that Eco-feminism is truly not a movement in the traditional sense and may now be, as Sale argued, the shared dramas that inform other traditional movements. Each vision comes out of the three groups out of which Eco-feminism emerged. Each of these visions is still differentiated and not well integrated into a collective view of Eco-feminism. On the whole, these groups remain separate and distinct because the saga is limited and unable to unite all of the fantasies of each under its umbrella. To some extent, this is because the basis of eco-feminist consciousness is built upon sharing fantasies that deny uniform, constraining thought.

This results in what is termed a "saga" but is indeed not operating at that level. Eco-feminism serves as a term of identity that may unite these groups at conferences, in books, and in the popular press, but does not create uniform commitment to a uniform mission. Certainly, the general theory of what is wrong and what should be is consistent among the visions, but there is little agreement on the specifics or how to get there. Eco-feminism is an identity umbrella, without a mission statement which could create commitment and concerted, collective action.

As such, Eco-feminism is left to operate as a midly unifying rhetoric for diverse interests and networks. And the same appears to be generally true of the different visions under Eco-feminism. All three tend to operate as a consciousness resulting in personal change, with a concern for the wider world. Because of the call for localized action, the feminist vision has the most opportunity to result in collective action, but, for now, their heroes are those who are operating on the local level to solve problems directly impacting them. While this seems to be step away from new social movements, those ascribing to the feminist vision in this collection are not those that they hold up as heroes. The writers give the theoretical view of what is and should be, and only utilize these heroes as what can be done. However, because they call for localized direct action, this vision is the closest to traditional collective action.

Conclusion

These new phenomena do operate as identity networks offering a philosophy for living. The focus is on raising a collective consciousness in order to fundamentally change the structure of the world. This is a new form of action which operates entirely at the symbolic level, and there are many such groups within the larger structure of the environmental movement. Rhetorical analysis proved useful in uncovering how this process works within groups.

The utilization of fantasy-theme analysis allows the researcher to uncover meanings and understand how they operate within the movement. The result is a better understanding of what Eco-feminism and the level at which it operates for those who identify with it. Also, this study provides a view into how other such movements may operate as identity and consciousness for participants.

Further study should focus on how other rhetorical methods can help inform an understanding of these movements. An exploration of the use of Foucault, Habermas, and other theorists of ideology would be useful. Also, it would interesting to attempt an explanation of why these new movements are growing so rapidly in response to society.

As a whole, this conception has promise of developing a method of understanding and analyzing these new phenomena. This study forges an important link with other fields where rhetoric is central and useful in discovering how the process of meaning operates in the creation of consciousness and identity.

Eco-feminist Perspectives

In Kenya, women of the Green Belt movement band together to plant millions of trees in degraded lands. In India, they join the chipko movement to preserve precious fuel resources for their communities. In Sweden, feminists prepare jam from berries sprayed with herbicides to offer a taste to members of parliament- they refuse. In the United States, housewives organize local support to clean up hazardous waste sites. All these actions are examples of a worldwide movement known by many as "Eco-feminism," dedicated to the continuation of life on earth.

Eco-feminism emerged in the 1970s at a time when consciousness of the connection between women and nature increased. The term "Eco-feminisme" was coined in 1977 by French writer Françoise d'Eaubonne, who called upon women to lead an ecological revolution to save the planet. During the 1980s cultural feminists in the United States injected new life into Eco-feminism by arguing that both women and nature could be liberated together. Liberal, cultural, social and socialist feminism have all been concerned with improving the relationship between humans and nature, and each has contributed to an eco-feminist perspective in different ways.

Multiple Facets

Liberal feminism is consistent with the objectives of reform environmentalism; to alter human relations through the passage of new laws and regulations. Cultural Eco-feminism analyzes environmental problems within its critique of patriarchy and offers alternatives that could liberate both women and nature. Social and socialist eco-feminists ground their analyses in issues of reproduction, the domination of women by men and how capitalist relations of production reveal the domination of nature by men.

Generally speaking, eco-feminists address contradictions between production and reproduction, while attempting to make problems more visible and propose solutions. For example, when radioactivity, toxic chemicals and hazardous wastes threaten the biological reproduction of the human species, eco-feminists view these threats as assaults on women's bodies and on those of their children and act to halt them. Household products, industrial pollutants, plastics and packaging wastes are viewed as invaders to the homes of women, endangering their lives. Likewise, direct access to food, fuel and clean water is imperiled by cash cropping on traditional homelands and by pesticides used in agribusiness. Such chemicals threaten women's lives by polluting their water and food systems, leading to disease and birth defects. Chemicals, some argue, promote the growth of export crops which draw women into a spiral of dependency, inevitably leading to soil nutrient depletion. Rather than addressing short-sighted, single ended production, the eco-feminist agenda demands attention to the cyclical processes that connect and sustain all living beings.

Women can combat such hazards by altering family consumption habits, recycling household wastes and protesting waste production and disposal methods. They act to protect traditional ways of life and reverse ecological damage from irresponsible multinational corporations and extractive industries. Through envisioning and enacting alternative gender roles, employment options and political practices, eco-feminists challenge the ways mainstream society reproduces itself.

Cultural eco-feminists hold that women are closer to nature than men because of their physiology and social roles. Women bring forth life from their bodies, and undergo the pleasures and pains of menstruation, pregnancy, childbirth and nursing. In a social sense, childrearing and domestic caretaking have kept women close to the hearth and thus closer to nature. Some cultural eco-feminists celebrate the relationship between women and nature by reviving ancient rituals centered on goddess worship, the moon and the female reproductive system. An eco-feminist vision by which nature is held in esteem as mother and goddess is a source of inspiration and empowerment to women. Cultural Eco-feminism embraces intuition, an ethic of caring and connective human relationships.

In contrast to cultural Eco-feminism, the social and socialist strands of Eco-feminism treat nature and human nature as socially constructed and subject to analysis in terms of race, class and gender. Some critics of cultural Eco-feminism think it fails to adequately analyze the role of capitalism in humans' attempts to dominate nature. Some critics dispute the assumption that women's essential nature transcends socialization, which implies that what men do to the planet is bad and what women do is good. The belief that women have a special relationship to nature, claim critics, makes it difficult to accept that men too can possess or develop a genuine ethic of caring for nature.

Examining Ethics

Many eco-feminists advocate some form of a nurturing, caring environmental ethic to confront the oppression of women and nature by men. Such an ethic recognizes and embraces the multiple voices of women differentiated by race, class, age and ethnicity. An eco-feminist ethical perspective grounded in care and nurturing is pluralist, inclusive and contextual and thus constrains traditional ethics that are based on rules and utilitarian gender roles.

An alternative eco-feminist perspective is a partnership ethic that treats women and men as collaborators with nature. Just as human partners must give each other space, time and care, regardless of sex, race and class, allowing each other to grow and develop within a supportive relationships, so should humans give nature the space, time and care it needs to reproduce, evolve and respond to human actions. By constructing nature as a partner, it is more possible for individuals to have a personal, compassionate relationship with nature as well as with people who are sexually, racially or culturally different. The partnership ethic avoids casting nature as a nurturing goddess, and transcends the notion that humans are but one part of a vast ecological web and, thus, morally equal to a bacterium or mosquito.

Conclusion

The eco-feminist perspective is not singularly defined. It is comprised of a multitude of stances which continually cross check and critique each other. It is a dynamic and evolving perspective which, like women, ought not be held to any single definition. The many strands of the eco-feminist movement are woven together by the concept of reproduction and the continence of life on earth. In this sense there is more unity than diversity in eco-feminist's common goal of restoring the quality of the natural environment and for people and other living and non-living inhabitants of the planet.

9

Women and the Movement for Environmental Justice

The people most affected by poor physical environments in the United States are women and children, particularly African Americans, Native Americans, and Latinas. Many women of color and poor white women are active in hundreds of local organizations campaigning for healthy living and working conditions in working-class communities, in communities of color, and on Native American reservations, which are all disproportionately affected by pollution from incinerators, toxic dumps, pesticides, and hazardous working conditions in industry and agriculture. This movement draws on concepts of civil rights, and its organization, too, has roots in the civil rights movements as well as in labor unions, Chicano land grant movements, social justice organizations, and Native American rights organizations.

Its tactics include organizing demonstrations and rallies, educating the public, researching and monitoring toxic sites, preparing and presenting expert testimony to government agencies, reclaiming land through direct action, and maintaining and teaching traditional agricultural practices, crafts, and skills. Specific organizations represent different mixes of these strands, depending on their memberships, geographical locations, and key issues. Examples include West Harlem Environmental Action, the Mothers of East L.A., the Southwest Organizing Project, and the Citizens' Clearinghouse for Hazardous Wastes.

Besides opposing hazardous conditions, the environmental justice movement also has a powerful reconstructive dimension, involving sustainable projects that intertwine ecological, economic, and cultural survival. The 4-H Urban Gardening project in Detroit, for example, coordinates well over one hundred small gardens citywide and relies on the expertise of local people, mostly elderly African American women, who raise vegetables, both for individual use and to supplement food prepared at senior centers, as well as crops for sale: loofah sponges, fresh herbs, honey, and worm boxes for fishing. Many of these women were brought up in rural areas in the southern United States where they learned about gardening before coming to Detroit for work in the 1930s and 1940s.

By drawing on local people's knowledge, these gardening projects provide fresh produce at little financial cost, contribute to the revitalization of inner-city communities, and give a sense of empowerment that comes from self-reliance. When people are outdoors working they also make neighborhoods safer by their presence, watchfulness, and care. An additional goal is to teach young people about gardening, strengthening connections between the generations and helping young people to become more self-supporting. Examples of sustainable projects in rural areas include the White Earth Land Recovery Project, a project that produces wild rice and maple sugar on Native American land in Minnesota, and Tierra Wools, a New Mexico worker cooperative of twenty people-most of them women-that owns some three thousand head of Churro sheep and produces high quality, hand-woven rugs and clothing and organically produced lamb. Their objectives include economic development and environmental protection, as well as cultural revival and conservation.

Women make up the majority of local activists in environmental justice organizations, sometimes because they have a sick child or because they have become ill themselves. Illnesses caused by toxins are often difficult to diagnose and treat because they affect internal organs and the balance of body functioning. Women have been persistent in raising questions and searching for plausible explanations for such illnesses, sometimes discovering that their communities have been built on contaminated land or tracing probable sources of pollution affecting the neighborhood. They have publicized their findings and taken on governmental agencies and corporations responsible for contamination. In so doing they are often ridiculed as "hysterical housewives" by officials and reporters who have trivialized their research as emotional and unscholarly.

By contrast, Lin Nelson honors this works as kitchen table science. In October 1991 women were 60 percent of the participants at the First National People of Color Environmental Leadership Summit in Washington, D.C. Many urban gardeners in northern cities are elderly women, while in rural areas women work on family garden plots, planting, harvesting, and processing fruit and vegetables for home use. As ethnobotanists, women know backcountry areas in great detail because they go there at different seasons to gather herbs for medicinal purposes. Among Mexican Americans, for example, curanderas-traditional healers-continue to work with herbal remedies. This detailed knowledge is learned from older people, as is also the case with some Native Americans and others who live in rural areas. Gender is significant for women in the environmental justice movement, but this is not a concept of gender divorced from race and class. Women activists see their identity as women integrated with their racial and class identities, with race and/or class often more of a place of empowerment for them than gender. Although they recognize their own subordination based on gender, they are not interested in separating themselves from the men in their communities and frame their perspectives, as women, in class- and race-conscious ways.

Eco-feminism does not seem relevant to these activists because it pays much more attention to gender than to race or class. Moreover, it is not a land-based movement, is not currently involved in promoting sustainable development, and is not directly involved in struggles for healthy living and working conditions, though there are individuals who define themselves as eco-feminists active on these issues. Some eco-feminist writers and the editors of eco-feminist anthologies have attempted to bridge this gap by including a few contributions by women of color. In an attempt to make connections, these editors inadvertently appropriate the activism of women of color whose work is marginal to collections that assume a unitary framework. Alliances in practice between eco-feminists and environmental justice activists still need to be made.

Devon Pena took me to meet farmers in the San Luis valley. Typically the farms include well-watered bottomland for pasture and crops and dry upland areas that seem to grow little more than sage. We sat in Joe Gallegos kitchen and talked; more accurately, they talked and I listened. One crucial issue was the fact that a gold mining company located in the hills, Battle Mountain Gold, was polluting the river with cyanide. The river feeds an intricate network of irrigation ditches-acequias-that link all the farms in the valley, They talked about the importance of clean water. They opposed "center pivot"irrigation systems that draw water from underground aquifers. This was the lunacy of living on capital-squandering a nonrenewable resource. They talked about the relationship between crops and wild plants that support birds, rabbits, and other small animals. They described the soils in the valley in a way never heard soil described before, the sensuous feel of sandy loam and Alamosa clay, what you need to know to cultivate them well. They explained why it's increasingly hard to make ends meet financially, despite working hard for long hours, and the traps and contradictions of rampant capitalism that is only interested in quick profits. They talked about their families working this land for seven or eight generations, from before it was part of the United States, always respecting that it is alive. I also listened to a lot of sexist talk and sexist assumptions, even chivalrous notions, about women's place and capabilities. Late at night, I finally said, "Yes, but you've got to think about gender.

The liberation of women and girls has to be part of a truly sustainable future. " And there are women in San Luis, of course, who are saying the same thing. The vagaries of the academic job market meant that I left Colorado, torn by the realization that connections between people, especially across lines of race, class, and culture, need time to develop and a real life context to grow in. This was a limitation of a project some years earlier: Woman Earth, a multiracial network of women who wanted to link spirituality and politics, with a focus on health, ecology, and peace. We also adopted the principle of racial parity, meaning that there should always be equal numbers of women of color and white women. A core group of eight women met and talked and met and talked. We invited a larger group to a four-day working meeting. We were long on ideas but short on making them happen. Ironically, WomanEarth was profoundly unecological in a very basic way: We were a bicoastal group, spread out across this vast continent from California to New York with no strong roots in a place. Like many would-be groups and partnerships, we found it hard to confront difficult issues between us for fear that the alliance would fall apart. It did, of course, but I still dream of a workable WomanEarth some day. This project was crucial to my developing understandings about race and my commitment to multicultural projects in the future. We had high hopes for WomanEarth. Like many tough experiences, it's been a source of seeds, some of which are still waiting for the right place, time, and people to sprout.

Building Alliances for a Sustainable Future

Given the widespread and profoundly serious nature of environmental degradation, environmental issues have great potential for bringing people together across lines of race and class. For such collaboration to work, people need to have some basis for knowing one another, some shared stake in the community, and the prospect for developing trust despite differences in culture, ethnicity, and class. There needs to be authentic connection based on honesty and mutual respect. Much has been written about building bridges across lines of difference in the past decade or so. One obstacle is ignorance-simply not knowing each other's experience as well as not understanding its significance-though people in oppressed groups always know more about dominant groups than the other way around. Other obstacles include treating other groups' concerns as less meaningful than one's own and a lack of trust between people separated by profound differences in class and culture. The bridges to be built are emotional as well as intellectual, making personal connections that reach across our segregated lives.

Alliances require conscientious listening, honesty, active compassion, and a willingness to be self-critical. Learning about others means being open to uncertainty and surprise, an ability to suspend disbelief, and a sense of ease with ourselves so that we can be fully present to each other. This requires settings and projects where people can work together to develop a shared political culture and language, providing a key role for individuals whose experiences and connections enable them to cross lines.

Women of color point out to white women that we conveniently ignore our privilege as white while emphasizing our oppression as women. To build bridges across gender and race for white feminists means understanding that women of color cannot separate race and ethnicity from gender, any more than we can ourselves. We have to make alliances with women and men of color and, in the process, may have to deal with what we consider to be sexist attitudes and behavior. White women need to acknowledge the ways we sustain, perpetuate, and benefit from racism, albeit often unknowingly-in itself an aspect of privilege. Those of us who write and teach about Eco-feminism need to remedy the class, race, and ethnic limitations of our perspectives so as to build authentic alliances that cross race and class lines. We need to use our privilege in the interests of social justice. It is important to make a distinction here between a politics of solidarity, implying support for others in struggle, and a politics of engagement where we are in struggle together.

In 1991 a group of community activists in Detroit started Detroit Summer, a multi-cultural, intergenerational youth program/movement to rebuild, redefine, and respirit Detroit from the ground up. It was based on Freedom Summer when young people from northern states went to the South to register people to vote. Detroit Summer invited young people to spend three weeks working on community projects, talking to community activists in their seventies and eighties as well as to their peers, visioning a new kind of community and economy, not based on the whims of corporate investors but instead on local projects that provide for people's basic needs. The young people painted houses, cleared trash from empty lots, made playgrounds, planted gardens, and painted a mural. But this was much more than a paint-it, fix-it summer program. It was a volunteer program with a clear agenda of political education.

On the last day the whole group toured the work sites and showed each other their handiwork. Less tangible, but equally important, was the fact that they had lived and worked together: white suburban teenagers and college students; African Americans and Latinos from the city, half of them young women; a few lesbian or gay.

Standing on Common Ground

Coalitions and alliances need practical contexts as well as processes where people can work together and grow in their knowledge and trust of each other. The following issues are just a few examples that have the potential to bring eco-feminists and environmental justice activists together in a much more concerted way than is happening currently.

Environmental Health

Working in toxic workplaces is a serious health hazard for women, especially women of color. Some industrial firms have kept women of child-bearing age out of the most hazardous work-often the best paid in the factory-or required that they be sterilized first, to avoid being sued if these workers later give birth to babies with disabilities. High incidences of lead posioning in young children, cancer clusters in various parts of the country, and environmental illnesses involving sensitivity to chemicals are just a few environmental health issues that can bring together women's health advocates and grassroots environmental groups.

Food Production

A specific example of environmental illness is pesticide poisoning of farm workers, many of whom are Mexicans and Mexican American. Contaminated produce is not good for consumers either. Middle-class mothers were very effective in getting the pesticide Alar banned in the United States in the late 1980s because it can damage children's health, but they showed no apparent awareness of or concern for farm workers exposed to it in the course of their work. In many areas mainly white, middle-class consumers choose to buy organically grown produce, which does nothing to improve conditions for farm workers. Much more needs to be done to build alliances between farm workers and consumers, for example by supporting farm workers' campaigns for better working conditions, shopping at local farmers' markets, investing in producer/consumer cooperatives, as well as by increasing public awareness of the dangers of pesticides.

Making Cities Liveable

The literature on Green cities emphasizes air pollution, auto congestion, urban sprawl, energy overconsumption, toxins, deteriorated buildings, and an absence of open space as key issues. These problems are seen in terms of the physical design of cities, which is based on cars. Though mention is sometimes made of political, economic, and cultural obstacles to ecologically sound cities, planners and architects tend to emphasize new or revamped architectural designs and transportation technologies. Other aspects of urban life-affordable housing, employment, amenities, environmental health, and personal safety-are equally critical. People organizing around such issues in urban neighborhoods, often women, understand only too well the connections between poor physical environments, poverty, and racism. As exemplified by Detroit Summer, this is a fruitful area for building alliances between eco-feminists and environmental justice activists.

Making Connections: The Process of Alliance-building

The following principles concern the processes of building aliances:

1. Know who you are, what is important to you, what your non-negotiables are. Know your strengths and what you bring to this shared venture. Recognize, accept, and honor the ways you are different from the others.
2. Figure out why you want to become allies with a particular person or group. What do they stand for? What are their values? What are they interested in doing politically? How do you know this? How do you find out? What is the purpose for coming together?
3. Commit yourself to communicate. Hold judgement until you understand what is going on. Ask the other person to say more. Listen, talk, and listen more. This may be accomplished through conversations, reading, films, events and meetings, and learning about each other's community.
4. Share the past. Talk about what has happened to you.
5. Be authentic and ask for authenticity from others. If this is not possible, what is the alliance worth?
6. Check out the person/group as the aquaintance grows. Are they who they say they are? Do they do what they say they believe in? Do you have reason to trust them? Judge them by their track record and what actually happens, not by your fears, hopes, or expectations that come from old experiences.
7. Keep the process "clean." Call each other on difficult issues as they come up-preferably with grace, teasing maybe, firmly but gently. Don't try to get to the bottom of things when it's impossible to do so meaningfully, but don't use externals (too late, too tired, too busy, too many other items on the agenda) to avoid it.
8. Be open to being called on your own stuff, even if it's embarassing or makes you feel vulnerable. Tell others

when their opinions and experiences give you new insights and help you to see things differently.

9. Do some people in the group take up a lot of space talking about their own concerns? Are they aware of it? What is the unspoken power dynamic between people? How does age, gender, class, or race play out? Can you talk about it openly?
10. What is the "culture" of your group? What kind of meetings and decisonmaking style do you have? If you eat together, what kind of food do you serve? What kind of music do you listen to? Where do you meet?
11. Look for the common ground. What are the perspectives, experiences, insights, and dreams we share?

Major U.S. progressive movements this century have emphasized specific injustices. In the 1930s it was class and labor rights; in the 1950s and 1960s, race and civil rights for people of color; in the 1970s and 1980s women's liberation; and in the 1980s and 1990s rights for gay men, lesbians, bi- and transsexuals.

Despite opposition, each movement made significant progress and then ran into limitations and contradictions. The challenge for organizers and activists is to recognize such limitations, to face them, and to respond in a way that is transformative rather than regressive, rethinking strategies and demands, building on their experiences, gains, and losses.

The next major social movement will need to incorporate demands from earlier movements, building a concerted oppositional politics in the United States that radically challenges white-dominated, patriarchal, global capitalism and includes transformative agendas and strategies for sustainable living. The work of creating livable communities is, at root, about taking on the whole economic system and the systems of power-personal and institutional-that sustain it. A broader-based, stronger environmental justice movement must integrate race, class, and gender, framing issues so that alliances can be made.

A vital aspect of building movements involves visioning the future, changing one's personal values and aspirations, rethinking and recreating one's place in the world, forging alliances across lines of difference and between generations, through art, song, ideas, and analysis, as well as shared projects. It means opening up a public debate that challenges and opposes the values and practices of this economic system-its hazardous production processes as well as its consumerist ideology. It means framing progress in terms of sustainability, connectiveness, and true security.

It involves promoting vibrant local economic projects so that people are not dependent on the whims of corporate investors and developers, building up communities where young people are needed, where they can develop skills and gain respect for themselves and each other through meaningful work and participation in community projects and decision making." It involves expanding and strengthening many existing, small-scale projects, including community gardens, farmers' markets, cooperative organic farms, seed banks to safeguard genetic diversity, and backyard gardening and composting; the designing and building of ecohousing that repairs, reuses, and recycles discarded materials, vacant land, and derelict buildings, especially in blighted postindustrial cities; and promoting technologies that rely on renewable resources. It involves creating a definition of wealth that goes beyond the material and includes health, physical energy and strength, safety and security, time, skills, talents, creativity, love, community support, a connection to one's history and cultural heritage, and a sense of belonging. Clearly, this is both a long-term agenda and something that is already happening in small ways through many local projects. We lead contradictory lives, navigating our way in this crazy capitalist world.

10

Chipko and the Rose-Colored Glasses of Eco-feminism

Chipko was an environmental and social movement in northern India in the 1970s which is commonly cited world-wide as a primary example of successful grassroots activism. The movement's iconic status has lead to drastically differing portrayals. Chipko is prominently described by eco-feminists as a reactionary rather than radical movement, which sought to end the exploitation of both nature and women. Key events in the Chipko movement involving women are described, and the romantic eco-feminist portrayal of the movement is problematized. This depiction of the movement alone has led to several unintended consequences which are in fact detrimental to the welfare of the women of northern India.

The Chipko movement, which gave birth to the concept of 'tree-hugging,' has been so frequently invoked world-wide as the example of successful grassroots environmental activism that it has gained iconic status and entered the realm of myth. A prominent facet of Chipko mythology is its portrayal as a women's movement. Many of the key players in the Chipko struggle were, in fact, women - but does that necessitate its classification as a women's movement, as eco-feminist thought would indicate? The Chipko story is a complex one of several narratives with varying or even contradictory themes - "there are in fact almost as many Chipkos as there are descriptions of the movement". This work will focus on the role of women in the movement's motivations and actions, and the problematic nature and unintended consequences of the eco-feminist portrayal of Chipko.

The movement originated in the Garhwal region of Uttaranchal, then the northernmost district of Uttar Pradesh, along the Indo-Tibetan border. Uttaranchal contains a portion of the Himalayas, buttressing the Tibetan plateau, including the highest mountains in the world, and the principal watershed for the fertile and highly populated Indo-Gangetic plain. The Himalayan mountain range is relatively young, and is characterized by earthquakes, highly erosive rivers, excessively steep valleys which are often unsuited to agriculture, and mixed monsoon forests. The area was populated by hill people to some extent for up to 1700 years, and is the location of several important shrines, including one at the headwaters of the Ganges.

In such a particularly difficult terrain, no single economic or agricultural activity is sufficient to sustain a household. A "basket" of various economic pursuits is necessary - such as cultivation, cattle rearing, gathering from nearby forests, or outside employment - which requires the disproportionately large participation of women. Food, fodder, fertilizer, fuel, and fibers, essential to daily life, are all collected in the forest. Unfortunately, deforestation in these areas has become especially apparent in the last century, spurred by a complex range of factors, including expansion of agriculture, commercial exploitation of forests, population growth, and urban spread. Village women rely on the forests and their tasks have become increasingly difficult to perform as the trees become fewer and the forests more distant. This decline in forest cover has tended to increase the time and energy that women commit to gathering forest products, decrease income from such products, and decrease time spent on cultivation, to the detriment of nutrition. The area is also plagued by joblessness, triggering a widespread emigration of more than half the male population to the plains in search of work during the last 125 years, leaving women as the primary caretakers.

The social and political environment of the area was ripe for the birth of a powerful social and environmental movement in the 1970s. Resentment against Uttar Pradesh's continuing program of commercialization and underdevelopment of Garhwal was pervasive. The preceding dozen years had been marked with repeated demonstrations against different state agencies, causing Guha to locate Chipko on a historical continuum of peasant protest. Particularly prominent was opposition to the widespread distillation and sale of liquor, led in the area by Gandhian Sarvodaya activists, and fueled by the participation of thousands of local women.

Harvest rights for timber and other forest products were increasingly auctioned off by the Forest Department to outside private contractors for lower prices than were charged to the smaller local forest labor cooperatives. To add insult to injury, the outside contractors preferred to employ the "more 'biddable' Nepalese and other migrants than local men". Then, an unusually heavy monsoon season in 1970 triggered the most devastating flood in living memory, covering an area of 100 km^2 with water and debris, washing away 6 bridges, 10 km of road, dozens of vehicles, 366 houses, and 500 acres of crops, spilling the banks of three river systems, and blocking irrigation to a further 95 lakh acres of land in eastern Uttar Pradesh. This flood made the link between deforestation and highly destructive landslides and floods obvious to the affected villagers. From this specific mix of turbulent circumstances, Chipko was born.

In essence, the Chipko movement was a series of demonstrations in the Garhwal region that varied in participation, methodology, and ideology. Chipko activists included village women and men, Gandhian activists (such as Sarla Behn, Mira Behn, former politician Sunderlal Bahuguna and his wife, Vimala, and Chandi Prasad Bhatt), members of forest labor cooperatives, students from leftist political parties, including self-described communists, and other activists. This wide variation in participation gave Chipko diverse strategies ranging from mass mobilization, the tree-hugging and confrontation of axemen that Chipko is known for, as well as more militant and agressive actions, such as setting fire to forest auction halls as in Naintal. Chipko presented a front that was anything but ideologically uniform, which is why, thirty years after the first demonstration, there is still no consensus about its classification.

The movement is varyingly painted by outside commentators as a peasant appeal to moral economy, a "path towards a green earth and a 'true civilization'", an "explicitly ecological and feminist movement" or concerned with social justice, political democracy, and a reformation of local agriculture. This picture is further complicated by the "differing and sometimes contradictory accounts written by major figures involved in Chipko". What follows is an account of a few of the many incidents that comprise the Chipko movement, with a special focus on those events that highlight the role of women. It should be noted that generally there is a greater amount of material available concerning such incidents, likely due to the attention given them by the large body of eco-feminist literature - a situation which would need to be rectified to get a more even-handed image of the movement.

Early in 1973, the Dashauli Gram Swarajya Sangh, a small cooperative of artisans in the Chamoli district founded and led by Chandi Prasad Bhatt, requested permission from the Forest Department to fell two ash trees from the forest near the village of Mandal, for the production of agricultural implements by its woodcraft unit. Their request was denied, and instead the allotment was auctioned off to Symonds Co., a firm located in faraway Allahabad that manufactured cricket bats. This spurred the DGSS to vow to prevent the Company from harvesting its allotment. To this end the DGSS organized several meetings in the area to plan possible responses. Many tactics were discussed, including torching the trees, felling and removing the trees themselves, or lying in front of Company trucks. Eventually the DGSS settled on the now iconic tactic of hugging the trees, expressed in Bhatt's famous words "Let them know that we will not allow the felling of ash trees. When they aim their axes upon them, we will embrace the trees". Thus the Chipko movement was given a name - chipko is Hindi for 'adhere' or 'stick to,' though "it is usually translated in a more 'feel-good' way as 'hug'". In April and June, the Symonds Company was twice denied access to their allotted trees, both near Mandal and the village of Phata Rampur, 80 km away, by demonstrating villagers, despite being offered five to ten ash trees as compensation. The Company retreated, empty-handed, and the opening battle of the Chipko movement was a success.

Following this success, Bhatt and the others made the critical decision to spread the word to other villages in the region of the Forest Department's auctioning plans and the success of Chipko. By "moving beyond their immediate local need to embrace a wider spatial and temporal perspective," Chipko became a "meaningful social movement with regional implications". One of the villages contacted was Reni. By the time Chipko workers had reached Reni, trees in the nearby forest had already been marked for felling, ironically by the villagers themselves who needed the government pay. A meeting was held where the activists urged the villagers to adopt their strategy. Women, seated at the rear of this meeting, were reportedly amused and "giggled" at the frequent usage of the word 'chipko', but, according to the dramatic flair of Weber, would soon "become the front-line soldiers" of the movement.

The Department scheduled the fellings for the last week of March, 1974. Fearing a repeat of the conflict at Mandal, the Conservator of Forests then arranged to meet with Chandi Prasad Bhatt in Gopeshwar on the 26th of March. On the same day, the men of Reni and nearby villages were called to Chamoli to receive long overdue compensation for lands used by the army after the Chinese invasion of 1962. The contractor's axemen were then free to proceed, and took a circuitous route to the marked trees. They were, however, spotted by a small girl, who then informed Gaura Devi, the head of the local women's circle. Gaura Devi mobilized some twenty-seven women to stop the laborers - according to Bhatt, "not caring for the odds against them, these women rushed to the forest and clung to the marked trees with angry tree-fellers threatening them with glistening axes". Eventually the workers were persuaded to withdraw. As recounted by Gaura Devi,

It was not a question of planned organization of the women for the movement, rather it happened spontaneously. Our men were out of the village so we had to come forward and protect the trees. We have no quarrel with anybody but only we wanted to make the people understand that our existence is tied with the forests. The demonstration at Reni marked the major entry of women into the Chipko movement.

The participation of women was well established in the events at Doongri-Paintoli, where "women defied their own menfolk as well as the Forest Department contractors in order to protect their forests". In 1978, the Forest Department came to an agreement with the all-male village panchayat, in which the Department would acquire the community forest and convert it to a potato seed farm, employing villagers and bringing improvements to the area, such as a road to the outside world, a health center, improvements to the local school, and electricity.

The loss of the community forest would have meant an additional 5 km walk to the forest for daily necessities by the village women; the women voiced their objections, but to no avail. Chipko activists came to the village to speak and incited the women, prompting the panchayat to ban Bhatt and his workers from the village. On February 9, 1980, a large meeting of local village women held a demonstration using Chipko methods, thereby preventing governmental felling. Nine days later, felling in the area halted.

Chipko, especially the events described above, is frequently highlighted in eco-feminist discourse. Eco-feminism is in turn based on the women/nature connection established by Sherry Ortner, though not without debate. Ortner makes this link to explain the universal subordination of women: "Since it is always culture's project to subsume and transcend nature," and women are considered closer to nature due to their physiology, social roles, and psychic structure, "then culture would find it 'natural' to subordinate, not to say oppress, them". Ortner goes on to say that the only way to escape this subordination is to more fully take up the cultural "projects of creativity and transcendence," and more fully align women with culture. Eco-feminism takes the woman/nature connection a step farther.

Vandana Shiva is described by Rangan as "the best known Indian eco-feminist in the world today," due in large part to "her repeated and wide-spread narration of the Chipko story". Shiva sees women, particularly rural Indian women, as "embedded in nature". Women are the custodians of Prakriti, nature or the feminine principle, which is the manifestation of Shakti, the divine feminine creative energy of the cosmos. Prakriti "seeks to nurture and maintain the harmony and diversity of the natural forests as a life source", and from which "men and developed industrial cultures are alienated" and must be recovered.

The shift from concern for the earth to concern for commercialism signals the death of Prakriti, which is for women, "simultaneously a beginning of their marginalization, devaluation, displacement and ultimate dispensability". Shiva makes clear that this death is triggered by the arrival of the masculinist, reductionist, industrial, colonizing forces of Western culture. Says Shiva,

An ecologically sustainable future has much to gain from the world-views of ancient civilizations and diverse cultures which survived sustainably over centuries. These were based on an ontology of the feminine as the living principle... Not merely did this result in an ethical context which excluded possibilities of exploitation and domination, it allowed the creation of an earth family.

Shiva disagrees with Ortner's assessment that women's liberation is linked with culture; Shiva terms this "the masculinization of the female", which, from the context of her work, is clearly undesireable. "Liberating nature from ceaseless exploitation" and women from "limitless marginalization" are seen by Shiva as simultaneous and identical ends. The eco-feminist discourse gives an interesting take on the motivations, actions, and origination of the Chipko movement. Shiva traces the beginnings of Chipko not to the confrontation at Mandal, but to a Bishnoi community in the northeastern state of Rajasthan 300 years earlier. Led by a woman called Amrita Devi, community members "sacrificed their lives to save their sacred *khejri* trees by clinging to them". She claims that the climatic nature of the Chipko movement "facilitates the appropriation of the movement by an individual or group who then erases the contributions" of the thousands of participants that have come before.

These appropriating individuals are then identified as the widely recognized male leaders of the movement, such as Chandi Prasad Bhatt, Sunderlal Bahuguna, and Dhoom Singh Negi, who, in 'reality' are the "students and followers" of the female leaders, such as Sarala Behn, Vimala Bahuguna, and Gaura Devi. This is supported by a quote from Sunderlal Bahuguna: "We are the runners and messengers - the real leaders are the women". In Shiva's eco-feminist narrative, Bhatt and Sunderlal Bahuguna, elsewhere portrayed as embodiments of the movement, are mentioned only in their 'messenger' capacity.

In this view, the basis for Chipko, the "women's special concern with forestry for survival," was only temporarily joined to "largely male" economic concerns. Shiva's account of the demonstration at Mandal makes no mention of the DGSS, or any economic concern, only that "when 300 ash trees... were to be felled in Mandal, the villagers Went to the forest beating drums. They declared that they would embrace the trees and not allow them to be cut". In Shiva's account of Reni, the laborers are spotted, not by a small girl, but by a cowherdess and her companions, who, surrounding the contractor's men, spoke of the forest as their mother and forbade the felling of the trees. The eco-feminist narrative of Chipko focuses almost exclusively on those events that took place in a forest setting, referring to the mass demonstrations at forest auction houses only as "expressions of popular discontent". In 1977, the two strains of Chipko thinking - the one feminine and life-enhancing which "emerged from India's ancient forest culture", and the other economic and life-destroying - clashed. The women of Chipko, who "of course, had always been the backbone," expelled those with economic concerns, making the movement "explicitly an ecological *and* feminist movement". In this new Chipko, the women continued to "struggle against the exploitation of the forests," whether the destroyers were outside contractors or their own menfolk, who had been "colonized," or brainwashed, by the commercial forestry system.

Perhaps not surprisingly, this portrayal of Chipko has its share of detractors. Locating Chipko's origin in the Bishnoi community of the sixteenth century is problematic, considering the physical and temporal distance to the activists of Garhwal. Also, though the Bishnoi religion, as a peripheral sect, does include a particular reverence for trees, there is no evidence that these ideas were widely shared as late as fifty years ago in nearby Sawar, much less in faraway Garhwal, or that they were widespread during pre-colonial times. The Bishnoi story was invoked by Sunderlal Bahuguna in his rhetoric, and so was well known by the early 1980s. Also, though large numbers of women were involved in Chipko, the leadership was predominantly male, and were "not always or only their 'students and followers', as Shiva maintains". Visible presence of women in the movement does not guarantee a concern with women's interests, or that women hold leadership positions. Says even dramatic Weber, "to call what we have known as the Chipko andolan a women's movement is only correct in a restricted sense. It may partly, or even largely, have been a movement of women - but not by women".

The cultural background from which Shiva's Chipko women are said to draw their motivations is misrepresented by Eco-feminism. The classical Indian texts that have been used to sustain this discourse are the same texts, written by elite, high caste men, from which come such idioms as "Woman is untruth," and "There exist no friendships with women. They have the hearts of hyenas". Shiva suggests that in accordance with Shakti and Prakriti, women were venerated, yet in Brahminical Hindu tradition, men's fear of Shakti is a major reason for the subordination of women. Neither are the ideas of Shakti and Prakriti as universal or enduring as Shiva portrays.

Furthermore, eliding the actions of hill women with the cultural motivations of mainstream Hindu women is questionable. Shiva's distinctions between the universal feminine principle, all women, Third-World women, Indian women, and mainstream Hindu women seem completely collapsible. Among hill peoples, women are relatively free, as evidenced by a higher divorce and remarriage rate; "it is the spread of mainstream Indian civilization which has imposed the constraints of caste society onto women". Neither is eco-feminist portrayal of ecological relations accurate. Mainstream Indian civilization, long before the colonizing influence of the British and modern science, was itself "established precisely by clearing forests for settled cultivation". The pre-colonial period was neither particularly socially harmonious, nor ecologically stable. By attributing the subjugation of women and nature solely to colonialism, Shiva is ignoring what were, in fact, "complex processes of gender subordination and environmental degradation".

The motivations assigned to the women of Chipko by Eco-feminism should also be examined. Though women often disproportionately bear the costs of environmental deterioration, it does not necessarily follow that their sole concern would be for the health of the forest. If a hill woman's needs and responsibilities for subsistence conflict with 'sound ecological practice,' then she will likely give priority to the more immediately pressing. Even this argument is based on the assumption that "if they were in a position to, women always and everywhere have both the knowledge and the desire to preserve the environment", and that is a large assumption to make indeed. Even when women do act in environment friendly ways, it can often by explained in terms of rational short-term benefit - for example only collecting dead, dry wood, so as to avoid carrying the heavier, green wood. More than a sense of communion, a woman's responsibility and need to supply subsistence for her household govern her relationship with the forests. The women of Chipko "fought to prevent the complete clearance of their forest as a functional livelihood strategy not because of a desire to retain or return to some pristine 'traditional' village life". By reducing hill women's attitudes and behaviors to biological attributes, eco-feminists ignore or devalue other explanations for their actions, such as structural location, personal motive, or agency.

It is clear that the motivations behind Chipko were rather more complex than portrayed by eco-feminist discourse. Both subsistence and commercial interests were at stake in the workings of Chipko, and they pertained to more than just the local women. Women had been feeling the burden of declining forests in the form of a growing firewood shortage before 1973, but the birth of Chipko required an economic incentive, like two ash trees and the DGSS. In Garhwal, the state held a policy of economic marginalization, while it continued to degrade the ecological base on which the embittered hill people depended. Additionally, each Chipko demonstration differed according to place, time, and participation - to assign one overall motivation, such as feminism, would be over-simplistic. The struggle at Mandal "centered on access to raw materials for small-scale industrial use," while in remote Reni, the women were protecting their major subsistence resource. Nor was Chipko primarily a reactionary movement, despite the eco-feminist portrayal: "We do an injustice to the vast majority of the women and men of Uttaranchal if we understand them to want to return to some idealized traditional past that is unlikely ever to have existed".

However, the eco-feminist reading of Chipko is pervasive, shaping the effect of Chipko on Uttaranchal and the world, even as it describes it. Chipko the myth has served as "an inspiration for activists both in India and elsewhere against social and environmental injustice". But Chipko's legacy on the ground is somewhat less than mythological. Its death can be traced to the enactment in 1981 of the 15 year moratorium on felling above 1000 meters in Garhwal. The ban was in fact a direct result of Chipko's agitations, and formed by the perception of Chipko as a strictly environmental movement. The ban was deeply resented by the hill people, who saw that Forest Department felling continued, while they were further excluded from the forest. As a result of the ban, and the 1988 amendment to the Forest Conservation Act which required permission from the Ministry of Environment and Forests for land use change in forested areas, 4,500 development projects all over Garhwal and Kumaon were stalled. According to Shamser Sing Bist, an activist in Garhwal, "the final act of betrayal came when a potentially radical movement for self-determination and self-management of our resources turned into a purely conservationist one".

To date, eco-feminist ideology has failed to end the marginalization of women, even in environmental management settings. Eco-feminist discourse mobilizes its depiction of the pre-colonial past, and the Chipko women as bearers and enactors of that ideal, as a "template for alternative development policy." As a result, most attention is being given only to efficient use of women in environmental projects. Indeed, the formation of new management institutions are entrenching gender inequalities. The romantic eco-feminist reading of the past is being used prescriptively, and has all the dangers of revitalizing old hierarchies, such as caste and gender; all over India, social activists "are looking to tradition for answers in various ways, including many who wish to 'revive the rich traditions of prudent use'".

The Chipko movement had several benefical outcomes, but little has changed in terms of gender equity. Village communities and government now share responsibility for forest management under the Joint Forest Management committees. But few women are members, in part due to structural constraints that allow only the head of the household to attend. Little account is taken of women's concerns in the all-male JFMs or village panchayats, often to the direct economic detriment of the women. Typically, this results in the women circumventing rules produced by these management bodies. Where they prove ineffective, women commonly form informal patrol groups, enhancing the efficacy of forest protection, but adding to "women's work burden and responsibility, without increasing their authority". The idealized representation of the past prevents the challenging of institutional and social constraints still felt by women, and allows inequities to persist in new environmental management institutions.

The problematic nature of the eco-feminist portrayal of Chipko has led to some unintended consequences, which could in fact damage the very cause that they sought to valorize. The many facets of Chipko, much like India, are much too complex to assign a single adjective and have any hope of conveying the entirety of the movement. This shifting quality of actions, motivations, and intentions has in fact made Chipko an excellent rhetorical tool - used to inspire, to shape policy, or to justify inequitable social structures.

11

Eco-feminism

Historic and International Evolution

Eco-feminism emerged in the 1970s and 1980s as myriad forms of feminist and environmental theories and activisms intersected. The term was introduced by Francoise d'Eaubonne in her book Le Feminisme ou la Mort [Feminism or Death] published in 1974. Some theorists, such as Ynestra King, name it as a third wave of feminism, while others place it in the general category of deep ecology. Eco-feminism acts in both and neither of these broad movements, simultaneously serving as an environmental critique of feminism and a feminist critique of environmentalism. Eco-feminist trajectories are varied; there is no one accepted or orthodox "Eco-feminism." Rosemary Radford Ruether, Ivone Gebara, Vandana Shiva, Susan Griffin, Alice Walker, Starhawk, Sallie McFague, Luisah Teish, Sun Ai Lee-Park, Paula Gunn Allen, Monica Sjöö, Greta Gaard, Karen Warren and Andy Smith are among the voices speaking from eco-feminist positions.

Eco-feminism asserts that all forms of oppression are connected and that structures of oppression must be addressed in their totality. Oppression of the natural world and of women by patriarchal power structures must be examined together or neither can be confronted fully. These socially constructed oppressions formed out of the power dynamics of patriarchical systems. In one of the first eco-feminist books, New Woman/ New Earth, Ruether, states:

Women must see that there can be no liberation for them and no solution to the ecological crisis within a society whose fundamental model of relationships continues to be one of domination. They must unite the demands of the women's movement with those of the ecological movement to envision a radical reshaping of the basic socioeconomic relations and the underlying values of this modern industrial society.

Ruether makes clear a central tenet of Eco-feminism: earth and the other-than-human experience the tyranny of patriarchy along with women. Classism, racism, sexism, heterosexism, naturism and speciesism are all intertwined.

Eco-feminism is multi-faceted and multi-located, challenging structures rather than individuals. By confronting systems of patriarchy, Eco-feminism broadens the scope of the cultural critique and incorporates seemingly disparate but, according to Eco-feminism, radically connected elements. Combining feminist and deep ecological perspectives - in and of themselves extremely varied ways of thinking about reality - is a complex, transgressive process that is often in flux. Eco-feminist positions reflect varied political stances that may be, and usually are, transformed through time and place. In other words, the political activisms and alliances stemming from Eco-feminism modify in relationship to the perceived justice issues being confronted in differing cultural and historical settings. Because of this constant morphing, Eco-feminism simultaneously challenges patriarchies from different angles. This is one of the myriad strengths of the fluid and radically diverse positions assumed by Eco-feminism.

Eco-feminism claims that patriarchal structures justify their dominance through categorical or dualistic hierarchies: heaven/earth, mind/body, male/female, human/animal, spirit/matter, culture/nature, white/non-white. Established oppressive systems continue to manifest their abusive powers by reinforcing assumptions of these binaries, even making them sacred through religious and scientific constructs. Eco-feminism posits that as long as any of the dualisms exist as an integral component of societal structuring and justification, they will all continue to serve as starting points to justify patriarchy. Therefore all dualisms and binary oppositional forms must be dismantled otherwise humanity remains "divided against" itself, a phrase that Griffin uses to describe the ideological impact of dualism.

As a justice advocate for the entire web of life, Eco-feminism resists dividing culture into these imbedded separate or dualistic arenas. In her introduction to *Eco-feminism: Women, Culture, Nature,* editor Warren asserts: What makes Eco-feminism distinct is its insistence that non-human nature and naturism are feminist issues. Eco-feminist philosophy extends familiar feminist critiques of socialisms of domination to nature.

Eco-feminism's constructive worldview replaces hierarchical dualisms with radical diversity and relationship, modeled on both biodiversity and the feminist emphasis on the strength of difference. Throughout the 1970s, few eco-feminists in academic settings designated themselves as such, though several engaged in similar theoretical endeavors linking feminist and environmental ideas. Early publications that analyze the woman/nature connection in light of the environmental crisis include Ruether's New Woman/New Earth, Mary Daly's Gyn/Ecology, Griffin's Woman and Nature and Carolyn Merchant's The Death of Nature.

Some of the earliest articulations of Eco-feminism analyzed the patriarchal underpinnings in religious and philosophical systems of the European and Mediterranean world. These cultural and geographical foci surfaced from the primarily European and Euro-American voices that constituted the initial eco-feminist conversations. Such scholars as Anne Primavesi, Carol Christ, Merchant, Daly and Charlene Spretnak examined cultural and religious systems from such areas as ancient Mesopotamia and Greece, as well as religious systems such as Judaism and Christianity. They proposed that patriarchal cultural structures revolved around layers of symbol systems that justified domination. For example, they interpret the creation stories in the book of Genesis, foundational for Judaism, Christianity and Islam, as demonizing both woman and animal.

These and other early eco-feminists analyzed pre-patriarchal cultures in the Mediterranean and old European worlds as well. Feminist historian Gerda Lerner and archaeomythologist Marija Gimbutas provided some of the groundwork for this analysis. Gimbutas' theories of Old Europe are based in her complex and widely critiqued archaeomythological reconstructions. Her theories suggest that life valuing, sometimes matriarchal and rarely militaristic societies existed before Indo-Aryan invaders slowly destroyed these cultures. Lerner's historical reconstructions focus on the shift from small Neolithic villages to city-based states with the accompanying rise of patriarchal cultural systems. Both theorists posit pre-patriarchal Mediterranean world religious cultures in which fertility goddesses and other nature symbolism figured prominently.

Gradually, patriarchal, militaristic sky gods replaced earth goddesses and gods. Most of the ancient symbols of power were subverted and remythologized as evil or chaotic. The mother goddess, whose body often birthed or constituted the earth, became the target of the powerful sky gods, as evidenced by such creation stories as the Babylonian Enuma Elish. The pattern of male deities killing female or animal deities in an effort to establish a patriarchal order and to control forces assumed to be chaotic repeats itself consistently. The snake, once a symbol of life, was trampled under the foot of the male deity and connected to evil. Hell was in the earth and Heaven was removed to the sky. Paradise lost its materiality and became a masculine, hierarchical projection.

Such theories raise many questions for scholars interested in the reconstruction of early human civilizations. For example, few archeologists accept Gimbutas' theories and suggest that they are projections of matriarchal and goddess myths. Still, some eco-feminists reference these historical reconstructions as alternatives to the commonly accepted patriarchal constructions that project historical progress. In other words, the idea of civilizations advancing from pre-agricultural to agricultural to industrial to post-industrial/technological might also be construed as a mythological projection. Applying feminist historical methodology, some academic eco-feminists reevaluate the patriarchal myth of progress, particularly its detrimental effects on the human-nature relationship. Carolyn Merchant articulates a version of this critique in *The Death of Nature*.

From the work of Griffin, Daly, Ruether, Merchant and others in the 1970s, grew a dramatic expansion of Eco-feminism in academic circles during the 1980s and 1990s. Activist movements, sometimes connected with but generally outside of the academy, also increased in the 1980s. Several conferences focusing on Eco-feminism were organized: "Women and Life on Earth: Eco-feminism in the Eighties", "Eco-feminist Perspectives: Culture, Nature, Theory", a group at the National Women's Studies Association. These efforts, along with other attempts to create sustainable organizations such as the Feminist Peace Institute and WomanEarth, led to the publication of several foundational anthologies. *Reclaim the Earth: Women Speak Out for Life on Earth*, edited by Stephanie Leland and Leonie Caldecott; *Healing the Wounds: The Promise of Eco-feminism*, edited by Judith Plant. All these volumes were edited by Euro-American eco-feminists but the editors included authors from various cultures. Petra Kelly, in her foreword to *Healing the Wounds*, proclaims a "global ecological sisterhood" and calls on the women of the Chipko Movement, the Greenham Common, the Krim Region and the Western Shoshone Indian Nation to "link arms" as global sisters. The practice of publishing anthologies with diverse voices rather than books representing just one voice exhibits the overall tendency among eco-feminists to value inclusivity and difference. Still these anthologies, while influential, were criticized for essentializing the woman/nature connection and for over-romanticizing or over-simplifying women in non-Western cultures.

Vandana Shiva, a physicist and environmental researcher/activist in India, published Staying Alive: Women, Ecology and Survival in India, which reflects the increasingly global nature of Eco-feminism during the 1980s. Shiva connects the "death of the feminine principle" with "maldevelopment," a term she uses to describe the introduction of Western, intensive agriculture to the "Third World." In her essay "Development, Ecology and Women" Shiva articulates the relationship clearly:

> Maldevelopment militates against this equality in diversity, and superimposes the ideologically constructed category of western technological man as a uniform measure of the worth of classes, cultures, and genders... Diversity, and unity and harmony in diversity, become epistemologically unattainable in the context of maldevelopment, which then becomes synonymous with women's underdevelopment, and nature's depletion ....

Shiva also published, with Maria Mies, a German, Marxist sociologist, *Eco-feminism: Reconnecting a Divided World*. In this book the authors connect the capitalist-patriarchal economic system with the oppression of women in both the northern and southern hemispheres. However Shiva, not unlike some other eco-feminists, has been criticized for essentializing women and nature in her work.

Another area of focus concerned the relationship of scientific worldviews to religion and culture. Eco-feminism suggests that the antagonism sometimes existing between religious and scientific worldviews has been detrimental, used by both approaches to advance their own hierarchical structures. The reductionist models of both Western theologies and many Western scientific ideologies project a material world that is not sacred, but mechanistic. This apparent disconnect between the material and the sacred, alleged by eco-feminists to be fostered by both religion and science, has been particularly detrimental when acted upon by European-American dominant cultures. The Christian eco-feminist theologian Sallie McFague, in her book *The Body of God: An Ecological Theology*, summarizes the situation:

> Moreover, and most significant for an ecological theology, this picture projected disembodiment: disembodied knowing and disembodied doing (internal human peace or forgiveness

of sins became the principal action between God and the world).

In The Death of Nature Merchant links this hierarchical, mechanistic approach to nature to the oppression of women. She argues that, whereas organic thinking and interdependence shaped European life through the Middle Ages, the "fathers" of the scientific revolution determined to dominate nature. Merchant quotes Francis Bacon extensively. He proposes to "hound nature in her wanderings" in order to "drive her afterward to the same place again." To disclose the "secrets of nature" Bacon suggests that "entering and penetrating into these holes and corners" of nature will lead to the uncovering of truth. During the same general time period, numerous European women were accused of witchcraft. The Malleus Maleficarum or Hammer of Witches, a manual on identifying and interrogating witches, instructed inquisitors to "penetrate" and torture witches in order to discover their secrets. Merchant argues that the feminine language used for "nature" and the parallel violent approaches of control assigned against unruly nature and unruly women are obvious.

Both Merchant and McFague emphasize the new, organic model of the cosmos developing in some areas of science and religion. The "common creation story" and the growing field of ecology, as well as some new cosmologies emerging from physics, provide fertile ground for eco-feminist entry into dialogue with the natural sciences.

The first volume of essays to focus on the topic of Eco-feminism and spirituality was Eco-feminism and the Sacred, edited by Carol Adams. Voices from various religious and ethnic perspectives were included, for example: Hindu, Jewish, Buddhist, Native American, Womanist, Christian. The volume combined voices from activist positions as well as from academic ones, with many contributors speaking from both simultaneously. Byllye Avery of the National Black Women's Health Project and Zoe Weil of ANIMALEARN, a division of the American Anti-vivisection Society, are two such contributors.

During the same three decades, eco-feminist activists engaged in myriad protests, boycotts and campaigns to bring attention to the interconnection of justice issues related to women and the environment as a whole. Feminism is politically activist at its core and feminist methodologies applied to scholarly work make political engagement requisite. Various scholars entered the activist arena via their intellectual contributions and various activists entered the academic arena via their commitment to justice-oriented endeavors. Many first generation eco-feminists encountered each other through antimilitarist and anti-nuclear protests during the height of the Cold War. In 1980 A Handbook for Women on the Nuclear Mentality, written by Susan Koen and Nina Swaim, used the word Eco-feminism as a foundational concept for action. The Women's Pentagon Actions and the Greenham Women's Peace Camp are two examples of eco-feminist, antimilitarization and anti-nuclear organizations.

The influence of the United Nations Decade for Women, with its many gatherings and coalition-building opportunities, on the development of Eco-feminism has not been adequately researched. Various international political conferences sponsored by the U.N. and international NGOs did impact eco-feminist activisms. For example, the U.N. Conference on Women in Nairobi in 1985 brought together eco-feminist leaders and provided them with further opportunities to connect with international colleagues. Other major international conferences that linked environmentalism and women's issues were the "U.N.'s Environmental Programme's Global Assembly on Women and the Environment" and the "World Women's Congress for a Healthy Planet," both held in Miami in 1991. While these international eco-feminist gatherings connected academic voices with activist voices, there are some eco-feminists whose focus has been activist and justice-oriented who deliberately separate themselves from the academic arena in general, and in particular from the Euro-American academy.

The issue of racism within eco-feminist, and feminist, dialogues has also been prominent. Though paying significant attention to diversity, white eco-feminists have often essentialized racial difference. For example, in the academic anthologies listed above, Shiva's voice figures prominently and seems to stand for all women who are not European or Euro-American. Few women of color have been able to remain in positions of leadership in activist or academic organizations for long periods of time. The political power of white women in these organizations undermines, often unintentionally, that of women of color. Even though such organizations as Woman Earth attempted to make racism an integral part of the eco-feminist conversation, racial tensions contributed to the eventual disbanding of numerous eco-feminist dialogue groups. Even the designations "white" and "of color" seem to maintain a binary within Eco-feminism as it tries to subvert all such labels.

Another outcome of issues connected to racism is the critique of the label "eco-feminist" by various activists from indigenous peoples. For example, Winona LaDuke, director of the Honor the Earth Fund and the White Earth Land Recovery Project, identifies herself as an activist for indigenous people rather than an eco-feminist activist. In an interview with Judith Plant Marie Wilson, member of the Gitksan-Wet'suwet'en Tribal Council explains her perspective on this issue:

At the risk of sounding scornful or derogatory I have to say that the Indian attitude toward the natural world is different from the environmentalists. I have had the awful feeling that when we are finished dealing with the courts and our land claims, we will then have to battle the environmentalists and they will not understand why.

Some of this tension grows from the appropriation of indigenous religious rituals by white people, including some eco-feminists. Andy Smith harshly criticizes such borrowing in her essay "For All Those Who Were Indian in a Former Life".

In the introduction Ruether notes that while Eco-feminism is not a "movement" in these large geographical areas, the global dialogue inspired by connections between the oppression of women and nature needs to be recognized. The contributors are all local/global activists and their work speaks to the globalization of Eco-feminisms. The Con-Spirando Collective in Chile collaborated with Ruether in developing the volume. Con-Spirando, translated as "breathing with" or "spiritual conspiracy," tries to "weave a network of women throughout Latin America who are interested in feminist theology, spirituality and Eco-feminism" while also holding women's rituals. This collective publishes a magazine by the same name and operates a women's center in Santiago in addition to focusing specifically on eco-feminist activisms and analyzes. Victoria Tauli-Corpuz, from the tribal community of the Igorots in the Philippines, reflects on the spiritual links between women and nature in Igorot culture. But the "introduction of high-yielding varieties of rice seeds" has disrupted women's spiritual leadership roles. Finally, Sarah Mvududu, with the Women and Law in Southern Africa Research Project in Zimbabwe, claims that "gender is also fundamental in understanding human interaction with the environment and with respect to natural resources". She explains this by analyzing Shona beliefs and woodland management. Spirit mediums, often women, are deeply involved with sustainable woodland development in Zimbabwe and their connection to sacred places where trees are protected is requisite for reforestation.

Eco-feminism has not been without critics, from eco-feminists themselves as well as from others. Some of the most ardent critics question the woman/nature link that is sometimes placed at the core of Eco-feminism, as evidenced in the title of such essays as Sherry Ortner's "Is Female to Male as Nature is to Culture?". Because of the strong woman-nature connection assumed and developed in some eco-feminist positions, various feminists distance themselves from Eco-feminism and suggest that it is essentialist in nature. Essentialism claims that cross-culturally and cross-historically those of a particular race, gender or other category share the same traits. Many expressions of feminism and Eco-feminism argue against all such essentialist constructions, while others expressions seem to maintain essentialism. Kate Nash, in her

1994 essay "The Feminist Production of Knowledge: Is Deconstruction a Practice for Women?" published in Feminist Review, clarifies the "tension" between the "deconstructive politics of feminism and the assertions, or constructions of unified identity that feminists are frequently called on to make on behalf of the category 'women' which gives the project its political specificity".

Various attempts at typologizing feminisms and Eco-feminisms have been made and are helpful for clarifying the diverse perspectives, though it should be noted that even these designations are understood differently by different eco-feminists. Cultural and radical forms tend to idealize the feminine whereas activist eco-feminists usually see their position as an analysis of a particular historical and cultural phenomenon. Some activist eco-feminists do engage in shifting political alliances that employ essentialist arguments functionally, but disengage from these alliances and reform others as requisite for effectively subverting patriarchal structures. One of the most helpful treatments of this continuing, sometimes heated, interaction among diverse manifestations of Eco-feminism is Noel Sturgeon's work *Eco-feminist Natures: Race, Gender, Feminist Theory and Political Action*. In addition to these groupings within Eco-feminism are ecowomanism, mentioned above, with a focus on race as the primary lens through which to view oppressions, and animal rights-oriented Eco-feminism. There are also those who consider themselves spiritual eco-feminists, such as Starhawk, embracing the religious, Earth-goddess based components of the position.

Deep ecology and Eco-feminism also engage in ideological debates. Many eco-feminists count themselves as deep ecologists and many deep ecologists count themselves as eco-feminists, while others might designate themselves as one but not the other. The background to the differences between some deep ecologists and some eco-feminists grew from the feminist critique of the androcentric tendency of deep ecology in its earliest, and often militaristic or violent, expressions such as those expounded upon in Edward Abbey's The Monkey

Wrench Gang. This approach has been dubbed eco-macho. Specific philosophical discussions took place under the auspices of the journal Environmental Ethics. Karen Warren and Michael Zimmerman published essays in this journal in 1987, both of which made explicit connections between feminism and deep ecology. In 1989, Warwick Fox's essay "The Deep Ecology-Eco-feminism Debate and Its Parallels" was published in the journal and followed by a response by Deborah Slicer in 1995 entitled "Is there an Eco-feminism-deep ecology 'debate'?" Though the intricacies of the discussion cannot be expanded here, recognition of this on-going tension (i.e. whether or not male-female dualism is the primary lens through which to analyze and critique destructive power relations) is requisite. One interpretation of Eco-feminism that shifts this analysis is Val Plumwood's Feminism and the Mastery of Nature. Plumwood's central relational model for abusive western power structures is master-slave rather than male-female.

Another area of Eco-feminism that needs to be addressed is the connection with animal rights activism, as noted previously. Adams has made explicit links between androcentric, patriarchal treatment of other-than-human animals, particularly focusing on the meat producing industries of the United States, and the exploitation of women. Her study, The Sexual Politics of Meat, provides the foundation for this field of inquiry. Greta Gaard's anthology *Eco-feminism: Women, Animals, Nature* includes several essays that analyze the mutual oppressions of women and non-human animals in patriarchal societies. A prominent activist presence in this field is the organization Feminists for Animal Rights whose co-founder, Marti Kheel, is also recognized as a leading eco-feminist voice.

However, these perspectives are countered by another prominent author, Mary Stange. She has referred to herself as an eco-feminist, though one who is critical of much that is usually assumed as central to Eco-feminism. Her books, *Woman the Hunter and Gun Women,* posit that women are natural hunters, therefore in a predatory relationship with animals. Stange suggests that the linkages between woman and other animals sometimes made by eco-feminists could justify continued essentialism and, therefore, continued domination of both women and other animals. Thus she claims that the woman-animal connection should be reevaluated.

As Eco-feminism continues to shift and grow, different positions will surely form and surface, while other positions and alliances will fade away or be replaced by more urgent connections. Diverse understandings regarding the nature of the web of relationships between various spiritual/religious traditions and Eco-feminism could persist. Eco-feminism and deep ecology may continue wrangling. Issues of racism, population growth and the valuing of some humans over others, or of all humans over other-than-human animals, will stir the thoughts and actions of eco-feminists on a global scale. Charlene Spretnak provides one perspective that summarizes eco-feminist ideological positions effectively:

An ontology based on dynamic and admittedly partial knowledge as well as awe toward the complexity of embodied and embedded existence would contribute substantially to the profound social transformation that is needed. And Wangari Maathai, while speaking at the World Women's Congress for a Healthy Planet in 1991, succinctly stated the activist positions of Eco-feminism: Things will not just happen...Women must do something.

12

Eco-feminism in Latin America

The Development of Feminist Theology in Latin America

Latin American feminist theology was born and matured within liberation theology, although today it is in critical dialogue with that theology. The evolution of Latin American feminist theology, which spans more than thirty years, can be divided into three stages paralleling the decades of the 1970s, 1980s, and 1990s. Feminist consciousness within Latin American theology evolved from the total identification of women theologians and biblical scholars with liberation theology, to a growing awareness of-and discomfort with-liberation theology's patriarchal mindset, to challenging the patriarchal anthropology and cosmology present in liberation theology itself and calling for a total reconstruction of theology from a feminist perspective.

Scholarship on this evolution continues to grow. However, three Latin American feminist theologians have systematic studies of this historical development: Mexican feminist theologian María Pilar Aquino, Costa Rican feminist scripture scholar Elsa Tamez, and Brazilian eco-feminist theologian Ivone Gebara. Aquino describes the first two stages in rich detail, using women's testimonies and women's group reflections throughout Latin America to substantiate her research. Tamez's periodization is the most systematic and succinct of the three; she describes each stage by setting it in the context of three congresses that gathered together Latin American women theologians in 1979, 1985, and 1993. In each stage she describes the political, economic, ecclesial, and theological context, the development of feminist consciousness, feminist hermeneutics, and the use of inclusive language. Gebara, while also describing the first two stages, concentrates on the third stage. Indeed, Tamez places Gebara's work on holistic Eco-feminism at the center of third stage of Latin American feminist theology.

The Schema of Elsa Tamez

Tamez first described the stages of feminist theology in Latin America in a lecture at the ecumenical congress of women theologians and biblical scholars and teachers held in Rio de Janeiro in December 1993. She continues to reflect upon and update her schema with rigor. While three fairly clear stages are observable in the evolution of feminist consciousness among women working in theology and biblical hermeneutics, Tamez insists: "It is important to recognize that the hermeneutical experiences of one decade do not cancel out those of another. Very often different, even conflicting experiences coexist, sometimes within the same person.... Nor is one phase to be treated as more important than another." Tamez describes the *first phase* of Latin American feminist theology as an exciting period that saw the emergence of left-wing political parties and grassroots movements of *campesinos*, workers, and neighborhood and solidarity groups.

In this same time period, however, the region's revolutionary struggles, which had coalesced a decade earlier, were severely repressed by military dictatorships in South America. Military governments were already in place in Nicaragua, Guatemala, El Salvador, and Honduras in Central America. These dictatorships were infamous for their use of torture, assassination, and disappearances. The Development of Feminist Theology in Latin America of activists. However, in the midst of this repression, there was an amazing growth in the number and strength of small Christian communities, whose members were mostly urban slum dwellers. They gathered together in their small communities to reflect on biblical texts from their own experiences as militants.

The book of Exodus, stories of the Babylonian captivity, and liberation texts from the Gospels were favorites. During this decade women theologians and biblical scholars were enthusiastically committed to liberation theology's method and practice. They saw women as historical subjects in their own right, capable of being protagonists of liberation. They also lifted up the double oppression women suffer, that is, both as women and as members of an oppressed and impoverished class. Tamez notes, however, that there was practically no dialogue with either secular Latin American feminist organizations or with first world feminist theologians. In those years most women working in theology saw feminism as simply another imperialistic invasion from the North, which could even be dangerous in that it diverted poor women from the primary contradiction of their economic and political oppression as a class.

Women were seen as an implicit part of the category of the poor; therefore, the option for the poor meant the option for poor women. Time was spent studying Old and New Testament stories in which women were leaders, or renowned for their subversive acts, or women like Hagar, who was triply oppressed because of her class, race, and sex, and yet was blessed by God, who allowed her son to found a new people. Tamez underlines how reflections on these selected texts of liberation nourished hope in a new society based on socialist ideals, where it was assumed that egalitarian relations between the sexes would fall into place.

However, in this period there was no awareness of the possibilities of inclusive language, and God was always addressed as masculine.

In the *second phase* Tamez notes that an uneasiness was beginning to be felt by Latin American women theologians and biblicists about the affirmation that women were implicitly included in the category of the poor, and they began to see the need to read the Bible from the standpoint of women.

In this decade the political context shifted to Central America, where the Sandinistas came to power in Nicaragua and left-wing revolutionary struggles made headway in El Salvador and Guatemala. At the same time, most of the dictatorships in South America were replaced with restricted democracies in which the military remained vigilant watchdogs. In these years it became more and more evident that the foreign indebtedness of Latin American governments was sucking the lifeblood out of their peoples-so much so that the 1980s is seen as "the lost decade" in terms of the region's development. This decade saw a right-wing backlash to liberation theology, especially from Rome. The Vatican's Congregation for the Doctrine of the Faith published a document warning against the dangers of liberation theology. Leonardo Boff, one of Latin America's most widely known liberation theologians, was summoned to Rome and subsequently silenced for a two-year period.

Theological reflection grappled with these realities by centering on themes of the kingdom of God and human history, a theology of life and of death, idolatry of the market, the discipleship of Christ, martyrdom, and a spirituality of liberation. At last, a dialogue began between male liberation theologians and their female counterparts on the oppression of women as women. Also, by the mid-1980s gatherings were taking place to reflect on black and indigenous theologies.

During these years more and more activist Christian women became involved in theological and biblical reflection. They gradually realized that liberation theology's discourse was tainted with androcentrism and patriarchal constructs, and they began to insist that theology done from the viewpoint of women's experience should reflect different cultural, biological, and historical experiences from those of men. Especially challenged was liberation theology's emphasis on economic oppression as it championed the option for the poor, often at the expense of cultural oppression and domestic violence. These were years of much creative theological production by women in liturgy, art, and poetry. Also, attempts were initiated to reach out to the region's feminist movements and to first-world feminist theologians.

With regard to hermeneutics, women began to search for female images of God and to refer to God as both mother and father. The Holy Spirit was seen as feminine. Women called not only for the practice of justice, but also for the need for tenderness, loving solidarity, and comfort toward those who suffer unjustly. Tamez, herself a biblical scholar, calls attention to three aspects of women's biblical work in these years. The first was the search for greater freedom in speaking about God, especially in the area of life's daily joys and sorrows. Second, there was a need for critical analysis of those biblical texts that were clearly patriarchal and discriminated against women. When a text did not allow for a more inclusive reinterpretation, it was dismissed as non-normative.This posture raised the question of the authority and inspiration of the Bible as the word of God. Third, there was also a need to affirm womanly virtues such as motherliness, unselfishness, and tenderness-virtues that historically society did not consider important. The virtues of commitment, resistance, and sacrifice were also seen as liberating. God-language began to change in some circles because of the influence of some Christian feminists who began to address God as both father and mother. However, the word *feminist,* although widely accepted in some areas, was still shunned by many as an import from the North. "Doing theology from the standpoint of women" and reading the Bible "through women's eyes" were more acceptable.

The *third phase* is characterized by a radical, anti-patriarchal hermeneutical approach that proposes a new, inclusive, and non-patriarchal theology, indeed, a total reconstruction of theology itself. Ivone Gebara calls this phase "holistic Eco-feminism."

During the 1990s progressive forces in Latin America were profoundly shaken by the collapse of the Communist governments of Eastern Europe and the demise of historical socialism. The defeat of the Sandinistas in Nicaragua also dampened the region's hope for an alternative to the capitalist order. Economically, the current neoliberal economic model, which gives supremacy to the demands of world markets, appears to be seen as the only viable alternative. Socially, once effervescent grassroots movements have stagnated, including the CEBs, which have gone into steep decline. On the other hand, the inroads being made by Pentecostalism throughout Latin America are indeed remarkable. (A common phrase heard among Latin American pastoral agents these days is, "Liberation theology may have opted for the poor, but the poor have opted for Pentecostalism.") All this has affected the vibrancy of liberation theology, a topic that will be treated more thoroughly below.

One bright spot in an otherwise dismal political landscape has been the rise of the indigenous movement as a result of the five hundredth anniversary in 1992 of the European invasion of the Americas. Indigenous theologians are calling for liberation theology's option for the poor to be expanded to include an option for the impoverished other, because the "otherness" of the continent's diversity needs to be taken into account along with economic disparities. For a growing number of women, it has not been enough to speak of the feminine face of God. They find current theological discourse androcentric and patriarchal to the core and see their task as reconstructing the whole of theology from a feminist perspective.

A major influence on these women has been the introduction of gender analysis into their theological and biblical work, along with new insights coming from feminist anthropology. In this area there is a much more open, welcoming attitude toward both Latin American feminism and colleagues in the first world. One of the most forceful new hermeneutical categories for this feminist theological and biblical scholarship is the body.

Concrete bodies of women and men are becoming a new locus for doing theology. Efforts are also being made to offer a nonsacrificial reading of redemption to free many poor women from accepting violence, especially domestic violence, as somehow "the will of God." New non-gender-specific names are emerging for the Divine, such as Grace, Compassion, and Energy. As Tamez concludes: "We are aware of the radical nature of this challenge, which means reworking, or rather reinventing, the whole of Christian theology. There is difficulty in re-reading the great theological themes such as Christology, the Trinity and ecclesiology because of their androcentrism. It is recognized that the development of feminist theology in Latin America is the implications of reconstruction take us beyond orthodoxy." She ends her overview by emphasizing that the priority for feminist theologians and biblical scholars and teachers in Latin America is always to link their work to the basic concerns of the poor.

The Schema of Ivone Gebara

While Gebara's systematization is not as detailed as that of Elsa Tamez, she also sees three stages in the development of Latin American feminist theology. She points out, however, that they are not necessarily chronological and that they often overlap, depending on historical circumstance and the level of feminist consciousness in a specific country or group. Gebara elaborated on this development in a course she taught in Chile in April 1993. When the course was finished, I interviewed her on these stages, focusing especially on the third stage. For Gebara, the *first stage* of feminist theology is characterized by women's discovery of their oppression as historical subjects-an oppression present in theology, the Bible, and the churches. She credits the secular feminist movement-not the churches-with nurturing this insight among Christian women.

In this stage women rediscovered many women in the Bible, such as Sarah, Hagar, Miriam, Ruth, Esther, Judith, Mary, Magdalene, and the women at the empty tomb, and reclaimed them as key actors in the history of liberation. For Gebara, this was important but not sufficient in itself. She says that women tended to overvalue the feminine during this stage and to fall into the patriarchal trap of lifting up those domestic qualities historically associated with women, such as motherhood and the double-duty workday. Gebara also challenges work done in those years to hold up women liberators such as Judith as models without questioning the violent patriarchal framework in which the book of Judith is situated. She also believes that during this stage, women tended to think that they were the "good" gender and somehow spiritually superior to poor, weaker men. There was also a certain desire to "even the score" with their male counterparts.

Gebara calls the *second stage* the "feminization of theological concepts." This was a time when women theologians worked to rediscover the feminine, maternal face of God in biblical texts. She also notes that during those years, women were given a voice within the churches and within liberation theology so they could present "the women's perspective." This pleased progressive male theologians and pastors and particularly male liberation theologians who had always insisted that their ranks were open to women theologians. However, according to Tamez, Gebara has pointed out that what women had been doing was "patriarchal feminist theology."

Gebara finds that liberation theology in general has not challenged the underlying patriarchal structure of Christianity itself. While she acknowledges that liberation theology offers a more collective understanding of God and stresses the social nature of sin and that God is a God of life and of justice who has a preferential option for the poor, she finds that its anthropology and cosmology remain riddled with patriarchy. Gebara situates the *third stage* of Latin American feminist theology in the postmodern paradigm and invites us to consider what she calls "holistic Eco-feminism."

The schemas elaborated by Tamez and Gebara are very useful in describing the development of Latin American feminist theology, although both Gebara and Tamez insist that these are not fixed periods; often two phases can overlap in the same country or area or church. The following section combines the insights of both.

The Three Phases of Latin American Feminist Theology

First Phase

Political/Economic Context:

- Effervescence of leftist political parties and popular movements
- Revolutionary struggles, which provoked military coups, followed by dictatorship
- Repression through massacres, disappearances, torture, generalized human rights abuse

Ecclesiastical/Theological Context

- CEBs spring up all over Latin America:
- Grassroots reading and interpretation of the Bible
- Option for the poor; texts read with the "eyes of the poor"
- Medellín and Puebla documents
- Ecumenism based on option for the poor, cutting through denominational lines
- Theology of liberation comes into its own with its methodology of reflection based on praxis
- The poor become the theological locus
- Key themes are the Exodus, the "valley of tears," the historical Jesus

Construction of Feminist Consciousness:

- Women theologians and biblical scholars identified totally with liberation theology
- Women seen as oppressed historical subjects in the Bible, in theology, and in the churches
- Women began to reclaim a more equal space within society
- Theological point of departure became the double oppression of women based on both sex and class
- A tendency to overvalue the feminine and a certain wanting to "even the score" by making women the "good gender"

- Almost no dialogue among feminist theologians from Latin America or between those from Latin America and the North Hermeneutics
- Biblical interpretation was both militant and grassroots-based
- Liberation texts were emphasized over other texts
- The task was to rediscover biblical women as key players in the history of liberation, which took place without awareness of the patriarchal context of the text itself

Inclusive Language:

- No awareness of sexist language
- A masculine divinity
- The word *feminist* is rejected as a foreign concept, imported from the North

Second Phase

Political/Economic Context:

- In Central America the Sandinista triumph, revolutionary movements in El Salvador, Guatemala
- In the southern cone dictatorships give way to restricted democracies
- Bush-Reagan era; Santa Fe documents
- Foreign debt becomes a crushing weight on the poor

Ecclesiastical/Theological Context:

- Ideological polarization becomes acute
- Vatican documents condemn liberation theology
- Liberation theologians become interested in the "women's perspective"
- Liberation theology becomes more receptive to the topic of "women" per se
- key themes are theology of life vs. theology of death; idolatry; martyrdom; spirituality of liberation

Construction of Feminist Consciousness:

- Growing commitmcent to see women's perspective at every turn

- Growing critique of all theology for its anthropocentrism and patriarchal mindset.
- Starting point in women's experience, bringing a different discourse to theology because of biological, cultural, and historical influences
- Efforts to rescue discourse related to God, for example, the maternal face of God
- Efforts toward the feminization of theological concepts
- Praxis of love and caring
- Lots of innovation in liturgy
- Openness to feminist contributions from both Latin American and northern feminists

Hermeneutics:

- Biblical interpretation sees every text from women's perspective
- Search for feminine images of God
- Commitment to feminize theology, to combine justice with tenderness
- Biblical work centers on valuing the ordinary, pleasure, play; reinterpreting of virtues traditionally linked to women such as maternity, tenderness, sacrifice, commitment
- Confrontation with patriarchal texts and insistence that they are not normative
- Reconstruction of texts and questioning of sources of biblical Authority

Inclusive Language:

- God as mother/father; as he/she
- Identification with the word *feminist* becomes more common

Third Phase

Political/Economic Context

- Fall of the Berlin Wall and withit, socialism as a model.
- Gulfwar invasion of Panama, defeat of the Sandinistas
- Neoliberal economic model firmly entrenched; market ideology reigns supreme

- state as benefactor of people is dismantled
- popular movements in general are weakened, lackluster interest in reform

Ecclesiastical/Theological Context:

- CEBs stagnate
- ecclesial crisis within both Protestantism and Catholicism
- Santo Domingo document is weak
- CLAI III document is weak
- amazing growth of Pentecostalism
- new energies coming from indigenous movement
- Chiapas becomes a rallying cry, "a society where all fit!"
- women's movement gains strength, as well as the black movement
- key themes are the market and the gods of sacrifice, the new evangelization, ecology and the land, dialogue with other religions
- option for the poor evolves into option for the impoverished

Construction of Feminist Consciousness

- feeling of being "boxed in" with no room to expand
- need to reconstruct all theology from a feminist perspective
- use of gender theory to analyze situation of oppression
- growing contributions from black and indigenous women
- new theories coming from the anthropology of symbolism
- challenge to confront the patriarchal structures latent in Christianity itself
- challenge to confront the patriarchal anthropology and cosmovision present in liberation theology
- calls for redefinition of both the human and the Divine
- openness to holistic Eco-feminism

Hermeneutics:

- body and the ordinary are considered hermeneutic categories

- call for a non-sacrificial reading of redemption
- key themes are the fiesta, joy, embodiedness, sexuality
- gender theory is applied to biblical texts
- creative reconstruction of texts to hear the lost voices of women
- major challenge is to reinvent all Christian theology in relation to the concepts of God, Jesus, Trinity, sin, and redemption, going beyond what is currently considered orthodox
- key question being raised is how to articulate a feminist hermeneutic that takes into account the basic problems of impoverished peoples

Inclusive Language:

- non-sexist names for the Divinity
- terms *feminist* and *eco-feminist* now commonly accepted

The Current Status of Liberation Theology

While Latin American feminist and eco-feminist theologies grew out of liberation theology, they now take a more critical view of several of liberation theology's key tenets. A review of the current status of liberation theology can be helpful. A heated debate is now taking place within liberation theology as to whether or not it is in crisis, given what appears to be the collapse of historical socialism. Some theologians, like Gustavo Gutiérrez, continue to insist that the end of the communist world does not affect liberation theology because its commitment was never to Marxism but to the poor. He argues that liberation theology is more urgently needed than ever in the face of neoliberal capitalism, which has aggravated the disparities between rich and poor.

Gutiérrez reaffirms the preferential option for the poor, reminding us that poverty has human and socioeconomic causes. While he acknowledges that liberation theology may have overemphasized economic factors, he insists that in its description of the poor as the "insignificant ones of history," women, especially poor women, as well as ethnic minorities were always implicitly included. He particularly welcomes current reinterpretations of the Bible from a women's perspective.

Juan-José Tamayo, a Spanish liberation theologian who has written and taught extensively on Latin American liberation theology for more than thirty years, is one of the more enthusiastic protagonists of including emerging Latin American theologies under the general heading of liberation theology. Tamayo believes that while at first liberation theology emphasized the socioeconomic aspects of poverty and class conflict, now, conscious of its own reductionism, it has opened itself to the new faces of the poor-marginal races and ethnic groups, cultures that have been overlooked, religions that have been outlawed, doubly and in many cases triply oppressed women, oppressed nature, abandoned street children, entirely excluded peoples and countries, and so on. Convinced that liberation theology must grapple with the major changes of the twenty-first century, he welcomes challenges coming from "new faces."

Tamayo is also aware of the discomfort feminist theologians feel about the androcentrism of much of liberation theology, and he lauds feminist theologians' use of the hermeneutics of suspicion to deconstruct categories that exclude women not only from theological discussion but from the Christian experience itself. He underlines the work feminist theologians are doing in initiating a post-patriarchal reconstruction of Christianity. Familiar with the eco-feminist posture of Con-spirando, he sees Eco-feminism as a logical development in the search to discover the root causes of women's oppression and the destruction of the Earth. Tamayo views these as exciting, viable themes that liberation theology must address, and he speaks of both feminist and eco-feminist liberation theology.

However, some leading Latin American liberation theologians are not as enthusiastically open to these new faces. Tension was evident at the theological congress sponsored by the Sociedad de Teologíay Ciencias de la Religión held in

Brazil in July 2000, where many of the "fathers" of liberation theology were present. It became evident during the congress that humanity is not only facing a major change in epoch but an end to a theological era "characterized by fragmentation and a search for new theological spaces, an enormously complex time in its pluralism, but at the same time promising and fruitful in its resources."

It was neither feminist nor eco-feminist theology that produced a heated debate at the congress, but rather Leonardo Boff's work in the area of ecological theology. In his presentation Boff expanded his definition of the option for the poor. In the 1960s, he said, liberation theology emphasized the economically and politically poor; in the 1970s the definition was extended to the culturally poor and included indigenous peoples, blacks, and other discriminated minorities; in the 1980s emphasis was given to the question of gender and the oppression of women; and now in the 1990s, liberation theology had begun to hear the cry of the earth, also impoverished because it is unjustly despoiled and exploited systematically. For each concrete oppression, we responded by developing a corresponding strategy and liberating pedagogy. Never has the Theology of Liberation fallen victim to an impoverished concept of the poor. It always tried to deepen its understanding of the complex reality of any poverty imposed unjustly.

The great "poor" at this time, then, is the Earth itself, which humanity can collectively destroy. We must change, or we will perish, Boff warns, using the metaphor of the spaceship with a few first-class passengers and many poor, the latter confined to the baggage department. But both groups depend on the welfare of the ship. There will be no Noah's ark this time round to save a few while the rest perish. Boff calls upon liberation theology to situate its reflection in the context of the new cosmology that has emerged from the latest scientific discoveries and that contemplates a broader understanding of evolution. He argues that all of us are being held hostage by a way of living and ways of production and by relations with the environment that imply systematic violence against persons, social classes, countries, ecosystems, and the Earth itself. He concludes:

> The option for the poor-the hallmark of Theology of Liberation-must be integral: all the poor with all their many faces, and the great poor one, the Earth, known as Gaia, Pachamama, and Great Mother. It is important to free all. But there are priorities. First is the urgent need to liberate the Earth through a real revolution in our paradigm of relationality with her.... This suggests a holistic paradigm based on reverence, respect and care for her biodiversity, integrity, and beauty.

Boff's expansion of the option for the poor to include the Earth itself caused a major altercation between him and his brother Clodovis at one of the plenary sessions. Clodovis Boff represents those liberation theologians who find Leonardo Boff's embracing of the new cosmology dangerous to liberation theology's traditional commitment to poor and downtrodden people. In Gustavo Gutiérrez's words, *Dónde dormirán los pobres?*. It is the poor majorities of Latin America who have always been the central focus of liberation theology. There is a growing fear among some liberation theologians that the concrete lives of the poor will no longer be the locus of their theology and that the issue of the poor seems to be losing its theological and ethical prominence. There is also fear that the traditional concerns of liberation theology will be watered down by new paradigms, such as the new cosmology. It seems likely that this debate will continue.

José Comblin, another of liberation theology's pioneers, is more blunt in his assessment of liberation theology's future: "Liberation theology is at a standstill," he says, "because Catholic theology and Christian theology in general are at a standstill; nothing new is coming out... there is no more interest in theology." Comblin is pessimistic about liberation theology's accomplishments. Now eighty, he feels free to be blunt. He says that the major reason there has been stagnation in people's willingness to participate in CEBs is the arrival of television. Even more pointedly, he says that the CEB movement arose not from the people but from pastoral agents who saw in them a new form of church and the promise of a new society. When such hopes were frustrated, pastoral agents often gave up. He finds the CEBs riddled with clericalism and therefore condemned to wither on the vine. He notes that Catholics, along with everyone else, are consulting other wisdom traditions and constructing their own belief syntheses.

Comblin believes that if liberation theology had been grounded in a strong autonomous culture, it too could have been autonomous. But given the current state of Latin American culture, he notes, such a situation is still a dream. He asks: "Where is Latin American liberation theology taught today? Who reads it? In Latin America, a tiny minority of the educated religious public. Rejection has produced an isolation, the upshot of which is that liberation theology is better known and more read in Europe and the United States than in Latin America itself." For Comblin, the value of liberation theology is that it questions theology as a whole. It directs Christian thinking beyond traditional Scholastic theology and the church's traditional social teaching inspired by that theology.However, he challenges some of liberation theology's most prized affirmations. For instance, he says that the "irruption of the poor" happened only in the sense that the church became aware of the poor.

He also argues that while liberation theologians and pastoral workers were proposing radical change, most of the poor simply wanted to improve their lives. The real revolution, in his opinion, took place in the second half of the twentieth century with the migration of millions of *campesinos* to the cities. That migration meant moving from one civilization to another. He also criticizes consciousness-raising as "injecting ideology into the mind of the popular classes: a task of instilling doctrine so that the people would learn to feel what the theory said that they ought to feel and to want what the theory said that they should want."

Comblin notes that the last stronghold of Christianity

was the family. But with the sexual revolution and the discovery of effective means of birth control, women were able to cut the cords of total economic dependency on their male partners. He marks other effects of the sexual revolution: the manifestation of those "repressions, fantasies, and taboos-an unconscious or semiconscious world that had never been brought to awareness.... For many women, the sexual revolution was-and still is-experienced as the most visible and most vital manifestation of personal freedom."

Comblin concludes that women, indigenous people, and blacks have been unwilling to be assimilated into liberation theology, and rightly so; the starting point for feminist theology has been a questioning of almost the entire history of humanity from the perspective of patriarchy. "For women, it is not enough to return to early Christianity: the solution will not be found there. And it is not very likely that the issue of women will be resolved through a theology, because it has much deeper roots which go beyond the domain of Christianity."

Comblin's frank evaluation concurs with what other analyses have pointed out. Although the problems of poverty, marginality, and inequitable income distribution have been exacerbated in recent decades, there is a growing shift in consciousness. The current situation does not result from capitalism alone but from a system, which today we name patriarchy, that goes back more than five thousand years. Although liberation theology has been persecuted by an increasingly conservative papacy, this is not the major cause for its apparent demise. The collapse of historical socialism has meant the loss of a utopian horizon, without which it becomes difficult to focus, mobilize, and sustain a struggle for a different, more just world. That world must be able to be imagined, and at this juncture of history, it cannot be.

No revolution can survive without a utopian vision, and today, the old words and symbols that once energized a generation of liberation theology activists no longer evoke such revolutionary energy. It appears that a deep historical shift is taking place. Some would see this shift as a call to go deeper and address issues neglected by liberation theology and to seek new paradigms and new sources of inspiration. Many liberation theologians see this as an enriching experience, while others maintain that questions coming from feminist and cosmological perspectives go beyond the basic commitment of liberation theology to the poor. New issues include analyzing not only neoliberal capitalism as the cause of oppression but also the older oppression of patriarchy; questioning the traditional theism of an omnipotent, anthropomorphic Creator; and addressing the lingering dualism that separates mind from matter, natural from supernatural, and the human from the rest of the life community.

At the same time it is important to stress that liberation theology has opened the door for those who have gone on to newer theological perspectives-indeed, it unveiled the possibility of dreaming in new ways. It is also necessary to acknowledge that the realities of poverty, injustice, and oppression that liberation theology addressed in the 1970s and 1980s have not gone away and that the blood of the martyrs still cries out. But the new millennium brings urgent new challenges and questions to be addressed:

- Can we speak of the poor and their children inheriting the Earth if it is devastated and poisoned, bereft of so many soulful presences?
- Can we live out an option for the poor without rediscovering our deep kinship with all living beings, our spiritual belonging to the wildly creative, deeply spiritual, unfathomably interdependent network we call the cosmos?
- Can we be of service to the Latin American poor, mostly *mestizos*, without more deeply imbibing the religious wisdom of their largely forgotten indigenous heritage?
- Can love for the people be sustained without a profound rediscovery of our bodies, of the healing and animating power of tenderness and sensuality?
- Can we expect the poor to be empowered while failing to deal with our gender issues, our hierarchical habits, our Western craving for control?

- Can our solidarity bear fruit if our allegiance is to an immutable anthropomorphic deity with a ready-made plan for the human future?
- Can the God-images of traditional theism fill us with the energy, the burning passion required to face these historic challenges?

The Feminist and Eco-Feminist Critique of Liberation Theology

Although Latin American feminist and eco-feminist theologians do not dispute their origins in liberation theology they are now experiencing varying degrees of ambiguity about whether they are still doing liberation theology, or if their criticisms of patriarchal theology place them outside this playing field. While most feminist theologians are increasingly critical of liberation theology's ingrained androcentrism, many first-generation liberation theologians-and most are clerics-have been the teachers of today's feminist and eco-feminist theologians. Thus there is a long history of friendship and a certain reluctance to criticize one's mentors. In addition to these strong personal relationships, feminist theologians still agree with much of liberation theology's analysis, especially regarding the devastating effects of the current neoliberal economic model on the region's poor. They ask, "What can feminist theology from Latin America and the Caribbean contribute to the knowledge, criticism, and defeat of this globalized, neo-liberal economy?" They also engage in theology from the locus of the poor, focusing on poor women and continually deepening their analysis of the feminization of poverty in a globalized world.

One of the severest criticisms feminist and eco-feminist theologians level against historical liberation theology is its avoidance of the issues of sexual and reproductive rights, especially as they affect poor women. Finnish feminist scholar Elina Vuola has examined this gap in her book *Limits of Liberation*. She charges that the stances of Latin American liberation theologians on sexual ethics have not moved from traditional Catholic teaching, which reflects the church's misogynist view of women. She notes, "One of the first causes of death for women of reproductive age all over the Third World, including Latin America, is the complications after an illegal abortion, but preventing the death of poor women has not been an explicit part of liberation theologians' 'agenda' of defending the poor."

Vuola views the concept of the poor in liberation theology as vague and homogenized. Until recently the poor were defined principally in economic terms and as productive and political subjects. She points out that "there has been a yawning gap in LT [liberation theology] which has to do with human corporality, sexuality and sexual ethics. The right of a female subject to her body and 'bodiliness' has been absent." There seems to be an inability to see "domestic" problems as "real" problems, given the supposedly more pressing survival struggles of the poor majorities.

Furthermore, the unequal power struggles existing between men and women have been largely ignored. This, Vuola charges, underlines liberation theology's disconnection between theory and practice: "Nothing is said of the reality of illegal abortions and the high rates of domestic violence and households headed by women, which are some of the most burning problems for Latin American women." She concludes that sexual ethics is an area in which liberation theologians are far from their stated ideals and method as a praxis-oriented theology that considers ethical reasoning and action key. She insists that defending poor women has not been part of liberation theology's priorities. The reason is that "'the poor' are seen mainly as productive subjects, understood in the framework of Marxist class analysis, and not as bodily, gendered, and reproductive subjects as well."

Mexican feminist theologian María Pilar Aquino argues the same point: The masculine theological focus has covered up the oppressive relations lived in the private area, and concealed relationships of domination exercised in the domestic sphere, where it is women who always endure the worse part. Ordinary daily life for an androcentric vision does not have epistemological value, nor does it form part of its attempts to understand the horizon of reality, that is, it does not influence the doing of theology. What, in effect, happens here is that the masculine theological focus grants a character of *naturality* to private, everyday life.

Criticism of liberation theology's androcentric vision has come to the fore in the third phase of feminist theology. Eco-feminist theologian Ivone Gebara argues that while feminist theology embraces liberation theology's critique of Euro-centered universalism, liberation theology is guilty of a similar masculine and androcentric universalism-the result of the education and formation of most male liberation theologians in Aristotelian and Thomistic philosophy and theology. This, she says, is where the two perspectives are most in conflict. Eco-feminist theology relies on different philosophical sources and conducts its research outside clerical circles and at the margins of ecclesial centers of power.

Liberation theology's frame of reference continues to be one of underlining the discontinuity between God's life and human life. Gebara argues that the fundamentally anthropocentric and androcentric character of liberation theology appears unquestionable. It speaks of God in human history, a God who in the end remains the Creator and Lord... It senses no need to reexamine the cosmological and anthropological foundations of the Christian faith. It reaffirms the goodness and justice of God's being without raising questions about the repercussions, throughout human history, of traditional or historically conditioned images of God.

Feminist Biblical Hermeneutics

There are two very clear currents within the third stage of Latin American feminist theology: holistic Eco-feminism and feminist biblical hermeneutics. The two are not exclusive and can indeed complement one another. But those feminist scholars working to reinterpret biblical texts from the standpoint of feminist hermeneutics are, perhaps, more committed than their eco-feminist counterparts to redeeming biblical traditions from their patriarchal interpretations. According to Colombian feminist biblicist, Carmiña Navia Velasco, feminist biblical scholarship is alive and well in Latin America. She reports that today it is not just a question of rereading texts with a critical feminist eye but also of searching for and examining the scriptures on topics that range from themes such as the body to violence and peace. She mentions feminist biblicists such as Alicia Winters, Tania Sampaio, Elsa Tamez, Irene Foulkes, and herself, among others, and cites the biblical journal *RIBLA*, published in Costa Rica, as a major publisher for their work.

Navia Velasco says that Eco-feminism in Latin America is especially rich in offering a more vibrant spirituality, including "a full reconciliation with one's being born a woman; a rediscovery of one's female genealogy and the role played by mothers, grandmothers, aunts, etc. in transmitting the faith; a joyful and full reconciliation with our bodies; a search for alternative forms of tenderness; and above all, a recovery and reworking of traditional symbols of the sacred." Here she mentions the contributions of Ivone Gebara and the Con-spirando Collective.

13

Masculinity, Nature and Eco-feminism

"Your masculinity is only as secure as your last competitive achievement. This fear of what nature might reveal is an endemic aspect of dominant forms of masculinity. It is built upon a denial of what cannot be denied, since it remains part of us" -Victor Seidler.

Bob Connell's attractive notion of 'exit politics' is only working for a very small minority with male profeminism typically a result of middle class / educational privilege and since the 1970s largely privatised to predominate in the sphere of personal relations. It is worth asking why there are no direct action groups of men, skilled in media exploitation akin to environmental groups, voicing public political protest against male dominance. Exiting from privilege may have caught on in terms of 'race'but the man who makes a concerted attempt to exit from traditional masculinity remains a rare and collectively unpoliticised figure.

Bob Connell refers to as 'hegemonic' masculinity. He defines this as "The configuration of gender practice which embodies the currently accepted answer to the problem of the legitimacy of patriarchy, which guarantees, or is taken to guarantee, the dominant position of men and the subordination of women". Connell's use of the word 'hegemonic' is intended to do two things, firstly to emphasis diversity in masculinities and secondly to imply that what ever hegemonic masculinity may be at a particular point in time, it is never total, but rather, open to challenge and change.

Moreover, for Connell, it is not enough to talk of diverse masculinities, but rather we must recognise the *relations* between these different masculinities that are "constructed through practices that exclude and include, that intimidate, exploit and so on. There is a gender politics within masculinity". I aim to contribute to this critique of hegemonic masculinity by discussing nature and briefly bringing in the philosophy of Eco-feminism as another worthwhile political critique for profeminist men to recognise.

The basic feminist premises that our dominant cultural institutions have been built upon and evolved along lines that embody and express hegemonic masculinity.

Seidler expresses this similarly, "With the identification of masculinity with reason, men become the protectors of and gatekeepers for this dominant vision of modernity. We set the terms on which others can be permitted to enter". The colonisation of the public sphere in this way puts forward a particular naturalised view of culture and humanity. Thus, if hegemonic constructions of masculinity have colonised what we have come to assume constitutes 'human nature' then a pro-feminist critique of hegemonic masculinity clearly also involves a simultaneous exposure of the arbitrary definitions of our dominant understanding of 'humanity'. This open up the idea that there is a similar degree of mythology and performativity to our 'human' identity, just as there is as we live through different genders.

Accepting that hegemonic masculinity is built upon the imperative to control all that is placed under the term 'nature'; new ecological practices can but only also simultaneously challenge patriarchy. Here we should understand 'nature' in an internal and external sense referring firstly to a man's own emotional and embodied life and then secondly, externally to the mastery of those human groups seen as 'closer to nature'- women, racialised groups, but *also* what we traditionally think of as nature- wilderness, animals and so on.

All this suggests that nature has been a decisive referent in constructing masculine identity. What strategies can be formulated to create alternative identities for men? If, as much eco/feminist theory suggests, we are talking about an interdependent 'web of oppression' involving class, gender, 'race' and nature it is possible to politically appropriate this interdependency. Each of these four dimensions has links to the other so it may be politically astute to pinpoint those areas of overlap. To give an example, a male involved in the environmental movement cares for things so that they no longer are 'things'.

In other words he begins to reverse the conceptual death of nature which constructs trees and/or non-human animals as objectified resources. He is impelled to care, to think emotionally about his relationship to nature. In doing so he can be said to be also at least partly practising something counter to hegemonic masculinity. He begins to break the link of interdependency that exists between hegemonic masculinity and those discourses which resource, objectify and expel nature. Single-issue movements are in reality only rarely 'single issue' so that those taking part have a good chance of being exposed to other emancipatory discourses. This was the case in Bob Connell's biographical study of Australian men involved in environmental protest who found themselves exposed to feminism through women on the protest.

It is obvious, that men being politicised for the first time are more likely to join other movements than profeminism and this is for a number of reasons. Importantly, the cultural stereotype of feminism is such to dissuade many young women from identifying themselves as 'feminist' so it is not likely to encourage many men. The public debate on gender remains rooted in essentialist assumptions, whereas that level of debate is largely antiquated within academic feminism.

Secondly, social movements associated around issues of class or nature retain an outward appeal that can be seen to bolster a particular form of romantic masculinity. In the case of class it is the heroic masculine romanticism of taking on the system and enforcing social justice. Whilst this form of masculinity can hardly be seen as wholly complicit with hegemonic masculinity neither is it typically open to sexual politics. In the case of environmental politics we perhaps find something different. Firstly, owing to the differing histories of environmentalism and so different influences, the male environmentalist is arguably more open to profeminism than the male who is first and foremost a socialist. Environmentalism in certain contexts threatens hegemonic masculinity more than socialism. This is illustrated in the mainstream response to male environmentalists who are sometimes seen as less manly, slightly emasculated. This is acutely captured in the case of male vegetarianism. Meat being one of *the* symbols of masculinity the male vegetarianism mounts a significant challenge to hegemonic masculinity, more so if the decision is taken for ethical reasons that then signify an empathy with non-human animals. The suspicion held against the male vegetarian can then translate into doubts about his heterosexuality.

One example from popular culture was a recent episode from *The Simpsons* in which Homer fears that his son Bart is gay. After mistakenly taking his son to a gay steel mill Homer takes Bart hunting in the wilderness to reestablish his son's manliness. In the style of *The Simpsons* this was all scripted with much irony but it remains significant that that scene could be chosen as one that would communicate to so many people. These are just a couple of examples that suggest that distance from, and domination of nature are an integral part of hegemonic masculinity. Whilst there are very many close links between class and gender, in terms of a strategy to encourage more profeminist men I would suggest that environmentalism at this point in time is a more fertile ground than purely class politics.

However, the long term liberationary intention has to be to make clear the interconnections between class, 'race', gender and nature and so to make less likely the existence of heterosexist socialists, patriarchal eco-warriors and humanist feminists and so on. To make clear that prioritising class, for example, over all other categories of oppression is unrealistic and only serves to re-impose a hierarchy of oppressions. This search for a better framework is where Eco-feminism comes in.

Eco-feminism, which has coalesced in the last thirty years, is a strategic response to the persistent Western association of women with nature. Now, feminist theorists have known for a long time that women have historically been associated with nature and that nature has often been feminised as in myths such as 'Mother Nature'. Gut reaction humanism meant that often this link was taken as degrading - indeed that is how the association is supposed to be taken. It is assumed that the oppressed along with the oppressor similarly regards the status of nature as inferior to all that is human so that a hierarchical system is imposed in which some people are thought of as more 'human' than others. Now the criteria over whether who can be regarded as human are liable to change over time to some degree.

During colonialism the Christian/Heathen distinction was of paramount importance. Since then the Rational/Irrational distinction has taken precedence. This new seemingly secular criterion is not wholly discontinuous from Christian definitions of the human. For example, a striking somatophobia, or 'fear of flesh' is retained in which the perceived ability to retain control of one's own body is given great weight in determining one's 'human' status. Thus, we can note how most oppressed groups in the Western context have had a 'lack of control' essence projected upon them think of oppression by gender, 'race', class, nature, age, disability, sexuality and so on. The perceived inability to control one's body takes many forms be it a lack of sexual restraint (though less of a problem if that happens to be 'normal' male heterosexual desire), or some other assumed physical 'weakness'. The 'human' in this perspective is one largely devoid of weakness, fragility and vulnerability.

However, as the eco-feminist philosopher Val Plumwood

suggests, you can not reduce all oppression to hegemonic masculinity. She believes that what is required is an understanding of a more complex dominator identity which she terms the 'master identity'. This term it can be argued allows us to think out the importance of other categories alongside gender. Just as we cannot reduce all oppression to class, we can neither reduce all to gender. It also makes a space for thinking how this identity, that has been formed through the complex system of dualistic associations that many liberation movements have problematised, does rather arbitrarily colonise what we have come to regard as 'human'. Eco-feminism is a decisive social movement since it is one of the first to coherently question this particular 'human'. Historically, emancipatory movements have been concerned with tackling de-humanisation.

Instead of taking the woman-nature connection as a degrading association for women, Eco-feminism takes a step back and considers how this association, which is the flip side of the 'men with culture connection', is part of many which stem from a whole legacy of Western dualisms. This is a legacy that not only informs gender, but also 'race', class and the separation of humanity from nature. To give just one example of it's structure it is not only women that have been historically associated with nature, but also 'non-white races' and the working classes, often through their animalisation, and more indirectly by associating these constructed groups with the body and emotions, but never reason or rationality.

Eco-feminism has intensified over the last twenty years. While it began by outlining the interconnections between the oppression of women and nature, it has broadened into a more intricate liberation theory picking out theoretical interconnections which it is hoped can ground political coalition/s. Sadly in academia feminism flexes it's own muscle by largely silencing Eco-feminism which is seen as threatening in some way. It is mistakenly stereotyped as essentialist by people still living off 1970s misunderstandings of what Eco-feminism actually is. It is prudent not to fall into the same stereotyping process. This usually consists of taking one problematic eco-feminist statement and pretending that it represents the entire philosophy of Eco-feminism. This is plain poor research or something more spiteful.

Most people still seem to think that Eco-feminism consists of the romanticisation and reproduction of the belief that women are 'closer to nature'. I refer to the reader to the 'further reading' that follows. Moreover, humanism remains a very important political myth for many with the spread of ethical concern to non-human spheres seen as a step too far or a misplaced priority instead of an important addition to liberation theory.

If the historical tradition in the West has been to associate women with nature, as Eco-feminism suggests, where does that leave the relation between masculinity and nature? How can men relate to nature in other than oppressive ways? Is it the fact of death and decay that nature represents which terrifies hegemonic masculinity as it disproves a fantasised-for omnipotence? One strategy for profeminist men has been to point out the ways in which patriarchy has also skewed the experiences of men. So we have as a consistent argument that we have lost out in terms of our emotional lives and that we have lost out also in terms of health, thinking ourselves too invincible to take care of our bodies. If this method of critiquing patriarchy holds true then it can also apply to men's experience of nature. To reconcile masculinity with nature would go some way to confessing male physical and emotional vulnerability and easing the stress and illness that goes with its denial.

The clear history and mythology of men 'returning' to nature, re-evoking what hegemony has encouraged them to repress, strongly suggests that many men have felt diminished by the relation to nature that hegemonic masculinity has provided. Such 'returns' are only partial and clouded in romanticism as long as hegemonic identity continues to be defined as so excluding of nature. Moreover, they are liable to be expressed through essentialism especially since men have in some contexts certainly been associated with nature. This relates to a point about dualistic associations in that they are never total and are liable to periodic reverse. Thus whilst the typical trend throughout the course of Western history has been to associate women and nature we can recount examples which do exactly the opposite.

When men have been associated with nature it has been the norm for this to be done in essentialist ways that have reinforced accounts of hegemonic masculinity as 'fixed in nature', and so presumably timeless and 'normal'. For example anthropomorphic accounts of certain 'wild' animals have been used to reinforce the supposedly inherent aggressive nature of men. Similar narratives are seen in everything from contemporary advertising discourse to romanticised accounts of man as 'the hunter'.

This is the very same trap that Robert Bly walks into when he attempts to revive the 'Wild Man' myth in his *Iron John*. This myth romanticises hunting and animal sacrifice as a way of male communication with nature. It is strange that hunting has been constructed in some discourses as a way of positive identification with nature since, at least in the UK, it is one of those very issues that have areas of overlap between different sources of power, being an intersection of class, gender and nature politics.

One of the reasons that makes it difficult to create truly positive ways of associatingmen with nature lies in the history of Western science's approach to nature. Thisapproach in its theory of knowledge and methodology has been orientated towardsdominating nature and constructing nature as an 'it', as already dead.

The controlling ethos has been expressed through the colonisation of Western Science by differenthegemonic masculinities that have been very resistant to change. This has been expressed by values that abstract, observe, isolate, control and yet keep at a distance that being examined. These values become so entrenched that they colonise areas of social life not directly related to Science. For example, we are taught to believe that observation or vision is the paradigm for accumulating knowledge to the neglect of other senses such as hearing, and our dominant cultural value to control our bodies speaks partly the scientistic distrust of flesh and emotion. New developments in gene technology and synthetic 'life' forms suggest that it's trajectory is striving for some form of pseudo-procreative ability, which would only appear to vindicate thecharge of 'womb envy' sometimes directed towards hegemonic masculinity. If, as I believe, there has been a clear link between hegemonic masculinity and theexploitation of the realm of 'nature' then I would like to leave you with the main argument of this article. Namely that ecological politics provides an important way in which men can subvert, albeit indirectly, hegemonic masculinity and then potentially create new, mutually enriching and non-oppressive conversations between men and nature. This claim should be accompanied with some warnings.

The area of environmental politics is not immune to male dominance or the unwelcome re-surfacing of hegemonic masculinity. Thus the whole arena of environmental activism would be strengthened rather than diluted by some thoughtful profeminism, that would then pave the way for an eco-feminist imagination that is adept at picking out interconnections between oppressions and so, in turn, arguing for interdependent oppositional politics.

The final warning for men specifically concerns falling into the various traps of feminising and/or romanticising nature, which historically have been indicative of dominating and/or repressed relations to nature and women. There are better relations to be had than these; ones that neither dominate, objectify, deny nor fear nature.

14

Eco-feminism in the 21st Century

Introduction

Since 'eco-feminism' was developed as a concept in the 1970s, there have been, arguably, major policy shifts in the fields of gender equality and environmental sustainability which warrant a consideration of the achievements of, and work outstanding for ecological feminism. This paper will assess the changing policy landscape to explore the extent to which this has structurally altered gender inequalities and societies' treatment of the environment, and the imbrication of these two processes. In order to do so, the rising profile of gender mainstreaming at the international, European Union and European national level; the application of the 'feminism' debate to environmental concerns; and the shifting of the 'radical edge' of eco-feminism, to explore future possible trajectories. The transformation of policy and development rhetoric to include gender (itself, arguably, a 'post-feminist' dilution of women's equality) masks a fundamental attachment to 'business-as-usual' where social roles, pay differentials, political representation and environmental degradation remain little changed. However, there is, sufficient evidence to identify the influence of eco-feminist thinking on major policy initiatives concerning the relationship between women, men and environment.

The central question, then, of this paper is whether Eco-feminism (as a distinct discourse, or as an amalgam of feminism and environmentalism constructed in different times and places in different ways) has changed the way in which Western society constructs the relationship between men, women and the environment. This, of course, is a problematic and speculative exercise and will follow from an analysis of how discourse and practice themselves have changed.

Eco-feminist approaches

It is tempting to use a retrospective to try to impose some sort of order on past intellectual activity and what I am attempting to do first in this article is to explore whether there is an intellectual trajectory, through a not necessarily coherent body of thinking and writing on gender and environment in the late 20th century.

In teasing out the possible relationship between women's position, gender relations, feminism, and the way in which Western society is seeking to control or manage the environment, eco-feminist writers in the 1970s and 1980s explored the relative importance of essentialism and social construction in these relationships.

The social constructivist analyses (which tended to dominate French and British writing, see, for example, Mary Mellor, 1992) drew from the Marxist and social feminist literature to show how women's position in society (as, for example, carers of children and other vulnerable family members, domestic workers, and low paid/status workers) derived from prevailing social and economic structures, which exposed them to a particular set of environmental incivilities. The specifically eco-feminist argument here proposed that, since the same social and economic structures also produced wide scale environmental damage, then women could, in some sense, 'share' this experience and were therefore better placed to argue on nature's behalf.

The essentialist argument that underpinned some of the North American and Australian analyses proposed that women had a particular relationship with nature by virtue of their biology and that this proximity to nature qualified them to speak more eloquently on nature's behalf. Different authors drew on each position to different degrees, and much of the critique of Eco-feminism over the past tWenty years has focused on the problems perceived with essentialism, and on the validity of a shared experience between the human and non-human.

Dennis Smith, in discussing the role of gender in peace and conflict, has argued that essentialism is often used as a tool to mobilize a group around a perceived characteristic which sets it apart, and certainly, cultural Eco-feminism did so. Its strength was to demonstrate the possibility of a way of thinking and being which reversed the normal hierarchy in which men stood at the peak; however, little academic feminist environmental thinking is currently framed in this way. Indeed, as Gillian Rose noted, to accept that women had an irreducible 'female essence' would be tantamount to admitting that others distinguished by 'difference' (such as minority ethnic populations, disabled people or gay men and women, and men more widely) could be driven to behave in similarly 'essential' ways, which, by definition, would be unchanging and unchangeable, an argument that social scientists have been working hard to refute for many years. The argument that informs this paper is based on an interpretation of Eco-feminism that is constructivist and it is certainly this strand that appears to have informed policy development over the past twenty years.

Changes in the Environmental Discourse: Policy

By 2001, a paper in the Journal of Gender Studies was taking as axiomatic that governments throughout the world were beginning to focus more attention on the subject of gender equality. The following reviews the extent to which, mainly inter/transnational policy has accomplished this transition, whilst Table 1 illustrates how both environmental policy and women's equality policy have been dialectically affected by each other.

Table 1: Strategies for Linking Women & Environment

Bringing gender into the environment	*Bringing the environment into gender*
1992 United Nations Conference on Environment and Development	1995 United Nations 4th Conference on Women and Platform of Action
2002 World Summit on Sustainable Development	
EU Gender Mainstreaming DGXI	

Environmental Justice Movement

One practice that has become much more widely embedded at national/international level from the early 1990s is gender mainstreaming. Framed within human rights and equality discourses that have informed the United Nations, it has become a plank of all UN conventions since the environment and women's conferences of the early-mid 1990s. Jointly, the outcomes of these two conferences have promoted the inclusion of environmental impacts and women's interests in other UN agreements, such as those concerning Habitat, Social Inclusion and Poverty. Whilst, arguably, the national machineries of the signatory states of these conventions are necessary as catalysts for promoting gender equality and justice, those same state structures are embedded in structural inequalities and it is sometimes difficult to see how they may be used to make anything other than superficial changes. Molyneaux distinguishes between women's 'practical' and 'strategic' needs, whereby addressing such 'practical' needs as better childcare (or, in environmental terms, reducing nitrogen dioxide or particulate pollution as a contributor to childhood asthma) does nothing to challenge existing power structures. However, strategic interests (such as challenging a society which values the macho image of much car driving/ownership) take on existing patriarchal 'paradigms of power'. Rai argues that an effective way of gender mainstreaming would be to frame women's interests in the wider interests of a just society rather than the commonly adopted additive nature of gender analysis.

The United Nations Conference on Environment and Development in 1992 was the first UN conference to be significantly informed by the non-governmental sector. Its centrepiece (or at least, the element that achieved the most publicity, and was least scathed by the Rio +5 evaluation, see Osborn and Bigg, 1998), Agenda 21, was a testament to the sustained lobbying by women's groups. The preparatory meetings took place across the globe for two years and ensured a reasonably coherent lobby from the women/environment movement worldwide, leading to the inclusion of a set of objectives defined in 'Global action for women towards sustainable development and equitable action'.

The link between women and the environment was consolidated, internationally, at the 1995 4th United Nations Conference on Women in Beijing. The resulting Platform for Action identified 'Women and Environment' as one of the critical areas of concern. UNED-UK's 'Gender 21' group subdivided this concern into: education; health; marginalised groups; planning, housing and transport; Local Agenda 21 and consumption and waste.

Ten years later, the World Summit on Sustainable Development did little to advance women's equality with respect to the environment, although the need to embed women's concerns was written more thoroughly into the Plan of Implementation. Few achievements had been noted in the intervening 10 years, for example, the UN had expressed frustration at the lack of progress on issues as wide as AIDS/ HIV, globalization, poverty, and health - all of which are distinguished by a gender dimension.

Point 20 of The Johannesburg Declaration on Sustainable Development commits to ensuring that "women's empowerment and emancipation, and gender equality are integrated in all activities encompassed within Agenda 21, The Millennium Development Goals and the Johannesburg Plan of Implementation". This plan variously refers to women, females, women and men, and gender, both generally (as in "the outcomes of the summit should benefit all, including women...”), and with reference to specific programmes. Such programmes include good governance, poverty eradication, eliminating violence, discrimination, health, economic opportunity, land ownership, water, agriculture, technology, energy and area specific programmes such as mountain areas and Africa. It also embeds gender considerations into the means of implementing the Plan, such as education, data collection, indicator provision, public participation and decision making. Such a thorough weaving of gender/women throughout the Plan for Implementation is, in some ways, an improvement on the targeted Chapter 24 focusing on women in Agenda 21, but it is too soon to establish whether it will have any effect on signatory states' treatment of women, particularly in relation to the environment.

Participants in the Women's Platform at the NGO Forum at WSSD had mixed reactions: both welcoming a more thoroughly embedded inclusion of women in plans and exasperation at the assumption in the main conference that ‘women's issues’ had already been dealt with at Rio.

There is some evidence that the women's groups were right to be suspicious as, in preparation for the WSSD, the UN Commission for Sustainable Development, in its own preparatory committee, identified the participation of women at all political levels as “still relatively low, and the level of participation at the international level is not adequately geographically balanced or adequately financed”.

Gender mainstreaming

On the basis of the women's groups involved in submitting evidence to the United Nations preparatory committees, it could be argued that the inputs into the UNCED and Beijing conferences were influenced by the eco-feminist debates from the 1980s onwards. As such, it is possible to see how constructivist Eco-feminism has been incorporated into policy governing gender relations, environment, and the linking of women and environment. One of these outcomes is ‘gender mainstreaming’. The United Nations pioneered ‘gender mainstreaming' which requested signatories of the 4th World Conference on Women "to mainstream a gender perspective into all policies and programmes, so that, before decisions are taken, an analysis is made of the effects on women and men". Nanavaty reports gains at this level and makes recommendations as to how to achieve the attitude shift which will enable this. The European Union accepted the principle of gender mainstreaming in 1996 and this has been formalised in the Treaty of Amsterdam, which commits member states to the "elimination of inequalities and the promotion of equality between women and men." For example, a recent investigation of the gendered impact of waste management practiceiv in selected European Union member states illustrates the scope for this and the limited amount of good practice that is beginning to emerge, although it is also clear that the European Union commitment, and subsequent UK commitment to gender mainstreaming through the Women and Equality Unit is not filtering down to the local level of waste management in anything but a piecemeal fashion.

The World Bank has identified practical reasons, consistent with its aims and practices, for incorporating gender equality into its programmes. "Gender is an issue of development effectiveness, not just a matter of political correctness or kindness to women. Evidence demonstrates that when women and men are relatively equal, economies tend to grow faster, the poor move more quickly out of poverty and the well being of men, women and children is enhanced."

Whilst most policy makers would not challenge these aims, eco-feminists do question the validity of pursuing economic growth, as much of this is likely to produce negative impacts on the environment. Their argument (see, for example, Mellor, 1992, Merchant, 1996, Plumwood, 1993) rests on changing our priorities whereby we may be driven more by quality of life issues, and that it is redistribution that should be at the heart of policy, rather than generating more growth. Eco-feminist literature suggests that women might be better able than men to effect this change, and that, therefore, it is not just a matter of equality within existing structures, but of changing the structures to reflect this mode of thinking, a point that will be developed when considering future trajectories of eco-feminism. Bhattar argues that gender mainstreaming, since the 1980s, has sought to integrate gender concerns as part of 'business as usual', and that part of this approach has been to raise the number of female appointments to decision making posts. Her reservations on this procedure are that this only works if women are able to "fundamentally re-orient the nature of the mainstream", which requires all policy makers to accept that there are "fundamental differences in the experience and interpretation of reality between women and men". Unless policy makers are aware of this in advance, no amount of gender mainstreaming initiatives will make any difference. She argues that a 'critical mass' of women is needed in decision making fora to create the possibility for women to support each other in policy initiatives, to be a catalyst for other women to be involved and to be in a position to allocate and control resources. A consensus seems to accumulate around a 30% to 35% minimum ratio of women to men to create critical mass.

Changes in Environmental Discourse: Environmental protest

Rai argues that civil society is essential to strengthen the resolve of government to gender mainstream, and to hold it to account. The degree to which any government is open to civil society scrutiny will determine the effectiveness of policy monitoring. Indeed, as the above discussion shows, the global environmental debate has recognized the importance of enabling women and men to participate meaningfully in environmental policy formation and decision making through civil society structures, as well as through more formal representative structures. Such participation requires the means to access information which, in the third world, means eliminating inequalities in education from primary level. At present, the global adult literacy rate for men is 85%, whilst that for women is 74%.

Public participation usually relates to forms of democratic challenge which are formalized and structured in relation to state decision making structures. Less formal expressions of political protest emerge when these formalized structures of participation are found wanting - when fundamental breaches of 'natural justice' are as much the result of governing structures as their neglect. Such protests are more likely to be organized by women, themselves on the margins of formal decision making, and this has characterized the grass roots environmental movement in disparate geographical locations. The early eco-feminist literature canonized 'movements' such as the Chipco in Himalayan India, The Green Belt in Kenya, Love Canal in New York State and drew attention to the role of women in dramatizing the links between environmental damage, the human impacts of this, women's relative lack of power and the strategies this lack of power has necessitated.

Wickramasinghe links the conceptual and practical aspects of Eco-feminism in her work in South Asia, arguing that this region, particularly in rural areas, has been at the centre of Eco-feminism and that this has helped women conceptualise the links between women and the environment. These inequalities- the gender gaps in education, and the distribution of rural work- have not been eased by "development but have been re-endorsed in newly created development paradigms".

What such movements lack in terms of financial resources, they make up for in imagination and commitment and social cohesion. Indeed, Seager claims that "at its best, feminist environmentalism rocks boats" in a variety of policy and philosophical areas. It combines theory and activism to "challenge and redefine foundational principles". In the United Kingdom, the Women's Environmental Network, founded to counter what was seen as a masculinist bias in environmental campaigningv, has taken on issues that particularly affect women in attention grabbing campaigns such as 'Getting Lippy', 'Real Nappies' (promoting the use of cloth nappies to reduce the 8 million disposable nappies that are discarded, mostly to landfill, each day) and Chocolate (raising awareness of the toxic pesticide residues of lindane which still exist in some non organic chocolate bars). Whilst the link between poverty and women is not explicitly made, Wen's work is founded on the understanding that women are not well placed to argue within business or government and this has been borne out through several public battles with advertisers. Both the establishment of Wen in 1988 and its current practice is informed by eco-feminism, which, through Wen's increasingly ought after policy advisory role, is indirectly finding its way into some UK government policy. In some ways, the example of Wen, illustrates the scope for more radical protest finding its way into public policy several years down the line. Their waste minimization campaign demonstrates this as well, as Wen is now called to advise central government and local authorities, and has made a significant corrective input in to the Greater London Authority's Waste Plan. The challenge for Wen, as a multi-issue campaigning organization is to combine working at the more radical eco-feminist edge, raising issues of salience to women, and often ignored in other policy fora, whilst retaining an ability to have an input into government policy. This apparent conflict of balancing the radical and incorporation is well explored by Neil Carter with regard to the environmental movement more widely.

Future trajectories for Eco-feminism

Environmental justice

The environmental justice movement has grown in scope over the past two decades, emerging primarily from analyses of environmental inequalities based on race/ethnicity and poverty. Whilst Eco-feminism has not claimed to be part of this, it clearly shares a number of its characteristics, not least, the fact that from the micro to the macro level, women are more likely than men to be classified as 'in poverty' the world over. The environmental justice literature, previously dominated by poverty and race issues, is just beginning to address gender. This is timely since there is accumulating evidence that gender is disproportionately associated with disadvantage in a number of ways. An Equal Opportunities

Commission funded report recently found that even when controlling for factors such as labour market status, age and number of children, household composition, and age, there was still a clear gender dimension to poverty, and that women who are single pensioners, unemployed, of Pakistani or Bangladeshi origin, teenage householders and/or tenants, are more likely than men with the same characteristics to be poor.

Such disadvantage has an impact on the extent to which these women are trapped in poor quality environments. It is also noticeable how women, compared to men, are disproportionately disadvantaged in both chronic and catastrophic environmental hazard situations. Fordham identifies how this is both as a direct result of the hazard, for example, in the 1991 cyclone in Bangladesh which killed almost 140,000 people, 90% of the victims were women and children, or indirectly. Here Fordham considers violence against women which increases in high stress situations, both in environmental catastrophes and chronically environmentally stressed situations, but which is largely ignored in the male dominated field of disaster management and development.

Much of the Eco-feminism literature refers to 'embodiedment'-or how women's bodies are particularly vulnerable to environmental pollution, and yet historically, safe chemical loads have tended to be calculated on the basis of men's body tolerance to exposure over an eight hour period. New European legislation (such as REACH-The European Registration and Evaluation Authority for the Restriction of Chemicals) and recent publications, are beginning to draw attention to the vulnerability of pregnant women, women more generally and women at different stages of their life cycle such as at puberty and menopause.

However, there are still relatively few instances of such recognition in the actual legislation. There is, consequently, significant scope to develop an environmental justice case along the lines that women are more vulnerable to toxic exposure both due to their social roles, which are more likely to consign them to poverty than men, and their biology. Recent publications on environmental justice are beginning to incorporate concerns about women into their analyses, and, more particularly, groups of women who are additionally marginalized by their income, occupation, ethnicity or disability. This is an important inclusion given that environmental justice issues are becoming more widely heard and argued in North America and Europe.

In 2003, two feminist/environmentalist writers published on the extension of feminist/environmental concerns into animal rights. Joni Seager argued that a shared structure of oppression, a feminist analysis of allocation of rights and gendered assumptions about the relationship between human and non-human species underpinned both Eco-feminism and animal rights. Seager goes further to suggest that both concerns share the problem of being consigned to a dualistic 'other' that, in reality, is more of a continuum. Such extensions of feminist/environmentalist concerns reach into debates into food production systems and recreational activities such as hunting, both of which can be enriched, she argues, by an eco-feminist perspective.

Likewise, Val Plumwood, who, in the 1990s argued for a dissolution of the dualistic way of seeing men and women, has extended this analysis to argue for a new 'inter-species' ethic as the only way in which to avert what she sees as an ecological crisis, born of human hubris, sado-dispassion, rationality and a dualistic culture which has separated 'Nature' and 'Culture' in the West.

Plumwood sees what/who she describes as the "Hero of Reason" as responsible for the "sado-dispassionate...cultural drama of reason and nature unfolding to choke the life from his planetary partner in his final sadistic act of mastery." Her aim is to provide "recipes for escaping this situation" and she uses most of the book to critique not only industrial and post-industrial approaches to the Earth and to what she variously refers to as Earth Others, supra-human, non-human and more-than-human (as alternative descriptors for life which is not classified as human), but also other spiritual traditions and approaches of deep ecology.

Conclusions

The relationship of the leading, or radical edge of any movement to the state is complex and increasingly well theorised. With regard to gender, Rai argues that, whilst it is important to work within the state, such a strategy cannot be used exclusively, as the radical edge identifies the future, possibly, currently less politically acceptable challenges. This 'radical edge' has a particular salience with regard to environmental feminism, as protest and community politics is sometimes seen as the only way in which women, as a minority in decision making arenas, can make their voice heard. This is as true within the academy (where both women, and feminist studies of one sort or another, are marginalized) as beyond.

In looking back, then, over the past thirty years of eco-feminism, it is argue that significant strides have been made to incorporate women's and gender issues within certain policy areas and both the global and the local level. The evidence for this, where this exists, lies in the campaigning groups who have informed international agreements and local practice. This is, of course, particularly so where the aims of these groups have coincided with the practical aims of international and aid agencies. However, real obstacles remain in making structural changes to social systems to ensure that equality and feminist concerns are routinely part of environmental decision making and eco-feminist theoreticians and activists continue to expose these concerns.

15

Toward a Queer Eco-Feminism

Although many eco-feminists acknowledge heterosexism as a problem, a systematic exploration of the potential intersections of eco-feminist and queer theories has yet to be made. By interrogating social constructions of the "natural," the various uses of Christianity as logic of domination, and the rhetoric of colonialism, this essay finds those theoretical intersections and argues for the importance of developing a queer Eco-feminism,

Progressive activists and scholars frequently lament the disunity of the political left in the United States. Often characterized as a "circular firing squad," the left or progressive movement has been known for its intellectual debates and hostilities, which have served to polarize many groups that could be working in coalition: labor activists, environmentalists, civil rights activists, feminists, animal rights activists, indigenous rights activists, and gay/lesbian/bisexual/transgender activists. Meanwhile, it is observed, the conservative right in the United States has lost no time in recognizing the connections among these various liberatory movements and has launched a campaign to ensure their collective annihilation. As a result, it seems the future of progressive organizing may well depend on how effectively scholars and activists can recognize and articulate our many bases for coalition. In theory and in practice, Eco-feminism has already contributed much to this effort.

At the root of Eco-feminism is the understanding that the many systems of oppression are mutually reinforcing. Building on the socialist feminist insight that racism, classism, and sexism are interconnected, eco-feminists recognized additional similarities between those forms of human oppression and the oppressive structures of speciesism and naturism. An early impetus for the eco-feminist movement was the realization that the liberation of women-the aim of all branches of feminism - cannot be fully effected without the liberation of nature; and conversely, the liberation of nature so ardently desired by environmentalists will not be fully effected without the liberation of women: conceptual, symbolic, empirical, and historical linkages between women and nature as they are constructed in Western culture require feminists and environmentalists to address these liberatory efforts together if we are to be successful. To date, eco-feminist theory has blossomed, exploring the connections among many issues: racism, environmental degradation, economics, electoral politics, animal liberation, reproductive politics, biotechnology, bioregionalism, spirituality, holistic health practices, sustainable agriculture, and others. Eco-feminist activists have worked in the environmental justice movement, the Green movement, the anti-toxics movement, the women's spirituality movement, the animal liberation movement, and the movement for economic justice. To continue and build on these efforts toward coalition.

"We have to examine how racism, heterosexism, classism, ageism, and sexism are all related to naturism," writes eco-feminist author Ellen O'Loughlin. Chaia Heller elaborates: "Love of nature is a process of becoming aware of and unlearning ideologies of racism, sexism, heterosexism, and ableism so that we may cease to reduce our idea of nature to a dark, heterosexual, 'beautiful' mother". But as Catriona Sandilands astutely comments, "It is not enough simply to add 'heterosexism' to the long list of dominations that shape our relations to nature, to pretend that we can just add queers and stir'". Unfortunately, it is exactly this approach that has characterized eco-feminist theory to date, which is the reason

I believe it is time for queers to come out of the woods and speak for ourselves.

The goal of this essay is to demonstrate that to be truly inclusive, any theory of Eco-feminism must take into consideration the findings of queer theory; similarly, queer theory must consider the findings of Eco-feminism. To this end, I will examine various intersections between Eco-feminism and queer theory, thereby demonstrating that a democratic, ecological society envisioned as the goal of Eco-feminism will, of necessity, be a society that values sexual diversity and the erotic.

Sexualizing Nature, Naturalizing Sexuality

The first argument linking Eco-feminism and queer theory is based on the observation that dominant Western culture's devaluation of the erotic parallels its devaluations of women and of nature; in effect, these devaluations are mutually reinforcing. This observation can be drawn from eco-feminist critiques that describe the normative dualisms, value hierarchical thinking, and logic of domination that together characterize the ideological framework of Western culture. As Karen Warren explains, value dualisms are ways of conceptually organizing the world in binary, disjunctive terms, wherein each side of the dualism is "seen as exclusive and oppositional, and where higher value or superiority is attributed to one disjunct than the other". Val Plumwood's 1993 critique of Western philosophy pulls together the most salient features of these and other eco-feminist critiques in what she calls the "master model," the identity that is at the core of Western culture and that has initiated, perpetuated, and benefited from Western culture's alienation from and domination of nature. The master identity, according to Plumwood, creates and depends on a "dualized structure of otherness and negation". Key elements in that structure are the following sets of dualized pairs:

- Culture/nature
- Reason/nature
- Male/female

- Mind/body
- Master/slave
- Reason/matter
- Rationality/animality
- Reason/emotion
- Mind, spirit/nature
- Freedom/necessity
- Universal/particular
- Human/nature
- Civilized/primitive
- Production/reproduction
- Public/private
- Subject/object
- Self/other

Eco-feminists have uncovered a number of characteristics about the interlocking structure of dualism. First, eco-feminist philosophers have shown that the claim for the superiority of the self is based on the difference between self and other, as manifested in the full humanity and reason that the self possesses but the other supposedly lacks. This alleged superiority of the self, moreover, is used to justify the subordination of the other. Next, eco-feminists have worked to show the linkages within the devalued category of the other, demonstrating how the association of qualities from one oppressed group with another serves to reinforce their subordination. The conceptual linkages between women and animals, women and the body, or women and nature, for example, all serve to emphasize the inferiority of these categories. But while all categories of the other share these qualities of being feminized, animalized, and naturalized, socialist eco-feminists have rejected any claims of primacy for one form of oppression or another, embracing instead the understanding that all forms of oppression are now so inextricably linked that liberation efforts must be aimed at dismantling the system itself. There is a theoretical gap, however, when we find that those few eco-feminists who do mention heterosexism in their introductory lists of human oppressions have still not taken the dualism of heterosexual/queer forward to be analyzed in the context of their vertical lists of dualized pairs, and consequently into the theory being developed.

In some cases, the same could be said for the dualism of white/nonwhite. This omission is a serious conceptual error, for the heterosexual/queer dualism has affected Western culture through its "ineffaceable marking" of these normative dualisms, according to queer theorist Eve Kosofsky Sedgwick. In her book, Epistemology of the Closet, Sedgwick finds that these normative dualisms actually subsist in a more unsettled and dynamic tacit relation according to which, first, term B is not symmetrical with but subordinated to term A; but, second, the ontologically valorized term A actually depends for its meaning on the simultaneous subsumption and exclusion of term B; hence, third, the question of priority between the supposed central and the supposed marginal category of each dyad is irresolvably nstable, an instability caused by the fact that term B is constituted as at once internal and external to term A.

Sedgwick's findings bear a neat resonance with Plumwood's theorizing of the linking postulates that connect such dualisms both "horizontally" and "vertically".

These linking postulates include:

- Backgrounding, in which the master relies on the services of the other and simultaneously denies his dependency.
- Radical exclusion, in which the master magnifies the differences between self and other and minimizes the shared qualities.
- Incorporation, in which the master's qualities are taken as the standard, and the other is defined in terms of her possession or lack of those qualities.
- Instrumentalism, in which the other is constructed as having no ends of her own, and her sole purpose is to serve as a resource for the master.
- Homogenization, in which the dominated class of others is perceived as uniformly homogeneous; Queers experience

backgrounding, radical exclusion, and incorporation. As Sedgwick argues, the heterosexual identity is constituted through a denied dependency on the homosexual/queer identity.

In terms of radical exclusion, queers find that the erotic is projected onto queer sexuality to such a degree that this quality is seen as the only salient feature of queer identities. When queers come out, heterosexuals frequently conclude they know everything there is to know about us once they know our sexuality. In terms of incorporation, it is clear that heterosexuality and its associated gender identities are taken as the standard in dominant Western culture, and queers are defined primarily in relation to that standard, and our failure to comply with it.

But the problem of oppression based on sexuality is not limited to the heterosexual/queer dualism. As queer theorists have shown, the larger problem is the erotophobia of Western culture, a fear of the erotic so strong that only one form of sexuality is overtly allowed; only in one position; and only in the context of certain legal, religious, and social sanctions.

The oppression of queers may be described more precisely, then, as the product of two mutually reinforcing dualisms: heterosexual/queer, and reason/the erotic. As Plumwood has ably demonstrated, Western culture's oppression of nature can be traced back to the construction of the dominant human male as a self fundamentally defined by its property of reason, and the construction of reason as definitionally opposed to nature and all that is associated with nature, including women, the body, emotions, and reproduction. Feminists have also argued that women's oppression in Western culture is characterized by our association with emotion, the body, and reproduction, and have responded to these associations in three different ways. Some have rejected these associations and attempted to align themselves with the public male sphere of rationality.

Others have reversed the valuation and embraced these

associations while devaluing the male rational culture. In contrast, eco-feminists have argued for a "third way," one that rejects the structure of dualism and acknowledges both women and men as equal parts of culture and nature. As a logical development of Eco-feminism, a queer eco-feminist theory would build on these analyses, using both queer theory and feminist theories about the oppression of the erotic. Though the reason/erotic dualism seems to be an aspect of the original culture/nature dualism, the heterosexual/queer dualism is a fairly recent development, as it is only in the past century that the concept of homosexual and heterosexual identities has developed. A queer eco-feminist perspective would argue that the reason/erotic and heterosexual/queer dualisms have now become part of the master identity, and that dismantling these dualisms is integral to the project of Eco-feminism.

Bringing these dualisms into the list of self/other and culture/nature dualisms offered by Plumwood is one step toward queering Eco-feminism. With this added perspective, eco-feminists would find it very productive to explore "vertical" associations on either side of the dualisms: associations between reason and heterosexuality, for example, or between reason and whiteness as defined in opposition to emotions and nonwhite persons; or associations between women, nonwhite persons, animals, and the erotic.

From a queer eco-feminist perspective, then, we can examine the ways queers are feminized, animalized, eroticized, and naturalized in a culture that devalues women, animals, nature, and sexuality. We can also examine how persons of color are feminized, animalized, eroticized, and naturalized. Finally, we can explore how nature is feminized, eroticized, even queered. The critical point to remember is that each of the oppressed identity groups, each characteristic of the other, is seen as "closer to nature" in the dualisms and ideology of Western culture. Yet queer sexualities are frequently devalued for being "against nature." Contradictions such as this are of no interest to the master, though such contradictions have been of great interest to feminists and queer theorists alike, who have argued that it is precisely such contradictions that characterize oppressive structures.

Before launching into a discussion of queer sexualities as both "closer to nature" and "crimes against nature," it is crucial to acknowledge that sexuality itself is a socially constructed phenomenon that varies in definition from one historical and social context to another. As scholars of queer history have shown, there was no concept of a homosexual identity in Western culture before the late nineteenth century. Until then, people spoke of individual homosexual acts, deviance, and sodomy; the persons performing those acts were always presumed to be "normal". Those homosexual acts were castigated as sinful excesses, moral transgressions of biblical injunctions. The shift from seeing homosexual behavior as a sin to seeing it as a "crime against nature" began during the seventeenth century. As early as 1642, ministers in the American colonies began referring to the "unnatural lusts of men with men, or women with women," "unnatural acts," and acts "against nature". "After the American Revolution," however, "the phrase 'crimes against nature' increasingly appeared in the statutes, implying that acts of sodomy offended a natural order rather than the will of God".

The natural/unnatural distinction had to do with procreation, but even "natural" acts leading to procreation could be tainted by lust and thus not free from sin. Procreative lust was preferable to "unnatural" lust, however. Finally, a third shift in the definition of homosexuality occurred toward the end of the nineteenth century. Through the work of sexologists such as Havelock Ellis, Magnus Hirschfeld, and Richard von Krafft-Ebing, the sexual invert became a recognizable identity, and the origins of sexual inversion were believed to lie in an individual's psychology. The word heterosexual first appeared in American medical texts in the early 1890s, but not in the popular press until 1926.

Today, nearly thirty years after the Stonewall rebellion, which launched the movement for gay liberation, the definition of queer identities is still evolving. "Homosexual" has changed to "gay," and "gay" to "gay and lesbian"; bisexuals have become more vocal; and most recently, transgender liberation has also reshaped queer community, changes that have prompted many organizations to replace "gay and lesbian" with "gay/lesbian/bisexual/transgendered" or simply "queer" in their self- definitions. The recognition of varying sexual identities and practices has inspired a rereading of not only straight history or queer history but the history of sexuality itself. Based on these historical developments, queer theorists have determined that queer sexualities have been seen as transgress in at least three categories: as acts against biblical morality, against nature, or against psychology. Thus, queer sexualities have been seen as a moral problem, a physiological problem, or a psychological problem. Though all three arguments are used against all varieties of queer sexuality today, the "crime against nature" argument stands out as having the greatest immediate interest for eco-feminists.

Queer theorists who explore the natural/unnatural dichotomy find that "natural" is invariably associated with "procreative." The equation of "natural" with "procreative" should be familiar to all feminists, for it is just this claim that has been used in a variety of attempts to manipulate women back into compulsory motherhood and so-called women's sphere. From a historical perspective, the equation of woman's "true nature" with motherhood has been used to oppress women, just as the equation of sexuality with procreation has been used to oppress both women and queers.

The charge that queer sexualities are "against nature" and thus morally, physiologically, or psychologically depraved and devalued would seem to imply that nature is valued - but as eco-feminists have shown, this is not the case. In Western culture, just the contrary is true: nature is devalued just as queers are devalued. Here again is one of the many contradictions characterizing the dominant ideology. On the one hand, from a queer perspective, we learn that the dominant culture charges queers with transgressing the natural order, which in turn implies that nature is valued and must be obeyed. On the other hand, from an eco-feminist perspective, we learn that Western culture has constructed nature as a force that must be dominated if culture is to prevail.

Bringing these perspectives together indicates that, in effect, the "nature" queers are urged to comply with is none other than the dominant paradigm of heterosexuality - an identity and practice that is itself a cultural construction, as both feminists and queer theorists have shown. There are many flaws in the assertion that queer sexualities are "unnatural." First among them is that such an assertion does not accurately reflect the variety of sexual practices found in other species.

For example, female homosexual behavior has been found in chickens, turkeys, chameleons, and cows, while male homosexual behavior has been observed in fruit flies, lizards, bulls, dolphins, porpoises, and apes. An examination of insect sexual behavior reveals that the female scorpion kills the male after mating, the black widow spider eats the male after mating, and the praying mantis may eat the male while mating.

Some animals are hermaphrodites, while other species are entirely female. Mating behavior also varies across mammal species. Some pairs mate for life, some are promiscuous. In some species, males and females travel together in herds, packs, or prides;in others, family groups are the basic unit;in others, males and females spend most of their time in same-sex groups and get together only for mating;in still others, all are loners who seek out members of their species only for the purpose of procreation.

The equation of "natural" sexual behavior with procreative purposes alone is conclusively disproven by both the evidence of same-sex behaviors and the observations of sexual activity during pregnancy, which have been reported for chimpanzees, gorillas, rhesus macaques, stumptailed macaques, Japanese monkeys, and golden lion tamarins. In his study of the bonobo, a species that, together with the chimpanzee, is the nearest relative to homo sapiens, Frans de Waal found that sexual behavior served a variety of reproductive and nonreproductive functions. In effect, research on non-human primate sexual behavior indicates that non-human primates engage in sexual activity far more than they need to from a reproductive point of view and thus much of their sexuality is nonreproductive". As Jane Curry concludes, "If we look to nature for models of human behavior, we are bound, are we not, to value tolerance and pluralism". This, however, is the second flaw in the assertion that queer sexualities are "unnatural": norms for one species cannot be derived from the behaviors and seeming norms of other species.

By attempting to "naturalize" sexuality, the dominant discourse of Western culture constructs queer sexualities as "unnatural" and hence subordinate. As Jeffrey Weeks writes in Against Nature, "appeals to nature, to the claims of the natural, are among the most potent we can make. They place us in a world of apparent fixity and truth. They appear to tell us what and who we are, and where we are going. They seem to tell us the truth". Arguments from "nature," as feminist philosophers of science have repeatedly argued, are frequently used to justify social norms rather than to find out anything new about nature. Attempts to naturalize one form of sexuality function as attempts to foreclose investigation of sexual diversity and sexual practices and to gain control of the discourse on sexuality. Such attempts are a manifestation of Western culture's homophobia and erotophobia. Returning to the list of dualisms that eco-feminists have shown to characterize Western culture, and examining how qualities are distributed across each side of the disjuncts to enhance that disjunct's superiority or subordination, we can see that the eroticization of nature emphasizes its subordination. From a queer eco-feminist perspective, then, it becomes clear that liberating women requires liberating nature, the erotic, and queers. The conceptual connections among the oppressions of women, nature, and queers make this need particularly clear.

Erotophobia and the Colonization Of Queer /Nature

The rhetoric and institution of Christianity, coupled with the imperialist drives of militarist nation-states, have been used for nearly two thousand years to portray heterosexuality, sexism, racism, classism, and the oppression of the natural world as divinely ordained. Today, although tWentieth-century Western industrialized nations purport to be largely secular, those countries with Christian and colonial origins retain the ideology of divinely inspired domination nonetheless. This section will first examine how Christianity has been used to authorize the exploitation of women, indigenous cultures, animals, the natural world, and queers. It will conclude by examining twentieth-century colonial practices.

Many feminists and eco-feminists who have examined Western culture's hierarchical and oppressive relationship with nature date the problem of human separation from nature back to 4000 B.C.E., the Neolithic era, and the conquering of matrifocal, agricultural, goddess-worshiping cultures by militaristic, nomadic cultures that worshiped a male god. The agriculturalists' view - that spirit was immanent in all of nature, that sexuality and reproduction were like the earth's fertility, and that both were sacred - was replaced by a worldview that conceived of divinity as transcendent, separate from nature, with humans and nature as God's creation rather than as equal parts of God. The female, bisexual, or hermaphroditic Goddess was replaced by the male, heterosexual God the Father, and the matrifocal trinity of Maiden, Mother, and Crone became the patriarchal trinity of Father, Son, and Holy Ghost. Thus, in searching for origins of the conceptual linkages among women, nature, persons of color, and queers, along with their collective oppression, many feminists and eco-feminists would argue that it is more relevant to look at the shift in social organization from matrifocal to patriarchal structures and values than to explore how a particular form of patriarchal religion (historically antecedent to that shift by centuries or even millennia) has authorized the subordination of women, nature, and their associates.

For other eco-feminists, however, the theories of a matrifocal past remain just that - anthropological theories rather than historical facts. So much of anthropology is based on a few pieces of broken pottery, scattered bones, and the remnants of buildings that some eco-feminists are reluctant to develop additional eco-feminist theory based too heavily on these interpretations alone. All eco-feminists who have addressed the topic of spirituality, however, have observed that Christianity has been used as both an authorization and a mandate for the subordination of women, nature, persons of color, animals, and queers - and it is this agreement that I will take as my point of departure.

Christianity originated as a small, ascetic cult, one among many such cults in the Roman Empire. It was, from the start, an urban religion, shaped in the context of urban, secular philosophies rather than in the context of earthbased, rural agriculturalism. The beliefs of the early Christians included the conception of Adam as both male and female, and of Christ as the restored androgynous Adam and the critical opposition between reason and passion, with the power of reason as the unique characteristic distinguishing humans from animals. Comparing some of those beliefs with the context in which they originated, one can surmise that the proponents of Christianity were influenced both by the beliefs of earlier, earth-based cultures and by the popular philosophies of their time, such as Stoicism and Gnosticism. Moreover, their ability to incorporate aspects of these other popular beliefs into Christianity may have enhanced its appeal and ensured its survival.

The early Christian perspective on sex and the erotic also suited the temper of the time. Christianity appeared during a time of increasing militarization in the Roman state. It was preceded by a "wave of grim asceticism". For Stoic and Epicurean philosophers of the period, sex and other erotic pleasures were seen as distractions from the contemplative life. Stoic morality held out chastity as an ideal, with heterosexual intercourse allowed only for procreation within marriage; other Greek and Roman writers also held that procreation was the only legitimate reason for intercourse. According to David Greenberg, "To be like the angels was to be spiritual; to be carnal, unspiritual. Sex was the essence of carnality, hence the antithesis of spirituality". During the first two centuries of Christianity, leading bishops and theologians required celibacy of all Christians, but later recanted and allowed limited sexual behavior within marriage for the sole purpose of procreation. From the second through the fourth centuries C.E., church leaders gave the topic of sex more attention and rejected it more vehemently than did the authors of the New Testament.

Thus, it would be inaccurate to argue that Christianity opposed queer sexuality per se; rather, Christianity opposed all sexual acts that were not purposely procreative. What distinguished Christianity from the many other ascetic cults of its time was the severity of its asceticism, its complete intolerance of other religions, and the high degree of organization among its adherents.

Hierarchy -the organizational structure and religious belief that characterized Christianity - may also have contributed to its survival, because this belief fit well with the Romans, who praised "the virtues of selfsacrifice to the state, obedience to hierarchical authority, and suspicion of pleasure and sex". As Elizabeth Dodson Gray has observed, the two accounts of creation in Genesis have been used in Christianity to legitimate both human/non-human hierarchy and anthropocentrism. Gray reminds us, moreover, that hierarchy itself means holy order. Her work shows that Christianity originally interpreted all social or economic ranking as reflecting a holy order, as the Apostle Paul explained: "Let everyone obey the authorities that are over him, for there is no authority except from God, and all authority that exists is established by God". The conceptual symmetry between Christianity and the Roman state made it possible for Christianity to spread gradually throughout the Roman army, where it incorporated additional elements of a contending religion.

Finally, under Emperor Constantine, "the cross was adopted as a military symbol and placed on shields and banners". In the fourth century C.E., the Roman Empire became the Holy Roman Empire, and the union of church and state as representing the reign of God's will on earth was sealed. The inferiority and subordination of women, animals, the body, nature, the erotic, and all their associates was proclaimed by law, decreed by religion, and relentlessly enforced. From the fourth through the seventeenth centuries, all those perceived as "nature" were persecuted through a series of violent assaults: the Inquisition, the Crusades, the witch burnings, and the "voyages of discovery." In his underground classic, Witchcraft and the Gay Counterculture, Arthur Evans writes of the similarities between the Inquisition and the witch burnings, particularly in their pursuit of victims.

From the fourth through the thirteenth centuries, the church was plagued with pagan influences, resurgences of the old religions attempting to combine with some of the tenets of Christianity: Gnosticism, Manichaeism, Massalianism, Bogomilism, Catharism, the Free Spirit, and others. According to Evans, these movements displayed five prominent features:

- belief in more than one deity;
- a prominent leadership role for women;
- a pagan sense of asceticism, including both self-denial and self-indulgence;
- hostility to the wealth and power of the church;
- a tolerance for Gay [sic] sex".

Unable to repress these continual resurgences, the church declared such beliefs heresy and commanded their eradication. The Holy Inquisition was created by Pope Gregory IX between 1227 and 1235, and in 1233 one of his famous bulls, the Vox in Rama, accused heretics of practicing sex rites that were "opposed to reason".

The Inquisition used the property of the accused to pay for the costs of trial and execution, and heresy hunting became a major industry in the Middle Ages. Economic motivations surely explain the persecution of a particular monastic military order of crusaders, the Knights Templars. In 1307, King Philippe of France brought charges of same-sex sexual behaviors against the entire order. Five thousand of its members were arrested, and over the next few years, those remaining free were hunted down all over Europe, until the order was abolished.

As Evans explains, the Knights Templars had accumulated vast amounts of wealth and had become the chief bankers of the Middle Ages: "Both Pope Clement and Philippe were in debt to them". In this first example of many, the church can be seen as using antierotic and homophobic rhetoric to mask the economic motivations of church and state.

If the Vox in Rama was the launching point of the Inquisition, the appearance of the Malleus Maleficarum in 1486 was surely the watershed for the witch burnings. Written by two Dominican monks, the "hammer of witches" explicitly links witchcraft to women and women's "inferior nature" claiming that women are "more carnal" than men. The spiritual practice of witchcraft was popularly seen as implicitly sexual: persons arrested on suspicion of witchcraft were always questioned about their sex lives, for witches were thought to hold wild and bawdy rituals that culminated in the witches kissing the devil's anus or having intercourse with the devil. Same-sex sexual behaviors and gender nonconformity were also conceptually linked to witchcraft: the phrase women with women recurs throughout the Inquisition's reports on witches' sexual behaviors, and because the majority of witches were women, the charge of "wild orgies" in effect suggests that women were engaging sexually with one another.

Men who engaged in same-sex behaviors were often strangled and burned on bundles of sticks called "faggots," which were tied and stacked in the kindling at the "witches' " feet. And in the earliest notorious example of what might today be called transgender persecution, nineteen-year-old Joan of Arc was burned at the stake as a witch in 1431, condemned to death for the sin of wearing men's clothing. Older, economically independent women, and those unprotected by a man, were especially vulnerable to accusations of witchcraft. Like those convicted by the Inquisition, their property and assets were seized and used to pay the cost of their executions. Estimates of the number of witches executed range between one hundred thousand and nine million; some say that approximately 83 per cent of those executed as witches were women.

What is known of the linkages between the "burning times" and the colonization of the Americas? Arthur Evans unequivocally asserts, "The widespread homosexuality of the North American Indians was given as an excuse by the invading Christian whites for their extermination". In Gay American History, Jonathan Ned Katz writes, "the Christianization of Native Americans and the colonial appropriation of the continent by white, Western 'civilization' included the attempt by the conquerors to eliminate various traditional forms of Indian homosexuality - as part of their attempt to destroy that Native culture which might fuel resistance - a form of cultural genocide involving both Native Americans and Gay people". And in his study of The Zuni Man-Woman, Will Roscoe finds, dating back to the sixteenth century, numerous reports on the "sinfulness" of native sexual behavior - the lack of inhibition, the prevalence of sodomy, and the tolerance or even respect for transgendered persons - all of which fueled the Spanish explorers' argument for the colonization of native peoples and their lands in the name of Christianity.

It is interesting that both the monarchs and the explorers felt the need to justify their colonialist desires for more land, more wealth, and more slaves. From medieval theologians, Christianity had inherited the message that the "fruits of any conquest could only be legitimate if the war that won them had been just"; conveniently, through the Crusades, Christianity developed the principle that "war conducted in the interests of the Holy Church was automatically just". Because the church had been engaged in persecuting the erotic since its inception, choosing the sexual behaviors of indigenous peoples as proof of their heathenism and lack of civilization seemed adequate justification for their colonization. Katz's valuable research in Gay American History offers numerous observations of native sexual practices, dating from the sixteenth-century explorers on. These records clearly express the explorers' erotophobic, imperialist attitudes. "The people of this nation the Choctawl are generally of a brutal and coarse nature," wrote Jean Bernard Bossu. "They are morally quite perverted, and most of them are addicted to sodomy. These corrupt men... have long hair and wear short skirts like women". "The sin of sodomy prevails more among them than in any other nation, although there are four women to one man,"wrote Pierre Liette about the Miamis in 1702. The role of the nadleeh, or transgendered person, particularly offended Western European sensibilities.

Of the Iroquois, the Illinois, and other tribes in the Louisiana area, Jesuit explorer and historian Pierre Franæois Xavier de Charlevoix wrote in 1721, "these effeminate persons never marry, and abandon themselves to the most infamous passions". When Jesuit Father Pedro Font found "some men dressed like women" among the California Yumas, he inquired about their clothing and learned that "they were sodomites, dedicated to nefarious practices." Font concluded, "there will be much to do when the Holy Faith and the Christian religion are established among them". The Franciscan missionary Francisco Palou reported with shock that "almost every village" in what is now Southern California "has two or three" transgendered persons, but prayed "that these accursed people will disappear with the growth of the missions. The abominable vice will be eliminated to the extent that the Catholic faith and all the other virtues are firmly implanted there, for the glory of God and the benefit of those poor ignorants". In the rhetoric of Christian colonialism, the Europeans filled the role of benevolent culture "civilizing" savage nature - and this "civilizing" involved taking the natives' homelands, eliminating their cultural and spiritual practices, and raping and enslaving their people.

A specific example of the role erotophobia played in authorizing colonization may be of use. In his book, *The Elder Brothers*, Alan Ereira reports on the Kogi, who live deep in Colombia's Sierra Nevada mountains, and who may be "the last surviving high civilisation of pre-conquest America". In 1498, the land around what is now the Colombian city of Santa Marta was discovered by the Spanish in their search for gold, and on June 12, 1514, a Spanish galleon arrived and began the process of colonization. That process involved reading a decree declaring the natives' new servitude to King Ferdinand and the Christian God, in both Spanish and Carib languages, although the native people did not speak either one. The Spanish conquistador Pedrarias Davila concluded his proclamation with the warning that if the native people did not submit to this rule :

> I assure you that with the help of God I will enter powerfuly against you, and I will make war on you in every place and in every way that I can, and I will subject you to the yoke and obedience of the church and their highnesses, and I will take your persons and your women and your children, and I will make them slaves, and as such I will sell them, and dispose of them as their highnesses command: I will take your goods, and I will do you all the evils and harms which I can, just as to vassals who do not obey and do not want to receive their lord, resist him and contradict him. And I declare that the deaths and harms which arise from this will be your fault, and not that of their highnesses, nor mine, nor of the gentlemen who have come with me here.

The Spanish invasion proceeded accordingly. As Ereira observes, gender and sexuality played a prominent role in the rhetoric and the justification of colonial conquest. "The Spanish could not endure the Indians' relationship between the sexes," he writes. "It was so fundamentally different from their own as to be an outrage. The men did not dominate the women". The Spanish were horrified, moreover, by the acceptance of homosexual behaviors and transgendered identities: "it was an inner fear, a fear of their own nature. And so they set out to eliminate sodomy among the Indians". After nearly a century of colonial enslavement and missionary zeal, the Spanish concluded their most vicious assault on the native population in 1599.

The governor of Santa Marta called together all the native chiefs at the base of the Sierras and told them he would put an end to their " 'wicked sinfulness' ". The native population planned a revolt, but news of their plans was leaked to the Spanish through two missionaries, and the Spanish were prepared. For three months, the Spanish carried out their own plan of torture and genocide against the indigenous people. When it was over, the governor declared :

> And if any other Indian is found to have committed or to practice the wicked and unnatural sin of sodomy he is condemned so that in the part and place that I shall specify he shall be garrotted in the customary manner and next he shall be burned alive and utterly consumed to dust so that he shall have no memorial and it is to be understood by the Indians that this punishment shall be extended to all who commit this offense.

Those persons "who wish to live" were required to pay a fine of "pacification" amounting to fifteen hundred pounds of gold. Gender-role deviance and the accepted presence of nonheterosexual erotic practices had become the rhetorical justification for genocide and colonialism. Not only did transgender practices and sodomy disturb the colonizers; even heterosexual practices devoid of the restrictions imposed by Christianity were objectionable. Among the Hopi of the Southwest, for example, those who had been successfully converted to Christianity were forbidden to attend the traditional snake dance because there, "male cross-dressing, adultery, and bestiality could be observed publicly". Missionaries objected to the heterosexual practices of the Pueblo Indians, calling them "bestial" because " 'like animals, the female placed herself publicly on all fours' ". What became known as the "missionary position" was advocated by the seventeenth-century Spanish theologian Tomás Sánchez, in his *De sancto matrimond sacramento,* as the "natural manner of intercourse.... The man must lie on top and the woman on her back beneath. Because this manner is more appropriate for the effusion of male seed, for its reception into the female vessel".

Sánchez likened the phallus to a plow and the woman to the earth; the missionary position would be the one most conducive to procreation and hence the most "natural." In contrast, the mulier supra virum position was "absolutely contrary to the order of nature". Appeals to nature have often been used to justify social norms, to the detriment of women, nature, queers, and persons of color. The range of colonial assaults on sexuality- from gender roles to same-sex behaviors to heterosexual practices - is the reason I name the colonizers' perspective erotophobic rather than simply homophobic. This colonial erotophobia remained intact through the arrival of the Pilgrims, the establishment of the United States, and the waves of westward expansion that followed. In the twentieth century, narratives of colonialism and exploration continue to bear the stamp of erotophobia, as feminist critiques reveal.

In her study of race and gender in international politics, Cynthia Enloe finds important connections between the conceptions of nationalism and of masculinity. In colonialist discourses of the nineteenth and twentieth centuries, the subordinated countries are feminized, the subordinated men are emasculated, and the colonized women are often depicted as sex objects by foreign men. One male writer described colonialism as the condition wherein a man's women are "turned into fodder for imperialist postcards. Becoming a nationalist requires a man to resist the foreigner's use and abuse of his women" in her study of U.S. polar expeditions, Lisa Bloom finds that "the explorations symbolically enacted the men's own battle to become men," and the recorded narratives left by the explorers present "U.S. national identity as essentially a white masculine one". Both Enloe's and Bloom's texts reprint popular colonial postcard images of naked or partially clothed native women reclining on the ground in what Bloom calls the "odalisque pose". Like the colonizers of three and four centuries past, the explorers and imperialists of the nineteenth and twentieth centuries have used the perceived eroticism of native peoples as a justification for their colonization. Serving as a foundation for all imperialist exploits, colonial nationalism offers a definition of identity that is structurally similar to the master identity.

Enloe defines a nation as "a collection of people who have come to believe that they have been shaped by a common past and are destined to share a common future. That belief is usually nurtured by a common language and a sense of otherness from groups around them". Nationalism, then, is "a set of ideas that sharpens distinctions between 'us' and 'them'. It is, moreover, a tool for explaining how inequities have been created between 'us' and 'them' ". Similarly, the editors of Nationalisms and Sexualities explain that "national identity is determined not on the basis of its own intrinsic properties but as a function of what it is not". Inevitably "shaped by what it opposes," a national identity that depends on such differences is "forever haunted by its various definitional others".

Looking at these definitions of nationalism from an eco-feminist perspective, it becomes apparent that national identity bears a structural similarity to the master model as defined by Plumwood. National identity participates in two of the five operations characteristic of the master identity -radical exclusion and incorporation. Colonialist nationalism, however, depends on all five operations of the master model, including the linking postulates of backgrounding, instrumentalism, and homogenization. Throughout the documents of explorers and colonists, native peoples are constructed as animal-like: they are perceived as overly sexual, and their sexual behaviors are described as sinful and animalistic. The indigenous women are eroticized, while the men are feminized - and all these associations are used to authorize colonization.

The feature of masculine identity that Enloe and Bloom seem to overlook and that Plumwood does not explicitly address is sexuality. Here again, feminist and eco-feminist theories fall short without a queer perspective. As Gayle Rubin has noted, "Feminism is the theory of gender oppression. To automatically assume that this makes it the theory of sexual oppression is to fail to distinguish between gender, on the one hand, and erotic desire, on the other". Queer theorist Eve Sedgwick argues that gender and sexuality are "inextricable... in that each can be expressed only in terms of the other... in twentieth-century Western culture gender and sexuality represent two analytic axes that may productively be imagined as being as distinct from one another as, say, gender and class, or class and race".

From a queer eco-feminist perspective, then, it is clear that notions of sexuality are implicit within the category of gender. Simply stated, the masculinity of the colonizer and of Plumwood's master identity is neither homosexual, bisexual, nor transgendered. Heterosexuality-and a particular kind of heterosexuality as well, a heterosexuality contained within certain parameters-is implicit in conceptions of both dominant masculinity and Plumwood's master model. In the preceding examples, the discourse of nationalist colonialism contains specific conceptions not only of race and gender but also of sexuality. The native feminized other of nature is not simply eroticized but also queered and animalized, in that any sexual behavior outside the rigid confines of compulsory heterosexuality becomes queer and subhuman. Colonization becomes an act of the nationalist self asserting identity and definition over and against the other - culture over and against nature, masculine over and against feminine, reason over and against the erotic. The metaphoric "thrust" of colonialism has been described as the rape of indigenous people and of nature because there is a structural - not experiential - similarity between the two operations, though colonization regularly includes rape.

Western eco-feminists have repeatedly argued against the feminization of nature in metaphors such as "mother nature" because of the subordination implicit in these gendered constructions, given the context of Western patriarchal culture. Elizabeth Dodson Gray may be the first eco-feminist writer to challenge the "tyranny of the straight white male norm," in her book *Green Paradise Lost*, when she shows how the "mother nature" metaphor leads to subordination. In patriarchal Western culture, Gray explains, masculinity is defined not only as independence but as "not-dependent." The process of socializing boys into men involves denying dependence on the mother; that dependence is then transferred to the wife. Male superiority is preserved by the social construction of a "wife" as "submissive... economically impotent, and in many other ways... inferior and non threatening to her man. In short, a wife is to be below her man, not above". According to Gray, the same transference is at work in Western culture's relationship with nature.

Men have done with Mother Nature this same dominance/submission flip flop. They have by their technologies worked steadily and for generations to transform a psychologically intolerable dependence upon a seemingly powerful and capricious "Mother Nature" into a soothing and acceptable dependence upon a subservient and non-threatening "wife." This "needs to be above" and to dominate permeates male attitudes toward nature.

Foundation of a Queer Eco-Feminism

Salient events in Western history reveal the foundations for a queer Eco-feminism. More than any other period, the sixteenth and seventeenth centuries clarify the conceptual links between the oppression of women, the erotic, and nature. As Carolyn Merchant, Susan Griffin, and Evelyn Fox Keller have so clearly demonstrated, in a patriarchal system that conceives of nature as female, there is a clear and necessary connection between the development of science as the rational control of a chaotic natural world and the persecution of women as inherently irrational, erotic, and therefore evil creatures. Such connections have provided the conceptual foundations for eco-feminist theories.

The foundations for queer Eco-feminism, then, are established by restoring and interrogating other aspects of that historical period: that women accused of witchcraft were accused not only for their gender but for their perceived sexuality and erotic practices; that such women were frequently burned with men who had sex with men; that the colonial conquest of indigenous peoples in the Americas was authorized partly on the basis of the natives' sexual behaviors. I am not suggesting that "co- occurrence equals causality"; rather, I am arguing that a careful reading of these several movements of domination - the persecution of women through the witch burnings, of nature through science, and of indigenous peoples through colonialism-which reached a peak during the same historical period in Western Europe, will lead to the roots of an ideology in which the erotic, queer sexualities, women, persons of color, and nature are all conceptually linked.

Today, all those associated with nature and the erotic continue to experience the impact of centuries of Western culture's colonization, in our very bodies and in our daily lives. Rejecting that colonization requires embracing the erotic in all its diversity and building coalitions for creating a democratic, ecological culture based on our shared liberation. To create that culture, we must combine the insights of queer and eco-feminist theories. As feminists have long argued, the way out of this system of endemic violence requires liberating the erotic - not in some facile liberal scheme, which would authorize increased access to pornography or child sexual encounters, but through a genuine transformation of Western conceptions of the erotic as fundamentally opposed to reason, culture, humanity, and masculinity. A queer eco-feminist perspective would argue that liberating the erotic requires re conceptualizing humans as equal participants in culture and in nature, able to explore the eroticism of reason and the unique rationality of the erotic. Eco-feminists must be concerned with queer liberation, just as queers must be concerned with the liberation of women and of nature; our parallel oppressions have stemmed from our perceived associations. It is time to build our common liberation on more concrete coalitions.

Bibliography

Andrews, Peggy. *Sisters Listening to Sisters: Women of the World Share Stories of Personal Empowerment.* Bergin and Garvey, 1996.

Awkward, Michael. *Negotiating Difference: Race, Gender, and the Politics of Positionality.* University of Chicago Press, 1995.

Bannerji, Himani. *Thinking Through: Essays on Feminism, Marxism, and Anti-Racism.* Women's Press, 1995.

Basu, Amrita, ed. *The Challenge of Local Feminisms: Women's Movements in Global Perspective.* Westview Press, 1995.

Butler, Judith and Joan W. Scott, ed. *Feminists Theorize the Political.* Routledge, 1992.

Carver, Terrell and Veronique Mottier, ed. *Politics of Sexuality.* NY: Routledge, 1998.

Chapman, Jennifer. *Politics, Feminism and the Reformation of Gender.* Routledge, 1992.

Chapman, Jenny. *Politics, Feminism and the Reformation of Gender.* Routledge, 1993.

Cocks, Joan. *The Oppositional Imagination: Feminism, Critique, and PoliticalTheory.* (out of print)

Elshtain, Jean Bethke. *Meditations on Modern Political Thought: Masculine/Feminine Themes from Luther to Arendt.* Penn State Univ. Press, 1992.

Fowlkes, Diane L. *White Political Women: Paths from Privilege to Empowerment.* Univ. of Tennessee Press, 1992.

Fraser, Nancy. *Justice Interruptus: Critical Reflections on the "Postsocialist" Condition.* Routledge, 1997.

Gottfried, Heidi, ed. *Feminism and Social Change: Bridging Theory and Practice.* Univ. of Illinois Press, 1996.

Hughes-Freeland, Felicia and Nickie Charles, ed. *Practising Feminism: Identity, Difference and Power.* Routledge, 1996.

Jones, Kathleen B., ed. *Citizenship in Feminism: Identity, Action, and Locale.* Indiana University Press, 1998.

Kenney, Sally J. and Helen Kinsella, ed. *Politics and Feminist Standpoint Theories.* Haworth Press, 1997.

King, Katie. *Theory in Its Feminist Travels: Conversations in U.S. Women's Movements.* Indiana Univ. Press, 1994.

Meehan, Elizabeth and Selma Sevenhuijsen, ed. *Equality Politics and Gender.* Sage, 1991.

Meyers, Diana Tietjens, ed. *Feminist Social Thought: A Reader.* Routledge, 1997.

Naples, Nancy A., ed. *Community Activism and Feminist Politics: Organizing Across Race, Class, and Gender.* Routledge, 1997

Okin, Susan Moller. *Women in Western Political Thought.* Princeton Univ. Press, 1992.

Pascall, Gillian. *Social Policy: A New Feminist Analysis.* 1997.

Pateman, Carole and Elizabeth Gross, ed. *Feminist Challenges: Social and Political Theory.* Northeastern Univ. Press, 1987.

Phillips, Anne. *Engendering Democracy.* Penn State Univ. Press, 1991.

Phillips, Anne. *Feminism and Politics.* Oxford, 1998.

Randall, Vicky and Georgina Waylen, ed. *Gender, Politics and the State.* NY: Routledge, 1998.

Rocheleau, Dianne, Barbara Thomas-Slayter, and Esther Wangari, ed. *Femininst Political Ecology: Global Issues and Local Experiences.* 1996.

Sapiro, Virginia. *A Vindication of Political Virtue: The Political Theory of Mary Wollstonecraft.* Univ. of Chicago Press, 1992.

Simon, Sherry. *Gender in Translation: Cultural Identity and the Politics of Transmission.* Routledge, 1996.

Sunstein, Cass R., ed. *Feminism and Political Theory.* Univ. of Chicago Press, 1990.

Thomas, Sue and Clyde Wilcox, ed. *Women and Elective Office.* Oxford, 1997.

Waring, Wendy, ed. *By, For and About: Feminist Cultural Politics.* Women's Press, 1994.

Warren, Karen J. and Duane L. Cady, ed. *Bringing Peace Home: Feminism, Violence, and Nature.* Indiana Univ. Press, 1996.

Wolf, Naomi. *Fire with Fire: The New Female Power and How It Will Change the 21st Century.* Fawcett Books, 1993.

Young, Iris Marion. *Justice and the Politics of Difference.* Princeton, 1998.

Young, Stacey. *Changing the wor(l)d: Discourse, Politics, and the Feminist Movement.* Routledge, 1997.

Zack, Naomi, ed. *American Mixed Race: The Culture of Microdiversity.* Rowman and Littlefield, 1995

Index